REROUTED

Embracing God's Plan
When Yours Falls Apart

ROSCOE HUNTER

Copyright © 2025 by Roscoe Hunter
All rights reserved.

No part of this book may be reproduced, stored in a retrieval system, or transmitted in any form or by any means—electronic, mechanical, photocopying, recording, or otherwise—without the prior written permission of the publisher, except in the case of brief quotations embodied in critical articles or reviews.

Scripture Credits:
Scripture quotations are from the Holy Bible, English Standard Version® (ESV®), copyright © 2001 by Crossway, a publishing ministry of Good News Publishers. Used by permission. All rights reserved.

Disclaimer
This book is intended for spiritual encouragement, personal reflection, and educational purposes. It is not a substitute for professional advice related to health, mental health, legal, financial, or other specialized services. Readers are encouraged to seek counsel from qualified professionals where appropriate.

Unless otherwise noted, all names and identifying details of individuals mentioned in testimonies or stories have been changed to protect their privacy. Any resemblance to actual persons, living or dead, is purely coincidental.

The author and publisher assume no responsibility for any outcomes that result from the application of concepts discussed herein. The views expressed are those of the author and do not necessarily reflect those of any affiliated organizations, publishers, or endorsers.

I dedicate this book to my late grandmother, Edith Hunter, who was the light that drew me to a relationship with Jesus as a little boy. Her witness and faithfulness I have carried with me through the completion of this book.

Author's Note

Why I Wrote this Book

I didn't write this book because I had all the answers—I wrote it because I lived the questions. The ones that haunt us in the quiet:

"Why am I here?"

"Is this all there is?"

"What does God want from my life?"

Rerouted: Embracing God's Plan When Yours Falls Apart was born out of the trials, missteps, breakthroughs, and moments of deep surrender in my own life. I've faced doors that slammed shut when I thought they should swing wide open. I've chased dreams that turned into distractions. And I've walked through seasons where success was loud, but my soul was quiet—and not in a peaceful way.

In particular, my early journey as an entrepreneur taught me something vital. I had ambition, talent, and drive. I pursued recognition, wealth, and the high of being "somebody." But somewhere along the way, I realized I was climbing a ladder that leaned against the wrong wall. Fame and fortune had promised fulfillment—but they never delivered. That revelation became a holy disruption, one that rerouted me back to the true source of identity: **God's purpose.**

This book is the fruit of that journey. It's not a theory. It's testimony and transformation. It's what happens when God strips away the false finish lines we set for ourselves and reveals the deeper race we were actually created to run. My race will not end until my last breath on this earth, and as you go through this book, know that you are not traveling this road alone.

How to Use This Book

I encourage you to read this book from cover to cover on your first pass. Let it speak to your spirit. Let the Scriptures, stories, and reflections wash over your mind and heart. Then, revisit it as a spiritual companion.

Many chapters include self-assessments, guided reflection prompts, checklists, and biblical frameworks to help you apply what you've learned. These tools are here for you to return to in moments of clarity—and confusion. Use them during your devotional time, your prayer walks, or whenever you feel the pull to realign with what matters most.

This is not just a book to be read. It's a book to be used.

Who This Book Is For

I wrote this for the **struggling Christian**—the one who believes in God but still feels lost in life.

I wrote this for the person who **knows they have a purpose** but can't seem to access it, define it, or live it out.

I wrote this for the **curious seeker**, someone open to the truth of Jesus and looking for clarity in a world that constantly offers counterfeit definitions of success and identity.

And I wrote this for those **led by the Spirit**—those who don't even know how they ended up with this book in their hands but can feel in their heart that God wants to speak through these pages.

If that's you, I believe this book will not only speak to you—it will **awaken something in you**. A reminder. A revelation. A roadmap.

Wherever you are on your journey, may this book encourage, equip, and guide you to walk boldly in the purpose God has placed on your life.

Let's walk this road—together.

**In purpose and grace,
Roscoe Hunter**

Contents

Introduction	1
Chapter 1 The Call to Purpose	5
Chapter 2 The Source of Purpose	19
Chapter 3 Uncovering Your Gifts and Talents	37
Chapter 4 Passion vs. Purpose	54
Chapter 5 The Role of Patience in Discovering Purpose	73
Chapter 6 Cultivating a Christ-Centered Mindset	89
Chapter 7 Staying Focused and Avoiding Distractions	103
Chapter 8 Committing to Your Purpose	119
Chapter 9 Why God's Purpose is Important	135

Chapter 10
Applying God's Wisdom in Leadership — 152

Chapter 11
Setting and Achieving Faith-Driven Goals — 174

Chapter 12
Fostering Unity Across Communities — 188

Chapter 13
Embracing a Life of Service — 207

Chapter 14
Overcoming Burnout in a Purpose-Driven Life — 224

Chapter 15
Measuring Impact and Success — 234

Chapter 16
Embarking on Your Purposeful Journey — 247

Chapter 17
Embracing Change as Part of Purpose — 261

Chapter 18
Navigating Challenges on the Path — 277

Chapter 19
Purpose-Driven Relationships — 290

Chapter 20
Learning from Spiritual Mentors and Leaders — 303

Chapter 21
Cultivating Humility in Purpose — 318

Chapter 22
Stewardship of Resources — 334

Chapter 23
Legacy and the Future   345

Chapter 24
Continuing Your Purposeful Journey   361

Chapter 25
Equipped for the Final Stretch –
Readiness in a Rerouted World   380

Epilogue
The Time is Now   389

Acknowledgements   391

Scripture References by Chapter   393

About the Author   425

What Comes Next?   427

Introduction

The Wake-Up Call

The morning light filtered through the blinds like a quiet intruder, illuminating the remnants of a dream I had spent years building—now reduced to silence. My office, once humming with life, lay still. No phones ringing. No staff laughing in the hallway. No deals being closed. Just the weight of failure pressing on my chest like an anchor I couldn't shake. In a matter of months, my business—my pride, my lifeblood—had unraveled.

I had done everything in my power to hold it together. Prayed. Hustled. Strategized. Sacrificed. But nothing could stop the collapse. I was left alone in the ruins with only one persistent question echoing in my heart:

"What now?"

And in that silence—beneath the grief, beneath the loss, beneath the noise of my ambitions—I heard it.

Not audibly. But clearly.

A whisper.

A pull.

A call to something deeper than success.

A call to purpose.

More Than a Self-Help Journey

This book isn't about recovering from failure. It's about uncovering the reason you were created in the first place.

Rerouted is a spiritual journey rooted in truth, Scripture, and soul-level honesty. It's about stripping away the layers the world has placed on you—titles, trophies, and expectations—and returning to the identity God gave you before you ever made a name for yourself.

This isn't a self-help manual. You won't find ten steps to instant success or quick-fix solutions for life's pain. What you will find is something better: a divine invitation to discover the blueprint that's already been written for your life by the One who knows you best.

We're in This Together

I don't know exactly what brought you to this book. Maybe you've experienced loss like I have. Maybe you're stuck in a career that feels hollow. Maybe you've accomplished everything you set out to do—only to find that the applause doesn't fill you the way you thought it would. Or maybe, like so many, you just feel like something is missing.

Wherever you are, I want you to know this:

You're not alone.

You're not crazy.

And you are absolutely not disqualified.

God still has a plan for you.

What You Can Expect

Each chapter of *Rerouted* is intentionally designed to walk you through a transformative process. You'll explore:

- The spiritual foundation for living with divine intent.
- The difference between passion and purpose (and why it matters).
- How to uncover your God-given gifts and activate them in the real world.
- How to navigate setbacks, resistance, and even burnout without losing your faith.
- The role of patience, community, humility, and leadership in fulfilling your mission.
- And how to leave a legacy that speaks long after you're gone.

You'll hear testimonies—real stories from people who've walked the same road. You'll dive into self-assessments, biblical examples, and reflection guides rooted in Scripture and relevant to modern life. This book is practical, prayerful, and prophetic.

But only if you engage with it. Fully.

A Purpose That Outlasts You

Here's the truth that changed everything for me:
Success isn't the goal. Significance is.

And significance only comes when you align with something greater than yourself. That something is God's purpose for your life—not just what you do, but who you become in the process.

Your life is not a random series of events. It is an intentional sequence, crafted by a God who knew your name before your first breath. That means nothing is wasted. Not your pain. Not your talents. Not even your detours. It's all part of the assignment.

So, if you're ready—really ready—to step into your calling with clarity and courage...

If you're tired of living by default and ready to live by design...

If you're done chasing validation and ready to walk in identity...

Then this journey is for you.

Let's begin.

CHAPTER 1
The Call to Purpose

The Collapse of My Business

As the first rays of dawn broke through the night, I found myself deep in contemplation. The once vibrant corridors of my business were now silent, each corner echoing the remnants of dreams that had abruptly ended. The emotional toll was significant; standing amidst the ruins I had lovingly built over the years was heartwrenching.

My heart ached with the weight of loss, a poignant reminder of the aspirations and sleepless nights poured into creating something lasting. Yet, even in this heartbroken state, I felt the subtle stirring of something profound—a growing realization of purpose, a divine whisper calling me toward a new path.

From Crisis to Clarity

The collapse of my business was sudden, unraveling over a mere three-month period against a backdrop of unrelated chaotic events that ultimately converged to dismantle my life's work to that point. However, this downfall marked a pivotal chapter in my life. Barely a week after confronting the void left by my shuttered doors, the recognition and clarity of my true purpose emerged, granting me both solace and direction, just as the chaos of failure began to dissipate.

In the quiet, desolate moments that followed the collapse of my entrepreneurial dreams, I embarked on a transformative journey marked by reflection and a profound search for deeper meaning. Once a young man striding confidently through the corridors of my creation—a business cultivated from a flickering idea into a vibrant enterprise—I now confronted the silent echoes of my ambitions.

Despite my desperate efforts—long nights troubleshooting and frantic days on the phone—everything still fell apart. Yet, amidst the ruins, the agitation of the past months gave way to the tranquil acceptance of a new calling. My struggle was not merely against external forces but against the inner comparisons of success equated with wealth—a metric I had unwittingly adopted.

The Seat Belt

Looking back, I realize that God was rerouting me long before I knew I needed a new direction. Sometimes, it's not the big spiritual revelations that wake us up—it's the split-second decisions that, in hindsight, were drenched in divine mercy.

I was in my early twenties, still moving through life on autopilot—chasing fun, avoiding consequences, and believing I had all the time in the world to figure out purpose "later." One night, some friends and I were out at a nightclub. Nothing too wild, just another night we told ourselves we deserved. It got late, and the group started to split up. Just two of us rode back in one of the cars—my friend was driving, and I took the passenger seat.

I remember being exhausted. I had been running on fumes all week, and by the time we got in the car, I was ready to crash—figuratively, of course. I leaned the seat all the way back, thinking I'd grab a quick nap on the ride home. But before I closed my eyes, I did something I normally wouldn't have if I were planning to sleep lying down: I clicked the seatbelt across my waist.

No fanfare. No "voice from heaven." Just a small moment—a quiet nudge, maybe—that said, "Buckle up." I didn't even think much of it. I just clicked in, adjusted the belt so it lay loosely over me, and dozed off.

Somewhere along the highway, I was jolted awake.

There was no time to process what was happening. One moment I was dreaming, the next—impact. A loud, sudden crash slammed into the front passenger side of the car. My side. Metal screamed. My body flew forward—until the seatbelt, loose as it was, caught me mid-air and slammed me back down into the reclined seat.

If I hadn't clicked that belt in—if I'd told myself I was too tired, or that it didn't matter because I was lying down—I would have gone through the windshield. That's not speculation. It's fact. The force was enough that even with the belt on, I was shaken to my core. Without it? I honestly don't know if I'd be alive to tell the story.

That night didn't just change my life physically—it began to shift something spiritually. I remember sitting in my room later, playing the moment over and over in my head, realizing just how thin the line was between continuing forward in my life... and ending it. And in that quiet moment, a thought settled over me like a whisper:

"You didn't save yourself. That was Me."

I hadn't earned that protection. I wasn't living righteously. I hadn't prayed for safety that night. But grace showed up anyway—uninvited, undeserved, but undeniably present. That seatbelt became a symbol of something bigger: a reminder that even in our sleep, even in our ignorance, God is watching. He sees what's ahead before we ever feel the impact. And sometimes He prompts us, even subtly, to take actions that protect us for reasons we can't yet see.

It would be years before I fully surrendered my life to Jesus. But that night planted something. It was a crack in my illusion of control. A moment where God reached into my recklessness and gently said, "Not yet. There's more for you to do."

Unveiling the Deeper Calling

My affinity for the entrepreneurial path was not a sin of greed but a misalignment of purpose, a truth unveiled in retrospective clarity. The relentless pursuit of entrepreneurial success had been a veil, concealing a more profound calling that urged me to listen beyond the noise of worldly metrics. My journey was not marked by failure for its own sake; rather, it was life's way of stripping away the unnecessary, revealing core truths with unyielding clarity.

Suddenly, I saw my entrepreneurial spirit not as an end but as a precious gift from God, a conduit for deeper service rather than mere financial gain. I understood then what had eluded me in stressful nights—my true purpose was whispered on the winds of a calling yet unexplored, a voice urging me to seek higher, to love wholly, and to live fuller.

Amidst the shadows of uncertainty and the echoes of what once was, I began to recognize that through the ashes of my ventures emerged a light—a new purpose. This transition from mourning to revelation happened not as a clear moment of epiphany but as a slow dawn, gently ushering me to see beyond my losses, to where the seeds of possibility awaited cultivation.

In my heart of hearts, beneath layers of ambition and societal benchmarks, I realized an innate resistance to materialism. Despite being in an environment that constantly touted money as the definitive measure of success, I recognized a profound inner yearning to redefine those metrics, to find joy and purpose beyond the paychecks and polished exteriors of success.

The Realization Moment

This epiphany was not a gentle nudge but a powerful upheaval, rejuvenating me with a zeal for authentic transformation. The seeds for a new journey—a path toward fulfilling my true purpose—were sown amidst the ashes of my past endeavors. And so, I embarked on what I called my "rerouted life," a journey steered by clarity and anchored in a purpose greater than myself, knowing that my true legacy would be not in things but in the transformations I inspired in others.

For me, the collapse of my business was both a devastating personal failure and an unexpected genesis. It was the crack in my meticulously planned life that allowed the light of purpose to seep in.

This chapter explores how such failures are often not the end but catalytic moments that lead us to our God given purpose. Through my experience, we see how life's disappointments can become the fertile ground for spiritual rebirth and reconnection with divine purpose.

As I grappled with the aftermath of my business's collapse, a pivotal moment of reflection emerged, echoing the profound insights of Jeremiah 1:5–10. This scriptural passage underscores key truths, offering a divine framework to comprehend my journey and to inspire those seeking understanding in their own adversities.

The Seven Foundational Truths for Purpose

1. **God Knows Us:** Even before we could understand or define our purpose, God intricately knew the plans for our lives. This divine knowledge offers comfort, reassuring us that we are fully seen and understood at all times.
2. **He has Set Us Apart:** Our personal failures do not define us but serve to refine and prepare us for unique purposes designed by God. Each individual's journey is distinct, highlighting a path filled with intentional significance beyond worldly success.
3. **He Directs Us:** Our paths unfold through divine guidance rather than personal determination, much like God's direction of prophets. This reassures us that He is intricately involved in leading us toward our intended destinies.
4. **He Delivers Us:** God's promise of deliverance remains constant, providing hope and assurance amidst self-doubt and despair. This divine support transitions us

from moments of apparent failure to achievements of spiritual success.

5. **He's Given Us His Word:** God's words empower us, becoming instrumental in pursuing our true calling. With this divine tool, we gain the conviction to articulate and follow the path destined for us.
6. **He's Given Us His Authority:** The spiritual authority imparted to us emboldens us to fearlessly pursue our goals imbued with divine intent. This authority accentuates that purpose-driven actions are rooted in divine will.
7. **He's Given Us the Ability to Do the Work:** God equips us for our mission, commanding us to "build and plant," transforming trials into testimonies. This empowerment affirms that with His guidance, every setback is a springboard to a remarkable new beginning.

Artist's Journey:

An acclaimed artist once found herself in a creative and emotional rut as her vivid canvases, bursting with life and color, repeatedly met rejection from gallery curators. This cycle of disappointment forced her to turn inward, questioning her value and purpose. In her solitude, she grappled with feelings of inadequacy, finding solace only in the art itself—a return to her roots of creation as self-expression rather than validation.

This introspective phase was catalyzed when she visited a local community center and witnessed a child's eyes light up at one of her pieces. It was this unguarded reaction, free from pretension, that sparked her breakthrough. The artist embraced authenticity, allowing her work to resonate on a more profound, personal level, eventually attracting an audience that stretched far beyond the confines of gallery expectations.

Corporate Executive's Journey:

In parallel, a corporate executive, Takahashi, navigated the intricacies of tradition versus innovation within a struggling Japanese manufacturing giant. Despite his outward success, the company's persistent internal crises left him feeling estranged and trapped in a stifling corporate culture that suppressed innovation. His struggle was not just professional but deeply personal, as he faced an internal crisis of cultural identity and loyalty.

The turning point arrived amid economic turbulence when he was tasked with restructuring efforts to survive growing offshore competition. Finding himself at odds with the rigid hierarchy, Takahashi experienced a liberating realization: rather than perpetuate outdated practices, he could lead through innovation. This marked his transformation, allowing him to redefine success by balancing his professional responsibilities with a renewed commitment to personal happiness and family. As the traditional corporate order faded, he evolved into a modern executive who valued personal fulfillment as much as professional achievement.

Let us now take time to dig deeper into a self-reflection guide to help you discover your divine purpose.

Self-Reflection Guide: Discovering Your Divine Purpose

Discovering one's divine purpose can be an enlightening journey that often begins with introspection, and journaling serves as a powerful tool in that process. By engaging with these prompts, readers can embark on a path of self-discovery, unveiling insights that align their lives more closely with their spiritual calling. Each prompt is designed to help individuals reflect deeply on personal experiences and divine guidance, fostering a clearer understanding of their unique path and purpose.

Journaling Prompts Inspired by Jeremiah 1:5-10

1. **God Knows Us**
- Reflect on a time when you truly felt known by God. What events or experiences affirmed your understanding that you are intimately seen and understood by Him?
- Journaling Prompt: "When has an experience made me feel deeply understood by God, and how does this knowledge shape my view of my purpose?"

2. **He Has Set Us Apart**
- Consider moments in your life when you felt unique or set apart for a specific purpose. How have these experiences shaped your journey?

- Journaling Prompt: "What skills, gifts, or circumstances make me unique, and how might God be calling me to use them?"

3. **He Directs Us**
- Recall a specific instance when you felt guided in your decisions. How did acknowledging this direction change your path?
- Journaling Prompt: "Describe a time when I felt God steering my decisions. What did this direction teach me about trust and obedience?"

4. **He Delivers Us**
- Identify circumstances from which you believe God has delivered you. How did these experiences strengthen your faith and resolve?
- Journaling Prompt: "What challenges have I faced where I clearly see God's deliverance, and how does this impact my current outlook?"

5. **He's Given Us His Word**
- Reflect on biblical verses or spiritual teachings that resonate with your current life phase. How do they guide your decisions?
- Journaling Prompt: "Which scriptures or spiritual messages continue to guide my life, and what actions do they inspire?"

6. **He's Given Us His Authority**
- Contemplate times when you felt empowered by divine authority to take action. How did this empowerment influence your achievements?
- Journaling Prompt: "When have I felt emboldened by God's authority in my pursuits, and how did this shape my actions and outcomes?"

7. **The Ability to Do the Work**
- Evaluate moments when you realized you had the necessary abilities to undertake difficult tasks. How has this realization motivated you?
- Journaling Prompt: "Describe an experience where God equipped me with the skills needed to accomplish His work. How did this recognition transform my approach?"

My story underscores a critical reminder: recognizing divine timing in life's setbacks requires active introspection. Such pivotal moments have served as quiet lighthouses that guided me through storms, illuminating a higher calling. For those of you facing disappointments, I can tell you from experience—reflective practices like journaling can reveal patterns and insights, while prayer and meditation open your heart to divine wisdom.

Consider, too, a corporate executive whose prestigious career left her feeling empty. She achieved success, yet each accolade felt hollow, disconnected from a deeper sense of purpose. A transformational turning point came during a volunteer trip, where she rediscovered joy in service. The clarity gained through acts of giving led her down a path that was not only successful by worldly measures but also spiritually enriching. Her story, like mine, reminds us that our greatest callings often arise from deep personal reflection and redirection.

Transformative Resilience: Embracing Adversity as a Path to Purpose

My story is not merely about a business collapse; it speaks to resilience—and the clarity that often follows adversity. That experience became an emblem for what I now see as a divine invitation to grow. What looked like failure was actually a redirection toward greater alignment with God's purpose for my life.

Just as my transformation has been pivotal, I'm reminded of figures like Joseph in the Bible, whose journey from despair to prominence in Egypt shows us a universal truth: our darkest hours can herald significant change and resurgence.

This truth prompts me to explore my own narrative—and I invite you to do the same. Are there recurring themes in your life suggesting a deeper calling? In what spaces can you foster growth and healing in the face of failure? These are the kinds of questions that helped me see beyond disappointment. They still help me, even now, to lean into introspection and embrace change as a sacred path toward purpose.

For those of you grappling with defining your purpose, I urge you—don't rush to conclusions. Let the questions do their work. The following chapters build upon the foundation of my journey, and I offer them with the hope that they will provoke deeper reflection and guide you toward a more profound understanding of your personal calling.

What the Research Tells Us About Purpose

Research indicates that adversity often acts as a catalyst for significant personal growth and transformation. A study from the University of North Carolina highlighted that experiencing adversity enhances one's ability to appreciate life, develop meaningful relationships, and foster resilience. This phenomenon, known as the "adversity effect," reveals that individuals often become more aligned with their inherent strengths and life's greater purpose after navigating tough situations.

The continued exploration of purpose suggests that embracing setbacks as part of a broader narrative enriches life. This aligns with findings from a 2018 study published in the Harvard Business Review, which posited that personal crises frequently lead to increased clarity and motivation toward long-term goals, ultimately fostering a stronger sense of personal fulfillment.

The Continued Journey

As you progress through the subsequent chapters, I encourage you to cultivate a mindset that sees setbacks as stepping stones to higher ground. My transformation is shared not to spotlight my pain, but to serve as both inspiration and motivation for your own journey toward authenticity and truth.

Each chapter that follows is an invitation to engage with the evolving landscape of your purpose. Know this: every failure makes room for resilience. Each question born out of adversity is a chance to grow intentionally and to hear more clearly the voice of God calling you forward.

May your journey through adversity lead to discovery, and may each challenge pave the way for spiritual and personal alignment. Embrace your unique path with confidence, curiosity, and faith, knowing that finding meaning is a journey filled with profound revelations and purpose-driven living.

As this chapter concludes, my story is not just about personal disappointment—it's a call. A beckoning to explore what lies on the other side of pain. I invite you to rediscover and realign with your divine calling. You are not alone on this path of spiritual discovery.

This closing sets the stage for the next chapter, "Chapter 2: The Source of Purpose," where we will delve deeper into understanding the origins of purpose and its diverse manifestations across life's many domains. What revelations await as we uncover the true wellspring of our intentions and desires?

Rerouted Truth: *God doesn't waste our detours—He uses them to expose the purpose that comfort could never reveal.*

CHAPTER 2
The Source of Purpose

On that crisp morning, as Lisa stood enveloped by the silence of the woods, she experienced an epiphany that shifted her entire perspective on life. In that moment of clarity, she realized that her existence was intricately woven into a greater divine plan, and her every step had been leading her toward this understanding. This was not merely a revelation about her life's direction; it was an awakening to the fact that her talents and passions were meant to serve a purpose beyond her own aspirations. Lisa understood that she was called to use her unique gifts in alignment with the divine will, contributing to the unfolding of a larger, sacred narrative.

This chapter explores the multifaceted nature of purpose. For those seeking fulfillment, purpose can be understood through three dimensions: Divine purpose, purpose within the body of Christ, and purpose within God's larger plan. Each aspect provides a unique layer of understanding, pulling individuals from isolation into the tapestry of community and ultimately, a universal mission.

GPS vs. Human Direction

Understanding God's purpose didn't just require surrender—it required me to admit that I wasn't the one with the best directions.

Before smartphones, before GPS apps that could pinpoint your driveway from space, we had street maps and gas station clerks. That was how we got around—and fortunately (or unfortunately), I got pretty good at it. Years of outside sales meant I spent half my life navigating unfamiliar roads, flipping through folded maps, highlighters in the glove box, street names etched into muscle memory.

So when my wife needed directions, she didn't call information. She called me.

"Babe, how do I get to North Point Plaza from the church?"

Sometimes I knew the route immediately. Other times, I'd dig out one of my beloved maps, trace the roads with my finger, and carefully write out step-by-step instructions—complete with landmarks, street names, and estimated turns. I'd hand them to her like sacred scrolls, fully convinced that she would arrive without a hitch.

But almost every time, I'd get a call halfway into her drive.

"Roscoe... I'm lost."

That one phrase carried enough tension to throw off both our moods. I wanted to help—but I couldn't see what she was seeing. I didn't know if she had missed a turn or misread a street sign. I didn't know which direction she was facing or how far off course she had drifted.

"I'm at a gas station next to a blue building," she'd say.

"What street?"

"I don't know... but there's a pizza place across from me."

"I need more than that."

"Can't you just tell me how to get back on track?"

I couldn't.

No matter how clear my instructions had been, I didn't have the real-time information to help her recover. And no matter how badly she wanted my help, I lacked the visibility to guide her from where she actually was—not just from where I thought she would be. The limitations of my knowledge became painfully obvious.

So when GPS finally became available to consumers, I drove straight to the store and bought her one. Not just because it was cool tech—but because it probably saved our marriage.

That little device could do what I never could: meet her exactly where she was. It didn't need her to explain landmarks or which way she was facing. It already knew. And better yet, it didn't shame her for missing a turn. It simply recalculated.

And isn't that what divine purpose is like?

We try to map out life, thinking if we get everything just right, we'll arrive where we're supposed to be. But then we make a wrong turn, lose the signal, or misread the signs. And suddenly, we're calling out for help, trying to explain to God where we think we are—when He already knows.

Jesus doesn't just give us a destination. He joins us in the journey. He doesn't need our perfect positioning to guide us. He's not asking for flawless execution. He simply says, "Follow Me."

That GPS taught me more about grace than I expected. Because while my instructions were conditional, His direction is constant. While my help was limited by my perspective, His help is anchored in omniscience. And while I was frustrated not knowing how to get my wife back on track, Jesus never panics when we feel lost. He simply reroutes us—mercifully, patiently, precisely.

I'm no longer trying to be anyone's personal GPS. But I've come to trust the One who sees the whole map. And when life throws me off course, I don't try to explain every wrong turn—I just ask Him to lead me again. And He always does.

The 3 Aspects of Purpose

1. Divine Purpose: Aligning One's Calling with God's Will

To begin with, divine purpose relates to personal calling—an acute awareness that emerges through spiritual relationship. It is the inner voice that aligns talents and desires with God's will, guiding life's journey along a path of fulfillment. Like Lisa's revelation, finding your divine purpose often feels like uncovering an intrinsic part of oneself, previously buried beneath societal expectations and self-doubt.

The foundational aspect of discovering one's divine purpose begins with recognizing that we are created with purpose by God. Jeremiah 1:5 (ESV) affirms, *"Before I formed you in the womb I knew you, and before you were born I consecrated you; I appointed you a prophet to the nations."* This scripture highlights the predestined nature of our individual callings. Aligning ourselves with God's will requires a commitment to seeking His guidance through prayer and immersing ourselves in His word. Proverbs 19:21 (ESV) reminds us, *"Many are the plans in the mind of a man, but it is the purpose of the LORD that will stand."* This alignment shifts our focus from personal ambitions to embracing God's divine plan, transforming everyday actions into acts of worship and devotion. This foundational understanding sets the stage for recognizing our integral roles within a larger divine community.

For much of my life, I believed purpose was something I had to chase down, wrestle with, or earn through achievement. I chased goals with tireless effort, only to find that my accomplishments, though fulfilling on the surface, left a lingering void in my spirit.

It wasn't until everything I built began to unravel that I was forced to listen more deeply. In the quiet that followed the collapse of my business, I stopped striving and started seeking. For the first time in years, I asked God not for results, but for revelation.

That shift—praying to hear rather than to be heard—marked the beginning of my understanding of divine purpose. I began to realize that God's plans weren't something I needed to architect; they had already been spoken over my life long before I was born. All I needed to do was yield.

2. Purpose in the Body of Christ: The Necessity of Each Person's Role in God's Greater Plan

Next, the purpose in the body of Christ invites individuals to recognize their roles as vital components of a larger community—God's living church. In fellowship, believers find strength, support, and grace that transcends individual capabilities. Just as various parts of the body work together harmoniously, each person has a unique role that complements and enhances the community's mission. This interconnectedness forms a powerful tapestry woven from shared love, faith, and purpose.

In the Body of Christ, each individual's role is crucial for the church's growth and unity. Ephesians 4:16 (ESV) states, *"From whom the whole body, joined and held together by every joint with which it is equipped, when each part is working properly, makes the body grow so that it builds itself up in love."* Similarly, 1 Corinthians 12:12 (ESV) explains, *"For just as the body is one and has many members, and all the members of the body, though many, are one body, so it is with Christ."* These passages illustrate the interdependency essential within the Christian community. Every believer's unique talents and callings—whether in teaching, healing, or encouraging—contribute to the church's mission. This interconnectedness ensures that each member uplifts one another, emphasizing the necessity of diversity in fulfilling God's plan.

Sunday School Teacher Inspiring Young Minds:

Meet Sarah, a vibrant Sunday school teacher whose passion for storytelling captivates her students. Every Sunday, Sarah transforms biblical tales into engaging adventures, sparking curiosity and wonder in young minds. Her storytelling is not just about imparting lessons; it's about planting seeds of faith. One day, she noticed a particularly quiet child, Liam, showing newfound interest and asking profound questions about the stories. This engagement encouraged Liam to express his thoughts and dreams in class, illustrating how Sarah's nurturing spirit helped him blossom. Her impact extends beyond the classroom, as students carry these lessons into their daily lives, embodying the values taught through her dynamic sessions.

Caretaker Providing Comfort to the Elderly:

George, a retired nurse, has dedicated his post-career life to volunteering at a local care home, where he offers comfort and companionship to the elderly. One resident, Mrs. Thompson, found solace in George's consistent visits and kind words. Despite her initial reluctance to engage, George's patience and humor eventually broke through her stoic exterior, revealing a lively storyteller with a treasure trove of memories. These interactions not only provided companionship but also allowed Mrs. Thompson to share her wisdom and stories, enriching the community's tapestry. George's role exemplifies Christ's love through action, bringing warmth and connection to those in their twilight years.

Community Leader Guiding with Vision:

In another part of the city, Pastor Miguel, a community leader, navigates his congregation through times of change with enduring vision and steadfast guidance. Under his leadership, the church has launched numerous outreach programs that address local needs, from food drives to youth mentorship initiatives. During one pivotal meeting, Pastor Miguel proposed a new initiative inspired by community feedback—a digital literacy program aimed at empowering both young and old in a rapidly evolving world. His ability to listen, adapt, and act on community input ensures that the church remains a beacon of hope and resilience, fulfilling its mission in alignment with divine teachings. His leadership not only guides the congregation spiritually but also mobilizes them into action, transforming individual talents into collective success.

Understanding this dynamic prepares us to explore our individual and collective contributions to the grand narrative of God's eternal design.

As I studied these scriptures, I began to see myself as more than an isolated individual trying to recover from a loss. I was part of something greater—an eternal body. Even though my business was gone, my ability to serve had not disappeared. God hadn't just gifted me with skills to create income—He had placed those skills within me to edify others.

I realized I had a role to play, not only in the church but in the lives of those God placed around me. This realization helped me move from shame into service. No longer was I focused on rebuilding a reputation—I wanted to contribute to something sacred.

3. Purpose in the Plan of God: Our Role in the Great Commission

Finally, understanding purpose within God's plan requires recognizing the broader perspective—our small but significant role in His eternal design. This divine view elevates personal purpose to one of universal significance, where each action contributes to a grand narrative authored by God. Like a master weaver designing an intricate tapestry, God's plan includes every thread, with each life shaping the larger story through its unique color and texture. Every personal calling, whether in ministry, business, or daily life, serves as a crucial thread in the expansive canvas of the Great Commission, intertwining our individual paths with the collective mission of spreading the gospel.

Ultimately, understanding our purpose involves engaging with God's global mission, as expressed in the Great Commission. Matthew 28:18-20 (ESV) charges, *"And Jesus came and said to them, 'All authority in heaven and on earth has been given to me. Go therefore and make disciples of all nations, baptizing them in the name of the Father and of the Son and of the Holy Spirit, teaching them to observe all that I have commanded you. And behold, I am with you always, to the end of the age.'"* This is further reinforced in 1 Timothy 2:4 (ESV), where Paul notes that God *"desires all people to be saved and to come to the knowledge of the truth."* These scriptures direct us to frame our lives around the mission of spreading the gospel, ensuring our everyday efforts reflect the larger narrative of God's kingdom. Engaging in this level of purpose demands an intentional life where actions and interactions consistently reveal our commitment to God's expansive plan.

Through these layers of purpose, individuals are invited to see their existence as an integral part of God's divine framework. This multidimensional understanding encourages believers to actively engage with their spiritual journeys, transforming personal growth into the collective elevation of the church and society at large. Whether one works in a church, hospital, school, or marketplace, aligning personal goals with the Great Commission enhances fulfillment and expands our reach, echoing the eternal call to spread love, wisdom, and salvation.

For example, an individual may feel led to pursue a career in healthcare. Though initially driven by a personal passion for healing, through prayer and reflection, they may begin to view their work as a ministry, caring not only for the physical but also the spiritual needs of their patients. In doing so, their personal ambition aligns with a greater purpose—contributing to God's plan of compassion and service, thereby weaving individual purpose into the fabric of a global mission.

The Power of God's Plan

Consider the story of a community revitalized through shared purpose. In a small town, local churches once divided by doctrine began collaborating on a community outreach program. This shared mission invited everyone to contribute according to their strengths—some managed logistics, others provided care, and still more spread words of encouragement and faith. Through this unity, the community prospered spiritually and socially, their combined efforts a testament to the power of working within God's plan.

From these narratives, we glean that purpose is a complex but coherent symphony of personal calling, community involvement, and divine orchestration. Readers seeking their own purpose might begin by listening closely to their heart's whispers—journaling insights often reveal patterns and desires. Engaging with community—participating in church activities, volunteer work, or faith groups—can offer new roles, while prayer and meditation provide spiritual alignment with God's wider purpose.

It took time, but I eventually began to understand that my life wasn't meant to be a self-contained success story. My experiences—the wins and the wounds—were meant to become testimonies that point others toward God.

What I had viewed as career failure was actually the beginning of ministry. Not a pulpit or a title, but a life lived in alignment with the Great Commission. I began to see how encouraging others, sharing my story, and offering guidance were all part of making disciples—of reflecting the hope I had found. Helping others to reroute.

This discovery lifted my eyes. I was no longer burdened by what I lost; I was compelled by what I could give. I wasn't just called to succeed. I was called to serve.

Reflection Exercise: Assessing Your Level of Purpose

In our journey of faith and purpose, it's essential to identify which level of God's purpose we're currently engaging with and discern where He might be leading us. This exercise is designed to guide you through personal reflection and evaluation, helping you uncover insights into your divine calling.

Preparation

Begin by finding a quiet space where you can relax and focus without interruptions. Have your journal and a pen ready to capture your reflections.

Step 1: Assessing Your Current Purpose

A. Divine Purpose

Reflect on your daily life:
- Think about your personal goals and desires. Do they align more with fulfilling God's will or pursuing your ambitions?
- Journaling Prompt: "In what ways does my current life reflect an alignment with God's divine plans for me?"

Realigning Desires

There was a season when I couldn't tell the difference between ambition and calling. I had goals, but they were shaped more by the pressure to succeed than by a desire to serve. As I began to surrender those ambitions in prayer, I noticed a shift. I started wanting what God wanted for me. My prayer changed from "Lord, bless my plans" to "Lord, reveal Yours." That's when I realized divine purpose wasn't a destination—it was a daily surrender to walk in His will.

B. Purpose in the Body of Christ

Consider your role within your faith community:

- Reflect on how you contribute to your church or spiritual community. Do you feel your gifts are being actively utilized for collective growth?
- Journaling Prompt: "How am I participating in the Body of Christ, and what impact does my role have on its function and unity?"

Finding My Role Again

After losing my business, I struggled with identity. So much of who I thought I was had been wrapped in what I did. But in the Body of Christ, I discovered that value isn't based on performance—it's based on purpose. I didn't need a title or a platform to matter. I began serving quietly in areas where help was needed: greeting newcomers, praying with someone after service. Little by little, God showed me that my role still mattered. I wasn't sidelined—I was repositioned.

C. Purpose in the Plan of God

Analyze your engagement with the broader mission:

- Contemplate your involvement in spreading the gospel and serving others. Are you actively participating in the Great Commission?
- Journaling Prompt: "What actions am I currently taking that align with Jesus's Great Commission to spread His teachings?"

Seeing the Bigger Mission

It hit me one day during a simple conversation with a young man who had just gone through a layoff. I shared what I had learned through my own failures, and by the end of our talk, he said, "You gave me hope." That's when I realized I was living the Great Commission—right there, in everyday moments. I didn't need a plane ticket to fulfill God's mission. I just needed a willingness to share what He had done in my life. That moment helped me see that purpose wasn't about platform—it was about people.

Step 2: Discern God's Leading

- Pray for guidance, asking God to reveal areas where He wants you to grow or shift.
- Journaling Prompt: "In which direction do I sense God leading me, and how can I prepare to follow this path?"

Learning to Listen Again

When I finally slowed down enough to pray without an agenda, I started to hear things I hadn't noticed before. God wasn't shouting—He was whispering. Leading me toward simplicity, toward healing, toward others who needed to hear the story I was trying to forget.

It wasn't just about where He was leading me—it was about who He was asking me to become in the process. I sensed that my next season wouldn't look like my last, and that was okay. I started journaling not just prayers, but questions. And in those questions, I began to see the new path unfolding.

God was calling me to walk lighter, to trust deeper, and to serve with what I had left—not wait until I had it all figured out.

Step 3: Actionable Steps

- Based on your reflections, consider what small, concrete steps can be taken to progress in each area. Identify at least one actionable step for each level of purpose.
- Journaling Prompt: "What specific step can I take today to align more closely with God's purpose in my life?"

Starting Small, Moving Forward

After those moments of clarity, I knew I had to do more than just feel inspired—I had to act. But the steps didn't need to be grand.

For divine purpose, I committed to starting each day with ten minutes of prayer before touching my phone. For my role in the Body of Christ, I volunteered once a week, even if it meant just stacking chairs or cleaning up after service. And for the Great

Commission, I began reaching out to one person each week—just to check in, encourage, or listen.

These weren't impressive actions, but they were intentional. And they helped me re-enter life with purpose. Obedience in the small things began to unlock bigger opportunities I never saw coming.

Conclude your session with a prayer of dedication, asking God for courage and wisdom to pursue His purpose more fully. This exercise clarifies your current position and encourages mindful progression toward a more spiritually aligned life. Regular practice can yield profound insights and renewed motivation to live purposefully within God's divine framework.

Returning to Lisa's moment in the woods, her story embodies the essence of discovery—personal revelation that expands when shared within a community. This reflection reaffirms that purpose, while deeply personal, gains richness and depth when lived in communion with others. As this chapter nears its closing, it not only inspires action toward discovering one's multifaceted purpose but also sets the stage for the next chapter, which will explore how uncovering individual gifts and talents enhances this journey of living purposefully.

Comparing God's Purpose: Sarah and Moses

The stories of Sarah and Moses from the Bible provide profound lessons on understanding and embracing divine purpose. Their journeys are rich with insights into how God calls and equips His people for unique roles within His divine plan.

Sarah's Journey: Embracing God's Promise

Sarah, originally named Sarai, embodies faith and the profound patience necessary to trust in God's promises. Her story, woven throughout Genesis, centers on her becoming the mother of nations despite years of barrenness. Imagine her laughter tinged with disbelief as she overhears God's promise: *"Is anything too hard for the Lord?"* (Genesis 18:14). Even after the detour of Ishmael's birth through Hagar, her heart clung to hope—a whispered promise that came to fruition with the birth of Isaac, fulfilling God's word. Her journey resonates with anyone who has faced delayed dreams, reminding us that divine purpose unfolds in its perfect time, even when doubt seeks to overshadow faith.

Moses' Mission: Leading with Divine Authority

Moses is a towering figure of divine encounter and transformational leadership, as seen in Exodus. Cast adrift as an infant to escape Pharaoh's decree, Moses' story is one of survival and providence. His encounter at the burning bush is charged with holy awe and hesitation. *"Who am I that I should go to Pharaoh?"* he questions, doubting his worthiness. God's response is clear and powerful: *"I will be with you"* (Exodus 3:11-12), a divine assurance that transforms his reluctance into resolve. Despite his initial self-doubt, Moses becomes a vessel of God's power, leading the Israelites to freedom. His story underscores the courage required to embrace a calling that seems beyond our means, illustrating how God's strength compensates for personal inadequacies.

Interweaving Themes of Purpose

Both Sarah and Moses experienced moments of doubt and reluctance but ultimately fulfilled significant roles within God's plan.

Their stories highlight interconnected truths about divine purpose:

1. **Divine Timing:** Both narratives emphasize the significance of God's timing. Sarah's eventual motherhood at an advanced age and Moses' emergence as a leader in the wilderness illustrate that God's purposes often unfold over lifetimes and through complex circumstances.
2. **Faith and Obedience:** Sarah and Moses teach us that fulfilling divine purpose involves faith and obedience, even when God's plans seem implausible. They demonstrate that divine purpose requires a shift from human doubts to God's assurances.
3. **God's Provision:** In both stories, God provides what is necessary to fulfill His plans—Sarah's eventual conception of Isaac and the signs and wonders Moses performed. This underscores God's faithfulness in equipping those He calls.
4. **Individual Purpose Within a Greater Plan:** Sarah and Moses played integral roles in a broader divine narrative. Sarah's role ensured the continuation of Abraham's lineage, while Moses laid the foundational laws for Israel. Their lives testify to the fact that personal callings contribute to God's larger story.

These stories inspire us to discern our purpose through trust in divine timing and reliance on God's provision. Each journey, marked by unique challenges and blessings, contributes to a grand narrative shaped by God's loving sovereignty. Engaging with our purpose involves patience, faith, and unwavering trust that God's plans, much like in the lives of Sarah and Moses, are unfolding as intended.

Prepare to journey deeper in "Chapter 3: Uncovering Your Gifts and Talents," where the focus will shift to identifying and embracing the unique strengths that God has placed within each of us, propelling us toward living out our fullest potential within His divine framework. Consider how your unique gifts might not only serve you but play a critical role in delivering God's message to the world around you. What talents lie within you, waiting to be discovered and aligned with your highest calling?

Rerouted Truth: *True purpose doesn't begin with your plans but with God's design for your life before you were even born.*

CHAPTER 3
Uncovering Your Gifts and Talents

In a quaint village nestled amidst rolling hills, there lived a young shepherd named David. Known for his ruddy appearance and the ever-present sling by his side, David was seen by many as merely a boy tending sheep. Yet, as dawn broke over the hillside, anxiety swept through the camp as the Israelites braced against the taunts of the fearsome giant, Goliath. The air was thick with tension, every breath sharp and heavy like an incoming storm.

On that day, amidst the clamor and unease, David's heart danced to a rhythm divinely orchestrated. The whispers he had long tuned into seemed to crescendo, surging in conviction. As he approached the trembling ranks of Israel, he recalled the whispers of his time alone tending his flock, *"Your servant has killed both the lion and the bear."* (1 Samuel 17:36).

Braving the doubtful gazes of his fellow countrymen and the disdainful glare of King Saul, David's resolve did not falter. "Let no one lose heart on account of this Philistine; your servant will go and fight him," he declared boldly. The chill of Saul's armor against his skin did little to comfort him—clunky and foreign, it was a poor substitute for the confidence etched on his heart by divine assurances.

Standing before Goliath, David's senses sharpened; the giant's voice boomed like thunder across the valley, laden with scorn. "Am I a dog, that you come at me with sticks?" Goliath sneered. It was then, with a steady hand on his sling and a stone cool in his palm, that David felt an exhilarating clarity. "You come to me with a sword and a spear, but I come to you in the name of the Lord Almighty," he retorted, his voice ringing clear and true.

In that moment of reckoning, David's arm swung back, each movement fluid, the stone released with prophetic precision; the air sang with tension. Thud. The giant fell, and with him, the doubts and fears of an entire nation crumbled, their echoes replaced by the jubilant victory cry that swept over the hills.

This narrative invites us to ponder: "Do you know what sets you apart?" As you reflect, consider the divine whispers in your life, echoes of purpose guiding each step, awaiting their moment to silence the giants before you.

Each of us carries unique gifts and talents, intricately woven into our beings by God to guide us along our purposeful paths. Identifying and embracing these gifts are crucial steps toward fulfilling our divine calling. Like David, discovering these talents involves a journey of self-exploration and faith. It requires us to listen deeply to our internal desires and to the subtle nudges that direct us toward activities where our hearts feel aligned with God's purposes.

For years, I thought I knew my strengths—strategic thinking, leadership, communication. These had been praised in business meetings. But when the business collapsed, I began to question whether those abilities were truly spiritual gifts or just marketplace skills I had refined over time.

It wasn't until I slowed down and started serving in smaller, quieter ways—encouraging someone after a prayer meeting, helping organize church events, mentoring a young man wrestling with direction—that something inside me awakened. I started seeing patterns. The feedback I got was less about performance and more about presence. People would say, "You helped me feel seen," or "You gave me clarity." That's when I began to understand that my gift wasn't just leadership—it was exhortation. God had given me a voice not just to direct, but to uplift.

This realization didn't come in a dramatic moment. It came in layers—each conversation, each act of service, each quiet moment confirming what the Holy Spirit was revealing. My gifts had always been there. I had just been looking for them in the wrong places.

The Mentor Story

Some gifts are discovered in silence, others through trials—but sometimes, they're uncovered through the kindness of someone who sees you before you see yourself.

It started the summer before my freshman year at Virginia Tech. I had taken a temp job through an agency that placed me at a downtown law firm. I was eighteen, green, and eager to make a good impression, but like most young people stepping into a new environment, I had no idea what I was walking into.

That's when I met Dennis.

Dennis was the manager I'd be reporting to, and from the moment we shook hands, something about his presence stood out. He carried himself with a quiet strength—kind but clear, confident but not arrogant. Over the next few weeks, I realized I wasn't just working a summer job—I was being mentored, even if I didn't yet have language for it.

One day, I made a bold comment in a meeting—something about how we needed to "make sure certain people got their act together so the rest of us could move forward." I said it casually, without malice, but it was immature. Dennis didn't scold me or embarrass me in front of the team. Instead, later that afternoon, he pulled me aside with a calm sincerity.

"Roscoe," he said, "I know what you meant earlier, and I appreciate your initiative. But as a leader—even a potential one—it's not just about calling things out. It's about calling people up."

That landed differently.

He wasn't correcting me to win a point. He was shepherding my thinking—guiding me not just in what to say, but how to see. That conversation lasted less than five minutes, but it left a permanent mark. Even now, when I mentor others, that memory comes back. It reminds me that redirection, when done with compassion, can be a doorway into transformation. And that leadership, in its purest form, looks a lot like discipleship.

Dennis and I stayed connected beyond that summer. The next year, after my freshman year, I returned to the same firm—and to his team. He welcomed me back, no questions asked, and continued to invest in me like I was more than just temporary help.

After my sophomore year, I needed full-time work. College was becoming increasingly expensive, and I was at a crossroads. Once again, Dennis made room for me. He didn't just find me a place on the team—he opened a door. That opportunity gave me the stability I needed, but more than that, it gave me a sense of identity. I was no longer just a student or an employee. I was someone being called higher.

Looking back, that relationship was more than mentorship—it was divine orchestration. God placed someone in my life who wasn't just ahead of me professionally but emotionally. Someone who reflected the love of Christ—not through sermons but through stewardship. Dennis didn't preach. He practiced. He paid attention. And in doing so, he played a pivotal role in shaping the direction of my life.

That season at the law firm became the nexus for my future business. The structure, the strategy, the client service mindset—it all began there. But even deeper than the professional skills I learned, I absorbed the posture of a servant-leader. That seed—planted in the quiet gestures of a mentor—would one day grow into the roots of this book.

Because when someone believes in you before you believe in yourself, it becomes easier to believe that God does, too.

Passion and Purpose: Complementary Forces for Fulfillment

Passion is the spark—the fervent drive that fuels what we love doing. It is often visceral, a deep-seated excitement that propels us forward. Purpose, on the other hand, serves as the compass; it is the reason behind our actions and the guiding principle that aligns our lives with a larger mission. While passion is tied to what excites us, purpose is connected to what fulfills us. Discovering both is essential for true fulfillment because while passion ignites our desire to act, purpose ensures those actions resonate with deeper meaning. Together, they create a harmonious balance where our endeavors are both joyfully pursued and meaningfully aligned. As we explore this integration further, consider how your own talents blend your passions with your divine purpose, leading to a life enriched by both enthusiasm and direction.

Success Stories: Uncovering Gifts and Talents

Story 1: The Visionary Artist

In a bustling city renowned for its creative vibrancy, Julia was a marketing executive whose life seemed fulfilled by professional success and a steady routine. However, an undercurrent of dissatisfaction gnawed at her, a pervasive sense that something essential was missing. Despite her achievements, she yearned for a deeper connection to her work. An unexpected gift of a watercolor set for her birthday became a pivotal moment of self-discovery. What began as a hobby soon transformed into a daily practice of painting, each brushstroke revealing a dormant passion she had long buried beneath conventional career expectations.

Julia's journey of uncovering her artistic gift was not immediate nor entirely smooth. Encouraged by friends who marveled at her creations, she began showcasing her work at local community centers. The overwhelmingly positive response revealed not only a latent talent but also a profound ability to evoke emotion and connection through her art. This revelation was empowering, redefining her self-perception from corporate professional to creator with a unique voice.

As she delved deeper into this newfound passion, Julia made the bold decision to pursue art full-time. This meant leaving the security of a corporate career and stepping into the uncertainty of the art world. Her commitment was not without challenges; however, it was rooted in an authentic understanding of her purpose—expressing beauty and exploring human experiences through her paintings. Over time, her talent became a bridge to other like-minded creatives, allowing her to foster a supportive community. Julia's story illustrates how uncovering innate gifts and aligning them with purpose can lead to personal fulfillment and community impact.

Story 2: The Transformative Teacher

Marcus had been a dedicated schoolteacher for nearly a decade, beloved by his students and respected by colleagues. Yet, something within him felt unfulfilled; he sensed a lingering call to impart more than standard curriculum knowledge. Driven by this intuition, Marcus began experimenting with interactive storytelling in his lessons, hoping to engage and inspire his students more deeply.

One day, during a discussion about conquering self-doubt, Marcus shared his personal story of overcoming adversity. To his surprise, the students were captivated, their participation enthusiastic, and their understanding of the subject deepened significantly. This method of teaching through personal storytelling resonated profoundly, encouraging students to express themselves more openly. Realizing the power of his experiences and storytelling abilities to inspire, Marcus refined this approach, integrating it formally into his teaching practice.

As a result, Marcus's classes transformed into a dynamic space where students discovered new perspectives and strengths within themselves. His innovative methods attracted attention from educational boards, leading him to develop workshops for other educators on integrating storytelling as an instructional tool. Through this, Marcus not only unveiled his unique talent for inspiring through narrative but also impacted the educational landscape, promoting a more engaged and compassionate approach to learning.

Uncovering Your Gifts

Both Julia and Marcus demonstrate that uncovering one's gifts and aligning them with purpose can lead to profound personal transformation and societal contributions. Their stories inspire readers to look beyond conventional paths, encouraging exploration and embrace of unique talents, enriching their lives and the communities they touch.

Self-exploration is a key component of this discovery. It begins with asking ourselves critical questions: What activities make time disappear? What tasks bring joy and satisfaction? Reflection through journaling or meditating on daily experiences can reveal patterns that point to individual strengths. Engaging in new experiences and pushing beyond comfort zones often uncovers hidden talents. Embracing our gifts in faith allows us to confront challenges with confidence and resilience.

The spiritual significance of recognizing individual gifts is profound. Each talent bestowed upon us is a thread in the larger fabric of God's creation, meant to serve not only our personal growth but the betterment of our communities. The biblical account of David illustrates this: his talents as a musician and a warrior not only defined his journey but shaped a nation. Similarly, our discovered talents can elevate not only our lives but those of others, reflecting God's glory through acts of service and love.

Just as biblical teachings reveal the divine nature of our talents, scientific exploration of strengths psychology offers insights that align seamlessly with this spiritual framework. Both perspectives underscore the importance of discovering and leveraging our unique abilities. By understanding the harmony between spiritual insights and scientific research, we gain a comprehensive view of our potential, guiding us to use our gifts effectively within both personal and communal contexts.

Scientific Insights on Uncovering Gifts and Talents

In the realm of uncovering personal gifts and talents, scientific insights offer invaluable tools that illuminate pathways previously obscured by conventional limitations. Understanding the science behind individual strengths empowers us to unlock our full potential, aligning innate abilities with purposeful living.

One foundational concept in this exploration comes from strengths psychology. Grounded in positive psychology, this field examines how individuals can identify and leverage their unique strengths—not merely to improve productivity, but to enhance overall well-being and life satisfaction. According to Dr. Martin

Seligman, a pioneering figure in this field, focusing on what people do well rather than their weaknesses results in higher levels of individual and collective fulfillment.

Psychological assessments, such as CliftonStrengths, offer systematic approaches to uncovering these talents. By analyzing responses to targeted questions, such assessments reveal dominant themes in personality and behavior. These insights allow individuals to consciously focus on areas where they naturally excel, fostering an environment of growth and self-improvement. This aligns with the narrative of discovering divine gifts within, providing a structured approach to understanding one's God-given talents.

Cognitive neuroscience sheds light on the mechanics of talent development. Research into neuroplasticity—the brain's ability to reorganize itself by forming new neural connections—suggests that skills and talents can be developed and strengthened throughout life. This scientific principle underlies the biblical assertion of developing one's gifts, as seen in the parable of the talents, where even small measures, when planted and nurtured, can yield substantial growth.

Moreover, studies in motivation and learning emphasize the role of intrinsic motivation—performing an activity for its inherent satisfaction—over extrinsic rewards. This intrinsic drive, often linked with a sense of calling or purpose, underpins our passion for nurturing our gifts. When aligned with spiritual objectives, this motivation becomes a powerful catalyst for innovation and perseverance, echoing the biblical narrative of using one's talents for a higher cause.

Notably, interdisciplinary research has demonstrated that environments rich in possibility and encouragement are crucial for talent development. Just as the parable advises that talents should not be hidden but invested, creating supportive communities encourages individuals to explore and expand their God-given abilities. These communities act as gardens where talents are sown, cultivated, and brought to fruition for collective upliftment.

Finally, the concept of deliberate practice, emphasized in psychological research by Anders Ericsson, highlights focused and sustained efforts to improve performance. This principle guides the notion that God-given gifts are perfected through dedication and perseverance—an idea firmly rooted in biblical teachings. Engaging in structured practice and seeking opportunities for feedback and reflection nurtures talents, preparing them for effective service in God's kingdom.

By integrating these scientific insights with spiritual truths, individuals are better equipped to uncover and cultivate their unique gifts and talents. This synergy empowers believers not only to flourish personally but also to contribute significantly to their communities and fulfill their divine purposes. This blend of science and spirituality provides a robust framework for understanding and developing personal gifts, reinforcing the journey toward a purposeful and enriched life.

Practical tools can aid in discovering personal strengths. Consider frameworks such as spiritual gifts tests, personality assessments, or feedback from trusted community members. These tools offer insights that might confirm what God has already placed in your heart. They act as mirrors, reflecting how others perceive your strengths, often validating intuitive hunches about talents waiting to be fully embraced.

Self-Assessment Tool: Discovering Your Gifts and Talents

As we embark on the journey of uncovering our unique gifts and talents, this self-assessment tool serves as a guide to introspect and reflect upon the innate abilities bestowed by God. Engaging with these questions will help you identify your strengths and align them with a meaningful and purpose-driven life.

Part 1: Personal Reflection

1. **Identify Joyful Activities:**
- When do you feel most alive and engaged? Reflect on activities that make time fly and bring you joy, as these often reveal your innate talents. Consider, "What activities have consistently brought me joy throughout my life?"

2. **Evaluate Natural Skills:**
- Think about moments when you experienced a transcendent sense of flow. These instances often highlight your natural abilities. Journal about a time when you easily accomplished a task or received compliments for a specific skill. Ask yourself, "What do I do effortlessly that others find challenging?"

3. **Acknowledge Your Passions:**
- Identify areas where your passions align with your skills. Passion fuels motivation, so clarify what excites you. Reflect on the question, "Which topics or causes evoke a deep emotional response in me?"

Part 2: External Feedback

1. **Gather Honest Opinions:**
- Seek feedback from trusted peers or mentors about your strengths. Often, others can recognize talents we overlook. Ask them, "What do you see as my key strengths and talents?"

2. **Analyze Past Experiences:**
- Review significant achievements and failures, as both can reveal skills you excelled in or developed further. Consider, "What skills have I honed through overcoming challenges?"

Part 3: Alignment with Higher Purpose

1. **Spiritual Alignment:**
- Reflect on how your talents can align with spiritual goals or community service to fulfill God's greater plan. Ponder the question, "How can my talents contribute to God's work in the community?"

2. **Visualize the Future:**
- Imagine your future self actively using your identified talents in ways that enhance both your life and the lives

of others. Write a vision statement that addresses how your talents can fulfill your purpose.

Action Steps:

After completing the self-assessment, you can take several practical steps to translate your insights into daily action, ensuring your talents are recognized and effectively utilized:

1. **Set Clear Goals:** Based on the talents and skills identified, establish specific, measurable goals that align with your insights. These goals should be actionable and time-bound, such as developing a particular skill, applying your talents in a community project, or starting a new personal initiative that harnesses your strengths.
2. **Develop a Plan:** Create a strategic action plan outlining the steps required to achieve your goals. This plan should include short-term actions, like enrolling in a relevant course, and long-term strategies, such as pursuing a career path aligned with your identified talents.
3. **Take Consistent Action:** Dedicate daily or weekly time to work on your goals. Establishing a routine not only reinforces commitment but also helps integrate new habits and skills into your daily life, ensuring that talent development becomes second nature.
4. **Seek Feedback and Adjust:** Regularly solicit feedback from mentors or peers to gain fresh perspectives and ensure you are on track. Be open to adjusting your plan based on this feedback and any new insights that arise.

5. **Reflect and Celebrate Milestones:** Schedule regular reflection sessions to review your progress, celebrate achievements, and identify areas for improvement. Reflecting on both successes and setbacks provides valuable learning experiences and motivation to continue evolving.

By following these steps, you can seamlessly integrate insights from your self-assessment into your everyday life, ensuring that your unique gifts and talents are fully leveraged for personal growth and divine purpose.

Recognizing Your Gifts

Michelle, a corporate leader, was recognized for her strategic acumen and ability to navigate complex business challenges. However, beneath her professional exterior lay a persistent nudge—a call to mentorship that she couldn't ignore. Despite her success, Michelle often questioned her capacity to genuinely impact others. She wondered, "Am I capable of leading others beyond profits and productivity?"

Her moment of doubt crystallized during a particularly demanding quarter, where pressures mounted, and she felt stretched beyond her limits. It was during a church retreat, amid the raw honesty and shared vulnerabilities of fellow attendees, that Michelle confronted her fears. "Why do I feel inadequate in guiding others when I'm dedicated to nurturing their growth?" she pondered aloud, feeling a mix of vulnerability and resolve.

A turning point came when she led a small group discussion at the retreat, sharing her insights and struggles. To her surprise, participants expressed how her words resonated deeply and inspired them. This unexpected response gradually dissolved her self-doubt. Encouraged by this experience, Michelle realized her gift for guiding others extended beyond the corporate world; it was a divine calling intertwined with her spiritual journey.

Embracing this revelation, she committed to mentorship more intentionally, not just in her professional environment but within her community. Michelle's transition involved setting clear goals for her personal growth as a mentor, seeking feedback, and cultivating a network of like-minded individuals who shared her passion for empowering others. Through this, Michelle not only enhanced her career but also enriched the lives of those around her, embodying the profound impact that true mentorship can have. Her journey invites us to reflect: "What fears must we overcome to fully embrace our gifts?"

The process of uncovering your gifts is not solitary. Community feedback is vital, as those around us often see our strengths more clearly than we do. Engaging in open dialogue within a supportive faith community can illuminate talents hidden in plain sight. Friends, family, and fellow believers provide invaluable perspectives that confirm, challenge, and expand our understanding of our own abilities.

Learn the Lesson

The lesson is clear: uncovering and embracing your gifts fosters a deeper connection to your divine purpose. These gifts are not random but divinely aligned with God's plan for your life. As you journey inward, listen to your heart, seek divine counsel, and engage with your community to see your talents come alive. This process enriches your journey and deepens your impact on the world around you.

Returning to David's story, we find a simple shepherd boy whose talents carved paths for leadership and legacy. His journey from shepherd to king inspires us to recognize that our gifts, however humble, are instruments in the divine symphony of life. Embracing your talents is an act of faith, transforming individual potential into purposeful action.

As this chapter closes, let it ignite in you the desire to explore your unique gifts with curiosity and courage. Prepare to venture into "Chapter 4: Passion vs. Purpose," where we will examine how the intertwining of these elements propels us further along our God-given paths, aligning passion with divine purpose to enrich our spiritual journey and impact. Reflect on the unique gifts you've discovered: How do they align with your passions, and how might these intertwined elements guide you toward a more fulfilling life? What paths may unfold as you embrace the synergy of passion and purpose in your personal journey?

Rerouted Truth: *Your gifts aren't random—they are spiritual tools assigned to you for the battles you were born to win.*

CHAPTER 4
Passion vs. Purpose

In a world where countless individuals chase fleeting ambitions, it often seems that many people chase passion more than purpose—driven by what brings immediate joy rather than what offers lasting impact. Yet, amid this perspective, a profound truth unfolds: passion and purpose, while distinct, are intricately intertwined, each essential for fulfilling a God-given calling.

Passion vs. Purpose: A Comparative Understanding

Passion ignites enthusiasm and excitement within us; it is emotion-driven, often leading us to activities that bring joy and fulfillment. This fervor propels us forward and keeps us engaged in the pursuits we love. Purpose, however, serves as our guiding compass, offering long-term direction by aligning our actions with a broader mission or goal. It provides a deeper sense of meaning, ensuring our daily activities contribute to an overarching objective.

While passion fuels our journey, purpose is the roadmap that keeps us on course, intertwining closely to help us achieve a life of both joy and impact. Reflect on how your unique gifts align with your passions as you prepare for the exploration in Chapter 4: Passion vs. Purpose. Consider this harmonious blend a pathway to genuine fulfillment and contribution.

I Was Confused for Years

For years, I mistook passion for purpose. I was driven—fueled by excitement, ambition, and the thrill of achievement. When I was building my business, every goal reached felt like confirmation that I was doing exactly what I was meant to do. But underneath the surface, something didn't sit right. I was busy, even successful by many standards, but I wasn't fulfilled. There was a persistent ache, a quiet question I kept pushing aside: Is this really it?

It wasn't until everything I had built began to unravel that I could finally hear God clearly. When the noise of performance and productivity faded, I realized I had been pouring all my energy into something that didn't feed my soul. My passion had led me to build, but my purpose—God's purpose—was calling me to serve.

God began showing me the difference in unexpected moments. Conversations where someone said, "What you said helped me see things differently." Situations where I was no longer striving for attention but felt compelled to pour into others, to listen, to encourage. That's when I understood—passion had been the fuel, but purpose was the direction. And for too long, I had been driving fast with no map.

Through prayer, reflection, and a lot of honest soul-searching, God revealed that my voice wasn't just meant for pitching ideas or rallying teams—it was meant to edify, to guide, to uplift. I began surrendering my need for outcomes and started embracing obedience. No longer chasing opportunities, I started asking God to place me where I could make the most impact—even if it didn't look impressive on paper.

"I Think I've Been Shot"

Sometimes purpose whispers. Other times, it breaks into your world uninvited, without warning, and leaves you stunned on a summer sidewalk.

I was ten years old, just a kid growing up on the south side of Alexandria. It was the kind of community where people looked out for each other. Not wealthy, not flashy—just honest families doing their best to make life work. My dad worked two jobs, and my mom picked up whatever side hustles she could find to help support the family. That summer, she was delivering phone books.

Now, this was the pre-digital era—no cell phones, no Google Maps, no way to "click here for the number." Back then, that thick yellow-paged phone book was your lifeline to everything: doctors, plumbers, churches, restaurants. And these weren't lightweight deliveries. Each book was like carrying a small encyclopedia. My mom would load stacks into the trunk and backseat of our old car, then hop out at each block, grab a few, and deliver them to the front steps or into small apartment buildings—one by one.

My siblings and I made a game out of it. We weren't delivering books, but we were her support team. We'd wait on the sidewalk while she went into a building, then when she came out for more books, we'd help move them closer to the next address. It was summer. No school. No schedule. Just the sun beating down on the pavement and the rhythmic hustle of my mom grinding to make ends meet.

We'd worked our way near the end of the block. My brother, sister, and I were standing in front of a four-unit apartment building, laughing about something only kids find funny, when I heard it:

POP.

Not a firecracker. Not a car backfiring. Something sharper. More final.

Instantly, a hot, jarring pain shot through my right leg.

I looked down, confused, rubbing my thigh through my polyester pants. That's when I saw it—a perfectly round hole in the fabric. My mind raced to make sense of it. Then came the thought that no child should ever have to consider:

"I think I've been shot."

I shouted for my mom, panic in my voice. She came sprinting out of the building she was delivering to, eyes wide with terror.

"What happened?" she yelled.

"I think I've been shot!" I said, trembling.

Without hesitation, she dropped everything and rushed to me. We ducked behind a parked car like we were in a war zone. None of us saw the shooter. We had no idea where the shot came from, or if another one was coming. All we knew was that we had to move. And fast.

We crept down the block, low and frantic, hiding behind cars as we went—like Navy SEALs trying to make it out alive. When we finally made it to our vehicle, my mom jumped in and drove like a woman possessed. No hesitation. Just pure, desperate love. She didn't know where the bullet had landed or how bad it was. She just knew her son was hurt and needed help.

Somewhere along the route, a police officer saw us speeding and pulled us over. My mom yelled through the window, "My son's been shot!" The officer immediately radioed for an ambulance, and within minutes, I was being rushed to the hospital.

Oddly, that neighborhood had never been known for violence. No gangs. No drug corners. It was quiet. Safe. Predictable. Yet, that day, something changed.

After the chaos subsided, detectives brought us back to the scene. They asked me where I was standing, how I turned when I heard the sound, and tried to trace the bullet's path. They knocked on doors, followed leads, and ran a full investigation. But it went nowhere. To this day, no one was ever caught. No explanation. No closure. Just a bullet that found its way into a ten-year-old boy's thigh.

When the doctors finally reviewed the X-rays, they explained the bullet had landed in the center of my upper leg. Miraculously, it hadn't hit any arteries or bones. It was just lodged deep in the muscle tissue.

They gave us two options: either cut through a lot of muscle to get it out immediately, or leave it in and allow the body to slowly push it to the surface over time. We chose the latter.

And so, the bullet stayed.

At ten years old, I wasn't thinking about theology or life lessons. But something in me changed that day. My world suddenly felt fragile. I realized how quickly everything could shift. And over time, as I grew older, I started to reflect deeply on that moment—not with fear, but with reverence.

God didn't just protect me that day. He marked me.

That bullet—still lodged in my leg decades later—became a constant reminder of divine preservation and unfulfilled purpose. It made me ask hard questions early in life: Why am I still here? What am I supposed to do with this life I've been given? What if that one shot was meant to wake me up before I even knew I was asleep?

There were seasons where I let that memory fade into the background. But God always found ways to bring it back—sometimes through a conversation, a sermon, or even an X-ray appointment. I still go in every five years or so to make sure the bullet hasn't moved. And it hasn't. Not one inch.

Some would call it coincidence. I call it a monument.

That bullet became more than just metal. It became a symbol. Not of trauma, but of calling. Not of tragedy, but of testimony. God used that moment—not to scare me, but to shape me.

Because purpose doesn't always knock gently. Sometimes, it arrives with a jolt that forever alters how you walk.

That shift changed everything. I still have passion, but now it's anchored in purpose. And that anchoring has given me peace, even when the path looks uncertain.

Aligning Passion with Faith-Based Purpose

Aligning your passion with a faith-based purpose is not about dividing your interests into secular and sacred, but rather integrating them so that your pursuits reflect and fulfill God's overarching plan. This alignment begins with deep introspection to discern where your enthusiasm intersects with God's calling for you, creating a unified pathway that honors both personal joy and divine mission.

To achieve this alignment, reflect on activities that instill a sense of deep fulfillment and joy. Consider how these activities might serve others or advance God's kingdom. Reflect on Proverbs 16:3: *"Commit your work to the Lord, and your plans will be established."* Here, 'work' symbolizes your passions; by dedicating them to God, you open avenues for those activities to transcend personal satisfaction and drive collective spiritual growth.

Recognize that your place in God's plan is inherently connected to the community. You are part of a network designed for His purpose, as emphasized in 1 Corinthians 3:5-10, where each person's role contributes to a greater mission. Consider how your passions can support or enhance the community's spiritual journey. For instance, if you have a passion for teaching, explore opportunities within faith-based education or spiritual mentorship.

Building a strong foundation in Christ is crucial to ensure your passions remain anchored in spiritual integrity. As you pursue this path, remember 1 Corinthians 3:10-15: *"According to the grace of God given to me, like a skilled master builder I laid a foundation, and someone else is building upon it."* By rooting your talents in

Christ, you not only fortify your purpose but also create a legacy for others to build upon.

Every journey with God involves sacrifices, depicted beautifully in Mark 12:41-44. Just as the widow gave all she had, aligning passion with purpose may require letting go of certain comforts or means of security to embrace a higher calling. Reflect on what you may need to surrender to let God lead your passions fully.

Surround yourself with wise mentors and supportive communities who share your faith-based vision. Proverbs 15:21-22 (ESV) states, *"Folly is a joy to him who lacks sense, but a man of understanding walks straight ahead. Without counsel plans fail, but with many advisers they succeed,"* highlighting the value of good counsel. Seek out church groups, fellowship gatherings, or professional networks that uplift your spiritual and personal goals.

The renewal of the mind, as mentioned in Romans 12:2 (ESV), *"Do not be conformed to this world, but be transformed by the renewal of your mind, that by testing you may discern what is the will of God, what is good and acceptable and perfect,"* is integral to aligning passion with purpose. Regularly evaluate your goals and aspirations, ensuring they continue to align with God's evolving purpose for you. Engage in prayer and scripture reading to stay attuned to divine guidance.

Lastly, stay vigilant about influences that might derail your spiritual journey, as Jesus warns in Matthew 7:15-20 (ESV): *"Beware of false prophets, who come to you in sheep's clothing but inwardly are ravenous wolves. You will recognize them by their fruits. Are grapes gathered from thornbushes, or figs from thistles? So, every healthy tree bears good fruit, but the diseased tree bears bad fruit. A healthy tree cannot bear bad fruit, nor can a diseased tree bear good fruit. Every tree that does not bear good fruit is cut down and thrown into the fire. Thus you will recognize them by their fruits."* Be open to constructive criticism and remain steadfast in your values, ensuring that your path is guided by truth rather than fleeting trends.

In essence, aligning passion with faith-based purpose transforms your pursuit of personal interests into a meaningful journey that glorifies God and enriches both your life and the lives around you. This alignment is a dynamic process that fosters growth, community, and profound personal satisfaction rooted in divine purpose.

Emily's Story

Consider the story of Emily, a dedicated nurse whose life trajectory seemed etched in her passion for healthcare. Her enthusiasm drove her through long hours and immense stress, bringing pride yet growing discontent. One particularly grueling shift, the feeling of purposelessness enveloped Emily as she tended to a critically ill patient. "Why am I here if my work only touches the surface of healing?" she wondered, grappling with an internal conflict between her love for nursing and a yearning for something more substantial.

This moment of doubt opened her eyes to the realization that passion alone wasn't enough. The energy she poured into her work was consumed without replenishing her spirit, leaving her questioning the deeper meaning behind her efforts. Her turning point came during a conversation with a chaplain, who encouraged her to consider the spiritual dimensions of care. Emily realized, in that instant, that her purpose was not just to heal bodies but also to mend souls.

Overcoming her fears of inadequacy, Emily began integrating holistic care practices, focusing on spiritual well-being alongside physical recovery. She embraced this new purpose with the understanding that true healing required more than medical knowledge; it demanded compassion, empathy, and a spiritual connection with those she served. This transition transformed her work from a series of tasks into a ministry of healing and hope, fulfilling her both professionally and spiritually. Emily's story illustrates a critical truth: passion ignites action, but purpose provides the framework that makes this action meaningful and aligned with divine intent.

In examining nuanced scenarios, there are instances where passion can conflict with purpose. Imagine someone who is passionate about climbing the corporate ladder but gradually realizes that this drive conflicts with their deeper calling to family and community service. Such conflicts demand reflection and discernment to align pursuits with an enduring purpose.

Addressing Common Misconceptions About Passion vs. Purpose

In the journey of aligning passion with purpose, common misconceptions can create roadblocks that hinder true fulfillment. By examining and addressing these misconceptions, we can develop a clearer understanding of how to pursue a life that reflects both personal enthusiasm and divine calling.

One prevalent misconception is that passion must align perfectly with one's purpose for it to be valid. Many believe that every passion should directly correlate with a career or a clear path in life. However, passions may not always translate into professional endeavors but can still be vital contributors to our overall purpose. For instance, a person may have a passion for painting while their purpose aligns more with community service. This does not invalidate their passion; instead, it offers an avenue for personal refreshment and expressions of God-given creativity, enhancing how they serve their purpose.

Another misunderstanding is the belief that purpose is static, whereas passion is dynamic and susceptible to change. This overlooks the truth that both passion and purpose evolve as we grow and encounter new experiences. Rather than seeing purpose as a fixed destination, it's more productive to view it as a guiding north star that reframes as we gain new insights and deepen our understanding. This changeability means that our passions can contribute to our purpose in varying and unexpected ways over time.

A third misconception is that following your passion will always lead to fulfillment. While pursuing what you love is important, without a grounding in purpose, this chase can sometimes result in burnout or emptiness. True fulfillment arises from passions intersecting with a purpose that serves others and glorifies God, as noted in scriptures like Colossians 3:23 (ESV): *"Whatever you do, work heartily, as for the Lord and not for men,"* which encourages us to do our tasks heartily as if working for the Lord.

Moreover, some believe that to live a purposeful life, one must abandon personal passions if they don't immediately fit into the perceived divine plan. This mentality can lead to unnecessary sacrifice and loss of joy. In reality, God often uses our innate passions as tools for the greater mission, weaving them into His intricate plans in ways we might not initially understand.

Understanding the Misconception

There's also the misconception that if you haven't discovered a life-defining passion or purpose by a certain age, you've missed your calling. This belief places undue pressure and an arbitrary timeline on spiritual growth. Discovering passion and purpose is a lifelong journey, and God's timing is perfect. Engaging in active exploration and remaining open to God's leading are key.

Understanding these misconceptions clarifies the relationship between passion and purpose, allowing individuals to pursue their paths with joy and conviction. It encourages a balanced perspective that honors personal enjoyment while prioritizing alignment with God's greater plan. This integration empowers believers to live fulfilling lives that honor God and contribute meaningfully to the community, reflecting the diversity and richness inherent in His design. By dispelling these myths, we pave the way for a more harmonious journey where passion and purpose coexist as interwoven facets of God's plan for each individual.

To help you distinguish between passion and purpose, consider the following reflection questions:

1. What activities leave you feeling fulfilled beyond momentary joy?
2. How do your passions contribute to a larger goal, especially in service to others?
3. In what areas of your life do you feel a deep, unshakeable calling, despite challenges?

Aligning passion with purpose requires introspective exploration of activities that bring joy and satisfaction, often pointing toward innate passions. Re-evaluate how these passions align with the greater good, considering faith and beliefs as guides. Engage community members for feedback, and seek counsel from mentors and faith leaders to discover paths where passion and purpose meaningfully intersect.

Returning to Emily's story, her transformation from a passion-driven to a purpose-guided life exemplifies the power of integration. It prompts us to evaluate our own lives: Are we merely chasing passions, or are we surrounded by a purposeful framework guiding our endeavors?

Testimony: Balancing Passion and Purpose

In the complex interplay of passion and purpose, stories of individuals who successfully navigate this landscape can provide valuable guidance. One such story is Lydia's, a vibrant individual whose life trajectory offers insightful lessons on harmonizing personal passions with higher callings.

Lydia appeared to be living a life driven by passion. From a young age, she immersed herself in music, captivated by its beauty and emotional depth. Music was not just a hobby; it was her lifeline, a form of expression that touched her soul. Her dream was to pursue a career in performance, and she was well on her way, performing in various local bands and gaining noteworthy recognition.

However, despite her achievements, Lydia sensed a lingering emptiness—an unmet yearning that the applause at her performances could not fulfill. Her soul craved something more substantive, something that transcended personal satisfaction. This realization marked the beginning of her journey from pursuing passion to seeking purpose.

Her journey from experiencing music as merely a passion to recognizing it as a profound calling was both transformative and intense. Initially, Lydia basked in the highs of performing, but an unshakeable feeling of incompleteness lingered, casting shadows on her achievements. Despite her successes, a quiet discontent simmered beneath the applause—a yearning for something greater that stirred restlessly within her soul. This emotional tug became undeniable during a pivotal mission trip, setting her on a new path.

The turning point came during a mission trip with her church, where Lydia was tasked with leading a worship session. In those moments, she experienced a profound sense of connection and clarity. This was more than just performing; it was an act of worship, a conduit through which she could channel her talents toward something greater than herself. Lydia began to see that her passion for music could serve a higher purpose—to inspire and uplift others, facilitating spiritual connection and communal worship.

As she prepared to lead a worship session, Lydia felt an unfamiliar blend of nerves and excitement. The atmosphere seemed charged with energy she hadn't encountered in her usual performances. When the first notes left her lips, a wave of warmth and peace enveloped her and those present. It was as if, in that moment, her music transcended personal expression and became a conduit for divine connection. Tears welled in her eyes, not from fear or nervousness, but from an overwhelming sense of purpose.

Recognizing this shift was both enlightening and daunting. Lydia faced the challenge of reconciling her ambitions with her newfound purpose. The decision to embrace worship music full-time meant stepping away from the potential for personal fame and acclaim in the broader music industry—a prospect that had once been her dream. She felt vulnerable, questioning if she had the strength to lead spiritually as well as musically.

Overcoming these challenges required deep introspection and guidance. Lydia turned to prayer and sought counsel from mentors within her church community, who encouraged her to trust in the gifts she had been given. With each small step, she began to embrace her role not only as a performer but as a facilitator of communal worship and spiritual connection. Her decision to join the church's worship team full-time marked a newfound confidence and clarity of purpose.

Lydia's journey shows that while the path to aligning passion with purpose may be fraught with doubt and sacrifice, it ultimately leads to deeper fulfillment and a more meaningful contribution to the world. Her story encourages others to explore their own passions through the lens of purpose, finding the courage to align their pursuits with a greater, divine mission.

Through her journey, Lydia teaches us that God's purpose often harnesses our deepest passions, transforming them into service for the greater good. Her story encourages others to reflect on their paths, realigning them to find a harmonious balance between what they love and how it can serve God's plan. In doing so, individuals can experience a fuller, more meaningful life, where passion and purpose are not at odds but beautifully woven together in God's intricate design. Just as scripture provides the foundation and inspiration needed for this alignment, practical steps translate faith into action, ensuring that our everyday lives echo divine intentions and purpose.

Step-by-Step Guide to Aligning Passion with Divine Purpose

Aligning your passion with divine purpose is a transformative journey that begins with introspection and leads to fulfillment. Here is a practical guide to assist you in aligning your passions with your spiritual calling, leading toward a cohesive and purposeful life.

Begin with Self-Reflection

- **Explore Your Journey:** Reflect on significant moments in your life. How have past struggles and successes shaped your passions? Consider asking yourself, "What obstacles did I overcome, and how have they deepened my understanding of what truly brings me joy?"
- **Capture Evolution:** Look at how your passions have evolved over time. Ask yourself, "How have my hobbies or interests changed, and what does that reveal about my current values and goals?"

Discern Divine Direction

- **Seek Clarity in Faith:** During prayer or meditation, reflect on moments of clarity that stood out amidst confusion. Ask, "When did I feel most guided by a deeper sense of purpose, and how did my faith illuminate my path?"

- **Align with Intentions:** Delve into how your convictions have influenced your passions. Consider, "How has my spiritual journey shaped the way I pursue my passions?"

Evaluate Core Values

- **Identify Innate Values:** Examine the core values that resonate most strongly with you. Ask, "Which values consistently guide my decisions, even when faced with difficult choices?"
- **Integrate Passions and Values:** Think about how your values can align with your passions to drive purposeful actions. Ask, "How can I ensure my passions are in harmony with my fundamental beliefs and values?"

Seek Counsel and Feedback

- **Embrace Perspectives:** Reflect on how feedback from trusted individuals has influenced your self-perception and direction. Ask, "What insights have others shared that reshaped my understanding of my strengths?"
- **Discuss Your Evolution:** Engage in dialogues about your evolving passions and purpose. Consider, "What questions can I ask my mentors to gain deeper insights into aligning my talents with a divine mission?"

Prioritize and Reassess Goals

- **Set Evolving Goals:** Establish goals that harness your passions and challenge you to grow. Reflect, "How can I set goals that push me beyond comfort while remaining aligned with my spiritual path?"
- **Regular Reassessment:** Revisit your goals regularly to ensure they remain relevant to both your passion and purpose. Ask, "How has my vision changed or expanded with my growth and experiences?"

Embrace Growth and Learning

- **Commit to Lifelong Learning:** Identify opportunities that can bolster your growth. Ask, "What areas can I explore further to cultivate my skills in alignment with my purpose?"
- **Reflect on New Knowledge:** After learning new concepts, ponder their impact on your journey. Consider, "How does this new understanding align with my passion and purpose?"

Reflect on Impact and Legacy

- **Consider Broader Impact:** Reflect on how your efforts extend beyond personal success. Ask yourself, "How do my passions and actions contribute to the community and serve God's greater plan?"
- **Define Legacy:** Clarify the legacy you hope your aligned passions and purpose will leave behind.

Consider, "What enduring impact do I want to make on the world, and how will it glorify God?"

Through these reflections, you continuously align your passions with a divine framework, ensuring that each step you take is rooted in personal joy and spiritual dedication. How do these insights shape your understanding of the journey from self-discovery to purposeful living?

As this chapter concludes, it positions readers to take actionable steps toward integrating passion with purpose, enriching personal journeys, and benefiting communities.

Rerouted Truth: *When passion fuels but purpose directs, your life becomes a divine force rather than just a busy pursuit.*

CHAPTER 5

The Role of Patience in Discovering Purpose

Under the sprawling skies of the Judean desert, the air is heavy with the scent of dust and distant rain as Abraham reflects on God's promise of a son. The vastness of the barren land around him mirrors the ebbs and flows of his hope, challenged by the relentless march of time. Each grain of sand slipping through his fingers echoes the years that have passed without the promise being fulfilled. In this solitude, a profound sense of anticipation and doubt envelops him, yet a steadfast faith illuminates his path like the morning sun breaking over the horizon.

Abraham feels the weight of uncertainty but senses an indomitable presence—a divine assurance that whispers to him through the rustling leaves and gentle winds. This connection to God carries him through his days of waiting, reinforcing the patience that defines his journey. His faith is not a passive act but a living dialogue with the Almighty, reaffirming his trust in divine timing despite the starkness of his surroundings.

This narrative underscores the significance of patience in a purpose-driven life, illustrating how rushing through the journey can obscure the intricate beauty of God's masterful design. As readers reflect on Abraham's story, they are prompted to ponder, "How does faith sustain you through the uncertainties of your own life?"

Patience is foundational in discovering and fulfilling one's divine purpose, serving as a crucial anchor for aligning with God's perfect timing. The scripture emphasizes that each phase of life carries its appointed time and purpose, necessitating trust in God's broader vistas.

Learning to Wait on God

After the collapse of my business, I found myself in an unfamiliar place: stillness. For years, I had moved fast, made decisions quickly, and thrived in environments where results were the measure of success. But in that season, the silence from God was unnerving. I prayed, I journaled, I even knocked on a few doors hoping one would open—but nothing moved. In those moments, I couldn't help but reflect on Habakkuk 3:2 (ESV): *"For still the vision awaits its appointed time; it hastens to the end—it will not lie. If it seems slow, wait for it; it will surely come; it will not delay."* My faith was shaken.

There were days when I genuinely questioned whether I had misunderstood my calling. I wondered if God had forgotten about me. I kept asking, *"Lord, did I miss something? Was all of that just me chasing passion and not purpose?"*

The hardest part wasn't the external quiet—it was the internal wrestling. I felt stripped of everything I used to draw identity and affirmation from. I wasn't leading anything, launching anything, or achieving anything. I was just waiting. But that waiting became sacred.

Over time, I realized that God wasn't being silent to punish me—He was preparing me. The delay wasn't rejection; it was refinement. He began showing me that patience wasn't weakness. It was actually an invitation to trust Him deeper than ever before.

I remember one morning, sitting on my porch, reading that passage in Ecclesiastes—and it hit me: this wasn't a pause; it was a season. And God had appointed it. That revelation changed my perspective.

Eventually, I stopped trying to force a breakthrough and started asking God to form something new in me. He reminded me that just because I wasn't moving didn't mean He wasn't working. I was being shaped for something greater than I had previously envisioned.

The Monkey Trap

That season of stillness also forced me to confront the things I had been clutching too tightly—things that were keeping me stuck. And oddly enough, what helped me understand it was a story about a monkey and a coconut.

You may have heard it. There's a traditional method used in some parts of the world for trapping monkeys. It involves a hollowed-out coconut tied to a tree, with a small hole just big enough for a monkey's hand to slip through. Inside, the hunters place fruit—berries, bananas, anything sweet and fragrant.

The monkey comes along, reaches in, grabs the food—but then gets stuck. The fist it makes to grip the fruit is too large to pull back through the hole. And here's the fascinating part: the monkey won't let go.

Even as danger approaches.

Even when it hears footsteps.

Even when escape is possible.

It holds onto what it wants—until that very desire becomes the trap.

That image haunted me.

Because I realized I had done the same thing.

I had my hand wrapped around what I thought life was supposed to look like. The business I built. The dreams I formed. The timing I expected. And even when everything was unraveling, I wouldn't let go. I prayed for deliverance, but I held on to my definition of what "success" had to be.

But spiritual growth requires surrender. Jesus didn't invite us to carry everything; He invited us to lay it down. And sometimes, we don't experience freedom because we're still clutching things God's already told us to release.

That's what the monkey couldn't grasp. Freedom was one decision away—but it would cost him the very thing he thought he couldn't live without.

In my case, it wasn't just about letting go of a career. It was about releasing my need for control, validation, and outcomes I had been idolizing. The patience God was cultivating in me wasn't passive—it was pruning. And part of that pruning was the invitation to loosen my grip.

I'm learning that God doesn't rip things from our hands. He waits until we trust Him enough to open them.

Now, looking back, I see that season of stillness as one of the most productive times in my life—not because I accomplished anything outwardly, but because God cultivated something within me: a rootedness, a resilience, and a peace that didn't depend on progress.

Biblical Case Study on Waiting on God

In the intricate mosaic of our lives, patience is a thread woven into the very fabric of faith. Ecclesiastes 3:1 serves as a profound guide, urging believers to trust in God's perfect timing. Patience is intrinsically linked to the discovery of our purpose, as the act of waiting fosters resilience and refines character. This process of anticipation and endurance prepares us for what God has planned, enabling us to appreciate and act upon our purpose with clarity and intention.

David's Long Road to Kingship: A Masterclass in Divine Timing

Among the biblical figures who embody the power of waiting, David's journey stands as a striking portrait of how patience shapes purpose. His story is not just about anointing and ascension—it is about the tension between promise and preparation.

When the prophet Samuel anointed David as king, David was still a shepherd boy, tucked away in the fields, overlooked even by his own father. The oil may have flowed, but the throne was far off. Between his anointing and coronation lay a long, uncertain road—one paved with betrayal, isolation, and prolonged injustice.

Initially welcomed into Saul's palace as a musician and warrior, David's favor quickly turned into a threat in Saul's eyes. Jealousy ignited a relentless pursuit. Forced into hiding, David spent years fleeing through caves and deserts. He was anointed—but not yet appointed. Called—but not yet crowned.

During these wilderness years, David faced repeated tests of character. He had multiple opportunities to kill Saul and seize the throne by force. From a human perspective, the path seemed clear—eliminate the obstacle and claim the promise. But David refused to shortcut God's process. "I will not touch the Lord's anointed," he declared, revealing a level of spiritual discipline rare for someone with power within reach.

Instead of rushing ahead, David chose reverence over revenge. He honored the process, even when the process was painful. He waited—not passively, but actively—allowing God to shape him into the kind of king who wouldn't just wear a crown but carry a heart after God's own.

Emotionally, the toll was real. His psalms echo with the cries of loneliness, betrayal, confusion, and divine silence. *"How long, Lord? Will you forget me forever?"* (Psalm 13:1). Yet even in his laments, David returned to trust: "But I trust in your unfailing love; my heart rejoices in your salvation."

The cave became a cathedral. The silence became a sanctuary. The delay became development.

By the time David finally ascended to the throne, he had become more than a leader—he had become a man forged by fire, defined not by the speed of his rise but by the depth of his surrender.

David's story teaches us that waiting on God is not wasted time. It is sacred ground. It is where warriors are made, leaders are molded, and hearts are purified. It is where calling is confirmed not just by what we accomplish, but by who we become in the process.

The Cost of Impatience vs. The Fruit of Patience

David's restraint stands in stark contrast to what happens when we rush ahead of God. The story of Abraham and Sarah choosing Hagar as a shortcut to God's promise is a sobering example of how impatience can introduce unnecessary pain into our journey. Had David chosen to kill Saul, he might have gained the throne—but lost God's favor.

Waiting is not easy. It tests our motives, tempers our pride, and clarifies our priorities. But it also proves our trust. And trust is the foundation of every great relationship with God.

David's life invites us to resist shortcuts and embrace the sacred stretch of time between promise and fulfillment. His journey reminds us that what God begins, He also sustains—and eventually completes.

The Power of Patience: Aligning Life's Timing with Divine Wisdom

Reflecting on the story of David, modern believers can learn the profound value of patience in our own lives. His life demonstrates that when we align our timing with God's, our lives unfold according to His divine purpose. Today, as we navigate the fast-paced demands of modern life, embracing patience can transform our journey. It encourages us to trust God's plan amidst uncertainty and readies us to fully receive His promises when they manifest. This timeless lesson calls us to slow down, trust in God's perfect timing, and find peace by aligning our lives with His eternal wisdom.

Cultivating patience requires intentional effort in our spiritual practices. Engage in faith by building trust and confidence in the invisible workings of God, understanding that He orchestrates our paths for His glory. Establish a consistent prayer life, nurturing ongoing dialogue with God to maintain clarity and focus amidst waiting. Reflection through meditation creates a sanctuary to align oneself with divine timing, fostering growth and readiness.

Embracing patience yields unparalleled rewards, often transcending worldly expectations. Those who wait on God discover blessings that intricately fulfill His grand narrative. David's life assures us that while we may wait, God is actively preparing our path to align with His sovereign plan.

As you reflect on David's journey, consider how your own waiting periods might be preparing you for a fulfilled purpose aligned with God's timing. Remember how David, through years of patient endurance and spiritual formation, fulfilled God's divine promise. When walking through the seasons of life, trust that God's timing is impeccable—for in every delay, there's preparation and an unfolding of His perfect purpose.

Examining David's life bears testament to the rewards of divine waiting. Though anointed in his youth, David waited many years before assuming the throne. His journey epitomizes patient preparation—enduring adversity, resisting shortcuts, and trusting God through uncertainty. Through it all, David's heart remained anchored in worship and obedience, reinforcing the power of abiding in God's timing.

Rushing into destiny without adequate preparation can lead to burnout and squander God-given opportunities. Impatience often blinds us to the lessons found in quiet moments, where God shapes and equips us. The delay of Jesus visiting Lazarus, as seen in John 11:5–6 (ESV): *"Now Jesus loved Martha and her sister and Lazarus. So, when he heard that Lazarus was ill, he stayed two days longer in the place where he was,"* exemplifies this divine pause, orchestrating miraculous outcomes beyond our immediate understanding.

Patience is Vital for the Journey

A modern example of someone grappling with impatience is Dorothy from the Warm Springs community. Initially, her life was marked by struggles with alcoholism, resulting in the loss of custody of her children. Her longing for a quick fix contributed to a cycle of setbacks. However, by entering and completing an alcohol treatment program, she realigned her life toward a more sustainable path. Dorothy's transformation, rooted in patience and perseverance, underscores the importance of a healthier, purpose-driven life. By investing time in rehabilitation and slowly rebuilding her life, she offers a powerful example for modern believers: embracing patience and the gradual work of change can lead to the fulfillment of potential and the restoration of lost opportunities.

Practicing patience is vital for a proactive, purpose-driven journey. Build unwavering faith by entrusting your path to God's grand design, anchored in the assurance that He who promises is faithful. Engage in regular prayer, nurturing your perception of God's timing and sustaining focus. Reflection during meditative practices merges your heart's rhythm with God's, prompting personal growth even while waiting.

The rewards of patient faithfulness to God's timeline often surpass immediate gratification. Those who embrace patience unlock grace and unexpected blessings woven into divine frameworks. Many biblical accounts demonstrate that waiting allows us to reap the fullness of God's intent.

In David's story, his eventual rise to the throne serves as a testament to how patience can sculpt our faith, ensuring that the realized purpose aligns with God's intent. As you embrace this lesson, remember that patience is not mere waiting; it is an active trust in God's orchestration of your life, a catalyst for readiness and profound alignment with His purpose.

The Long Hiatus

The truth is that shaping process takes a while.

After my business collapsed, I found myself in a spiritual and emotional stillness I had never experienced. And instead of rushing into the next hustle or "figuring out the next move," something in me said—**don't move yet.**

Not this time.

What followed was a long hiatus—one that, at first, felt like failure but eventually revealed itself to be holy.

I slowed down. Really slowed down. I got married. Started my family. Became a father. These were always things I had dreamed about, but honestly, they had taken a back seat to my relentless ambition. For the first time, I had space to be present with the people I loved and with the God I claimed to follow.

This wasn't just a break. It was a recalibration.

I didn't launch anything. I wasn't leading teams or pitching vision. I was learning how to sit still long enough to actually hear from God—not just talk at Him. In that quiet, I began to heal. I began to understand what it meant to commune with Him without an agenda. I became more mature in my thinking. Less reactive. More reflective.

That season also gave me time to pour into others in ways I hadn't been able to before—friends, family, young people just starting their journeys. I became a better husband, a better father, and even more surprisingly... a better listener.

And here's the thing that humbles me every time I think about it:

Rerouted would not exist without that season.

If I had never slowed down, I would have never been able to receive what God was really trying to show me. I would've stayed caught up in the cycle of chasing success while calling it purpose. But God, in His mercy, pulled me out of the driver's seat—not to punish me, but to protect me.

I've learned that there are seasons when God tells us to run. And there are seasons when He tells us to rest—not because He's forgotten us, but because He's forming us. That long hiatus wasn't an interruption in my story. It was the preparation for the part that mattered most.

Spiritual Readiness Assessment: Based on Romans 8:28-31

As you navigate your spiritual journey, discerning God's timing—whether to wait calmly or act boldly—is vital. Using Romans 8:28-31 as a foundation, this assessment aims to guide you through deliberate reflection to determine your current season.

1. Recognize Current Circumstances (Romans 8:28)

Begin by contemplating Romans 8:28, which assures us that "all things work together for good, for those who are called according to His purpose." Reflect on whether recent events in your life feel aligned or misaligned with this divine assurance. Are you witnessing clear signs of progress and opportunity, or does everything seem to be on pause? Write down instances where you see God's hand orchestrating outcomes or feel a call to patient waiting, trusting in His ultimate plan.

Action Step: Set aside time each day for a week to journal about your recent experiences and feelings. As you write, note any patterns or insights that suggest God's influence or areas needing patience. At the end of the week, review your entries to identify where God may be working in your circumstances, encouraging you either to wait or to act.

2. Evaluate Purpose Alignment (Romans 8:29-30)

These verses highlight conformity to Christ's image and our role in God's broader narrative. Ask yourself: "How is my current situation molding me to reflect Christ more deeply? Am I experiencing growth that aligns with the divine plan?" This reflection will help determine if God is calling you to act or if you're in a season of inward preparation. Consider how your talents and efforts contribute to God's overarching purpose and whether you're being sculpted for something greater.

Action Step: Create a personal mission statement that encapsulates your understanding of how your life aligns with reflecting Christ's image. Regularly review this statement, especially when making decisions, to ensure your actions align with your divine purpose and communication with God's bigger plan.

3. Assess Support and Opportunities (Romans 8:31)

Recognizing that "if God is for us, who can be against us?" evaluate the support you have and the opportunities presented to you. Are trusted advisors encouraging you to move forward, or are they guiding you toward reflection? Examine your current network to determine if you have the encouragement to take action or if there's a stronger call toward introspection and waiting for God's guidance. Journal about the people and resources surrounding you—are they facilitators of progress or anchors for deeper spiritual development?

Action Step: List the key people in your life and how they influence your decisions. Arrange conversations with those who play a significant role in guiding you, asking for their observations about the opportunities and supports you should consider. Compare this feedback with your reflections to discern your next steps.

4. Reflect on Spiritual Fruits

Consider the presence of the Spirit's fruits—peace, patience, and wisdom—in your daily life. Abundant fruits often signal readiness to act, whereas a scant presence might suggest a period of further spiritual cultivation. Note moments when these fruits are particularly strong, indicating readiness, or when they seem absent, suggesting a call for more growth.

Action Step: Monitor your daily interactions and decisions for signs of the Spirit's fruits. Record each instance in a journal, no matter how small, where you feel peace, patience, or wisdom. Use these entries to assess your spiritual maturity and readiness to pursue specific goals.

5. Examine Prayer Life

Your prayer life serves as a vital channel of communication with God. Reflect on the messages and impressions received during prayer. Are they calls to immediate action, or do they beckon you to further trust and patience? The clarity and nudges you receive in prayer may define a season of action or waiting, aligning your path with divine will. Record guidance you've perceived, corroborating themes of readiness or introspective growth.

Action Step: Dedicate a specific time each day for prayer focused on seeking clarity and guidance. Keep a prayer journal to document any impressions or themes that emerge. Periodically review these notes to discern any patterns indicating whether to wait or take action.

6. Identify Divine Signs and Insights

Seek out any spiritual signs or insights gained from scripture, circumstances, or people in your life. Are there recurring messages that push toward a notable shift or affirm your current state? Reflect on the themes and signals present in your spiritual experiences and journal these insights to discern God's direction.

Action Step: Collect and review scripture passages, circumstances, or advice from trusted individuals that consistently resonate with you. Dedicate time weekly to meditate on these signs, considering how they guide you toward readiness or further preparation.

7. Review Past Experiences

Reflect on how past periods of waiting have contributed to your spiritual resilience and preparedness. These reflections can highlight God's timing and reassure you of His perfect plan, informing your understanding of whether you're being called to wait or act now.

Action Step: Reflect on past seasons of waiting and acting by drafting a timeline of significant events, noting the outcomes and lessons learned. Consider how these insights can inform your current situation and your sense of God's timing.

8. Internal Alignment and Readiness

Ultimately, readiness isn't solely about external markers but internal alignment with God's purpose. Use these prompts to evaluate your internal peace, wisdom, and purpose-driven impulses, helping you align with God's best plan for you. Whether you find yourself in a season of waiting or action, rest assured that each phase sets the stage for God's divine purpose, actively participating in a journey beautifully orchestrated for His glory.

Action Step: Conduct a self-audit of your current state of peace and sense of alignment with God's purpose. Use tools like questionnaires or feedback from spiritual mentors to reinforce your understanding of your readiness for action or continued preparation.

As we conclude this chapter, let us reflect on the role of patience in discovering our purpose. Consider this question: "In what areas of my life might impatience be clouding my perception of God's perfect timing and purpose?" Take with you the understanding that patience is not a passive state but an active engagement with God's timeline. This chapter emphasizes the importance of trusting divine timing and nurturing a mindset that supports spiritual growth and peace. As we transition into the next chapter, "Cultivating a Christ-Centered Mindset," anticipate exploring how a mindset grounded in Christ enhances our patience and spiritual journey.

Rerouted Truth: *Waiting is not wasted time—it's God's training ground for the weight of what's coming next.*

CHAPTER 6
Cultivating a Christ-Centered Mindset

"Mindset shapes destiny." This provocative statement lays a profound foundation for understanding how aligning our thoughts with Christ's teachings is essential for both spiritual and worldly success. In the journey toward fulfilling one's divine purpose, cultivating a Christ-centered mindset serves as a vital underpinning for all endeavors.

As we explore the transformative impact of a Christ-centered mindset on our destiny, consider the journey of Alex. By reorienting his life around Christ's teachings, Alex exemplifies how this mental and spiritual shift can lead to both fulfillment and tangible success. His story illustrates that when our thoughts align with Christ, our path to destiny becomes clearer and more enriching, underscoring the truth that "mindset shapes destiny."

Alex, a corporate executive known for his strategic acumen and leadership prowess, faced a personal void despite his success, realizing his achievements lacked deeper meaning. During a transformative leadership retreat infused with spiritual teachings, Alex encountered Christ's lessons anew—principles of servitude, humility, and genuine love resonated deeply, prompting a life-altering shift in his mindset. By recentering his professional and personal decisions around Christ's virtues, Alex found not only success but profound fulfillment, transforming his perspective from personal gain to service-oriented leadership.

This narrative highlights how a Christ-centered mindset is pivotal for aligning everyday decisions with eternal values. Such a mindset embraces virtues like humility, service, and love, fostering personal growth and nurturing professional and relational dynamics, all contributing to genuine fulfillment as defined by divine principles.

Alex's insight illustrates how a mindset shift rooted in Christ-centered principles can reshape leadership styles and personal fulfillment. By realigning his aspirations and leadership approach with virtues of humility, service, and love, Alex transformed his business outcomes and found profound personal satisfaction. Embracing these virtues made his leadership more authentic and impactful, demonstrating that true fulfillment lies in aligning personal actions with God's overarching purpose.

From Control to Surrender

There was a time when I approached every challenge as something I needed to fix, lead, or overcome on my own. My default mindset was: "What can I do to solve this?" It wasn't that I didn't believe in God—it was that I functioned as if everything depended on me. I thought faith was about asking for God's help while still holding the reins.

But when my strategies failed, and my best plans unraveled, I found myself in unfamiliar territory: powerless. That's when God began to expose just how much I had been leaning on my own understanding. I wasn't cultivating a Christ-centered mindset—I was cultivating a me-centered survival strategy dressed in spiritual language.

The turning point came in a quiet moment of prayer when I finally admitted that I didn't know what to do next. I confessed that I was tired of appearing strong while crumbling inside. And in that space of vulnerability, the Holy Spirit gently reminded me: *"You don't have to carry this alone. Fixing is not your job—faith is."*

From that moment, I started to shift. I began to trade frantic planning for consistent prayer. I replaced internal pressure with surrendered trust. My thoughts—once filled with control and contingency plans—began to realign with Christ's invitation to abide in Him.

This didn't mean I stopped using wisdom or taking action—but now, I lead from a place of rest, not anxiety. I seek clarity through Scripture before I chase outcomes. My mindset became less about success and more about obedience. And that shift has changed everything.

The Typing Class

I actually began learning about obedience and disciplined thinking long before I had language for it—back in high school, in one of the most unlikely places: typing class.

It was the 10th grade, and I was sitting in my guidance counselor's office discussing college prep courses. She looked over my schedule and then made a recommendation that, at the time, felt completely out of left field.

"You should consider taking a typing class," she said.

I gave her the proverbial side eye. In those days, typing class wasn't filled with future tech professionals—it was mostly girls. And to be honest, I didn't see how punching keys on a giant IBM typewriter was going to help me become the leader I aspired to be. But she was persistent. She saw something coming that I didn't. The computer age was right around the corner, and she had the foresight to prepare me for it.

So I signed up.

Sure enough, I was the only guy in the class. And yes, I felt awkward. But none of that mattered to Mrs. Williams, our teacher. She didn't cut me any slack. In fact, she may have been harder on me than the others. Her mission was clear: teach us how to type the right way—by learning the home row keys and never looking down.

And let me tell you, that was hard.

Every instinct I had screamed to peek at the keys. It was so tempting to cheat the process. But every time I did, Mrs. Williams would catch me. Sometimes, she'd even hit the side of the typewriter with a ruler—not to punish, but to remind me: trust what you're building. Obedience matters more than speed.

I didn't fully understand it then, but something profound was happening. She was teaching me discipline. Training my mind to operate without crutches. Cultivating a habit that, over time, became so natural I can now type entire documents without ever looking at the keyboard.

That skill has served me faithfully for nearly four decades.

What started as resistance became mastery. What once felt foreign became second nature. And that's how the Holy Spirit often works in us. He trains us to operate from trust rather than reaction. From rhythm rather than impulse. From obedience rather than self-reliance.

God often brings us into spiritual "typing classes"—where we feel uncomfortable, unsure, and tempted to go back to old habits. But if we stay the course, something powerful forms beneath the surface. New instincts. New alignment. New readiness.

We don't always see the value of what God is teaching us in the moment—but in time, we find ourselves moving through life with a confidence we didn't even know we had. And when others wonder how we manage to navigate with such grace and focus, we know: it started when we stopped looking down and started trusting the process.

Cultivating a Christ-Centered Mindset through Transformation

The transformation of the heart and mind to align with Christ's teachings offers profound examples of change rooted in faith. Let's explore the narratives of two individuals whose lives vividly illustrate the power and process of developing a Christ-centered mindset.

Thomas' Story

Consider the story of Thomas, a young professional in the bustling world of finance. Initially defined by ambition and the relentless pursuit of success, his life spiraled into chronic stress and dissatisfaction. Despite achieving milestones admired by peers,

Thomas felt trapped in an emotional web, plagued by doubts about the true value of his achievements and fears about a future devoid of meaning. During this tumultuous period, at his girlfriend's urging, he began attending a local church group, albeit with skepticism.

During a small-group session, Thomas encountered a transformative message: the story of Zacchaeus from the Bible. Zacchaeus, wealthy yet despised, found redemption not through status or wealth but through an encounter with Jesus that redirected his life's focus. This story resonated with Thomas's unspoken need for a foundational shift from self-driven goals to a purpose anchored in Christ's love and teachings. This moment of recognition spurred him to immerse himself in scripture and prayer, seeking to understand and embody the values taught by Christ. Gradually, his outlook and priorities realigned significantly. He began volunteering with a financial literacy program at the church, channeling his expertise to empower those facing financial insecurity. The joy he experienced in helping others confirmed a new sense of purpose and fulfillment previously absent from his career-driven life.

Mary's Story

Similarly, Mary's journey highlights transformation through a Christ-centered mindset. As a single mother juggling work and raising children, she felt overwhelmed by daily challenges. Her interactions were often marred by anxiety and impatience as she grappled with the immense responsibility of providing for her family. Fear of inadequacy haunted her restless nights. A friend's invitation to a women's Bible study group introduced her to teachings that emphasized the peace and rest found in Christ.

Through these gatherings and countless hours of reflection, Mary learned to prioritize prayer and scripture as daily anchors. The supportive community helped her internalize lessons of grace, patience, and reliance on God's strength rather than her own. A specific turning point occurred during a study session focused on God's promise to provide for all needs, which resonated deeply during a particularly trying financial month. Slowly, Mary developed a serene confidence, enabling her to navigate life's challenges with newfound resilience and joy. This internal shift was palpable; her children and colleagues noticed the peace that now underscored her interactions.

Both stories illustrate that cultivating a Christ-centered mindset is not an instantaneous overhaul but a gradual process of aligning thoughts, behaviors, and life choices with Christ's teachings. Transformation requires openness to change and a commitment to practices like prayer, fellowship, and scripture study, which collectively renew the mind and cultivate enduring spiritual change. Through their narratives, Thomas and Mary remind us that true transformation reshapes how we approach life, enabling us to live with purpose, peace, and compassion.

Their journeys encourage readers to reflect upon their own lives, challenging them to invite Christ's teachings into every facet, thereby uncovering the potential for growth and fulfillment waiting in a Christ-centered life. Through Thomas and Mary's testimonies, we see faith's potential to ignite profound change, inspiring others to embrace a path defined by divine love and guidance.

To integrate Christ-focused thinking into daily life, establish routines that prioritize spiritual practices. Begin with dedicated prayer each morning, seeking guidance for facing daily challenges with grace and faith. Reflect through scripture meditation, drawing both inspiration and practical instruction from Christ's teachings to realign daily actions with divine purpose. Consider journaling your reflections to capture growth and areas needing additional alignment.

Danielle's Story

A real-life example of someone who successfully integrated prayer, scripture meditation, and journaling into their daily routine is Danielle, a working mother and small business owner navigating a season of professional uncertainty and personal burnout. Feeling overwhelmed by competing demands, Danielle knew she needed more than time management tactics—she needed spiritual renewal. She began each morning in quiet prayer, seeking guidance and peace before the chaos of the day began. Afterward, she would meditate on a scripture verse, often choosing passages related to wisdom, perseverance, or rest. These moments became a sacred pause that realigned her perspective and calmed her spirit.

Danielle also took up journaling—not just to record events, but to process how the Word was intersecting with her life. Through writing, she identified patterns of fear, control, and people-pleasing and began to surrender those struggles in prayer. Slowly but powerfully, her mindset began to shift. The demands of her business didn't disappear, but she approached them with a new sense of clarity and peace. Her decisions became more rooted in discernment than urgency. Her home life grew calmer as she modeled grace over stress, and her team noticed the change in her leadership style—more collaborative, less reactive.

Danielle's transformation reveals how spiritual practices, when made a daily habit, can become tools for internal healing and external impact. Her journey underscores that integrating prayer, scripture, and reflection doesn't just change how we feel—it changes how we lead, love, and live.

Practical Strategies for Maintaining a Christ-Centered Focus in Difficult Times

Navigating life's challenges while maintaining a Christ-centered mindset requires deliberate strategies that reinforce faith and perspective. Here are several practical approaches to help ground yourself in Christ's teachings during difficult times.

Firstly, establish a consistent prayer routine. Prayer serves as a lifeline to God, providing guidance, solace, and clarity amidst chaos. By dedicating time daily, whether in structured prayer or brief moments throughout your day, you create a rhythm that keeps Christ at the center of your thoughts. This practice not only aligns your heart with Christ's but also infuses your day with purposeful spirituality, fostering peace and direction.

Another strategy is to immerse yourself in scripture. Regular Bible study deepens your understanding of God's promises and reminds you of His faithfulness in every circumstance. Focus on passages that speak to perseverance and hope, writing them down or memorizing them for quick recall during moments of doubt. Engaging deeply with scripture can serve as a powerful anchor, providing comfort and reaffirmation of your path, much like a guiding star in tumultuous times.

Community engagement is also essential for sustaining a Christ-centered mindset. Surround yourself with a supportive network of fellow believers who can offer encouragement and hold you accountable. Participating in small groups, Bible studies, or church activities creates opportunities for mutual support and shared growth. These interactions reinforce your faith through collective worship and shared testimony, fortifying your resolve and reminding you of the broader body of Christ to which you belong.

Incorporate acts of service into your routine. Serving others shifts the focus from personal struggles to Christ's call for compassion and generosity. Engaging in volunteer work, reaching out to those in need, or simply being attentive and caring can refresh your perspective, reminding you of the joy found in serving with love. Acts of service not only reflect Christlike behavior but also cultivate humility and grace, foundational aspects of a Christ-centered life.

Meditation on the teachings of Christ helps maintain focus during trying periods. Take regular moments to pause and reflect on Christ's words and your current experiences, prayerfully aligning them with divine teaching. This practice encourages discernment and helps center your responses on faith-driven actions rather than immediate emotional reactions, fostering resilience and a deeper trust in God's plan.

Balancing life's demands while keeping your focus on Christ involves setting priorities that align with His teachings. Evaluate where you invest your time, energy, and resources, ensuring they foster spiritual growth and reflect Christ's example. Simplifying your commitments, if necessary, allows for a greater focus on what truly matters, nurturing a fulfilling spiritual life even amidst worldly challenges.

Finally, draw inspiration from faith-based literature and worship music. These resources can rejuvenate your spirit, provide new insights, and uplift your heart. Music and literature resonate deeply, offering encouragement and reinforcing the message of Christ's enduring love and support. Whether through hymns, contemporary worship songs, or inspirational books and devotionals, these tools provide a backdrop of spiritual encouragement that aligns perfectly with living a Christ-centered life.

A Mindset Rooted in Faith

By integrating these strategies into your daily life, you nurture a mindset rooted in faith, guiding you through inevitable challenges with steadfastness and grace. These practices serve as a testament to living faithfully and purposefully in alignment with Christ's teachings, regardless of external circumstances. This journey is a continuous process of growth and commitment, drawing you closer to Christ and His transformative love.

During times of spiritual dryness or discouragement, maintaining a Christ-centered mindset requires a deep commitment to spiritual disciplines designed to reinforce faith and perspective. Establish a resilient routine of prayer, scripture, and service to navigate these challenging periods. By consistently dedicating time to prayer, you open a channel to God's guidance and assurance, offering clarity and peace amidst turmoil. Delve into the scriptures, focusing on passages that emphasize hope and perseverance, which act as anchoring truths during uncertain times.

Engaging in a supportive faith community provides encouragement and accountability, reminding you of the shared strength in collective worship and testimony. Additionally, embracing acts of service shifts your focus from personal struggles to the needs of others, reflecting Christ's love and cultivating humility and grace.

These practices collectively nurture resilience and a deeper trust in God's purpose, fostering a mindset aligned with Christ even amidst life's storms.

Daily exercises for fostering Christ-centered thoughts include reflective scripture reading, seeking guidance through contemplative prayer, and engaging in community discussions that challenge and refine your thought processes. Sharing experiences with a faith community opens you to new insights and collective growth grounded in scriptural truths.

Returning to Alex's journey, his transformation through Christ-centered thinking exemplifies tangible benefits—personal fulfillment paralleled by enhanced professional success and enriched personal relationships. His story reinforces the transformative power that comes when our mindset aligns with Christ's teachings, opening vistas for growth and enriching our spiritual journey.

Daily Devotional Plan for Cultivating a Christ-Centered Mindset

Begin Your Day with Prayer and Reflection

- Find a quiet space free from distractions.
- Engage in prayer, expressing gratitude and seeking guidance for the day.
- Set an intention to invite God's presence into your thoughts and actions.

Dive into Scripture

- Read a chapter or select verses that resonate with your spiritual journey.
- Focus on the teachings of Christ, wisdom in Proverbs, or comforting Psalms.
- Meditate on the readings and journal insights and applications to your life.

Midday Check-In

- Pause for a moment of prayer or a quick review of the morning scripture.
- Recalibrate your focus to align with Christ's teachings.
- Offer any stresses or achievements back to God, maintaining a dialogue throughout the day.

Engage in Worship

- Listen to praise music during routine tasks or commutes.
- Sing along or absorb the music, inviting joy and spiritual connection into your day.

Evening Reflection and Prayer

- Review the day, noting God's presence in your experiences.
- Seek forgiveness where needed and express gratitude.
- Consider reading a devotional book or inspirational literature to close the day.

Incorporate Weekly and Monthly Activities

- Attend church services and participate in Bible study groups.
- Engage in community service programs to reinforce teachings and serve.

By following these structured steps, you maintain a consistent and growing relationship with Christ, preparing to navigate challenges with grace and focus.

As this chapter concludes, it encourages readers to reflect on a pivotal question: "How can I begin cultivating a Christ-centered mindset today?" By integrating prayer, scripture meditation, and intentional community connections into your daily routine, this mindset shift promises profound impacts, creating positive ripples across all facets of life. As we transition to Chapter 7, "Staying Focused and Avoiding Distractions," we'll explore strategies for maintaining clarity and steadfastness amidst life's inevitable distractions. This next chapter will ensure that your journey remains purposeful and aligned with your divine calling.

Rerouted Truth: *A Christ-centered mindset doesn't just change how you think—it transforms how you live, lead, and love.*

CHAPTER 7
Staying Focused and Avoiding Distractions

Imagine a lighthouse standing resolutely on a rocky shoreline, casting its beacon of light through a chaotic storm. Ships navigate the tumultuous seas, guided by this unwavering light toward safe harbors. Such is the role of focus in our lives; it directs us safely through the storms of distractions, keeping us on the path toward fulfilling our God-given purpose.

Much like a lighthouse's guiding beam, maintaining focus amidst daily distractions ensures safe passage through life's challenges. Losing focus can be likened to a ship adrift without a lighthouse, exposing us to the hazards of distractions that steer us away from our intended course and endanger our pursuit of a Christ-centered life. By standing firm against these distractions, we safeguard our journey toward realizing our divine purpose.

Maintaining focus is essential for achieving one's purpose. However, numerous distractions can impede this journey in our daily lives. Recognizing these distractions and deliberately cultivating focus and discipline are central to navigating life's challenges.

Learning to Guard My Focus

Distraction has always been one of the enemy's most subtle tools in my life—not through obvious temptations, but through good things that weren't God things. I used to mistake activity for progress. My calendar stayed full. I was constantly meeting, planning, and starting something new. But in hindsight, much of that noise was keeping me from clarity.

There was a time when I said yes to almost every opportunity that came my way. Speaking engagements, collaborations, side projects—they all felt important, and in some ways, they were. But I didn't realize how scattered I had become until the fruit started thinning out. I was busy—but I wasn't bearing the kind of fruit that remains.

The shift began when I finally paused and asked: *"What has God actually called me to focus on in this season?"* That question exposed a lot. I had allowed approval, performance, and fear of missing out to drive my decisions more than purpose and obedience.

God started pruning. Doors I once considered opportunities began closing. Some relationships shifted. At first, it felt like loss—but over time, I saw it as protection. In that quieter space, I began to focus on what mattered: building, mentoring, writing, serving. I started asking God, *"What's mine to carry?"* instead of trying to do it all.

Now, I guard my focus with intentionality. I plan in prayer. I evaluate every opportunity through the lens of assignment. And when distractions rise up—and they still do—I return to what God told me last. That's where my focus finds its footing again.

Addressing Emotional and Mental Distractions: Fear, Doubt, and Anxiety

In nurturing a Christ-centered mindset, emotional and mental distractions like fear, doubt, and anxiety can act as powerful deterrents, pulling us away from our spiritual focus. Understanding and addressing these distractions not only strengthens our faith but also deepens our commitment to living in alignment with Christ.

Fear often manifests as an immobilizing force that prevents us from stepping out in faith or pursuing our God-given purpose. This anxiety is frequently rooted in uncertainty about the future or a lack of trust in God's plan. One way to counteract fear is to embrace the truth that God's power is made perfect in our weaknesses, as Paul speaks of in 2 Corinthians 12:9. By acknowledging that we move forward through Christ's strength, we can confront fear with the knowledge that we do not journey alone.

Doubt, a close companion to fear, often enters uninvited when our faith is tested or when life's challenges seem insurmountable. In moments of doubt, it is crucial to turn to scripture for reassurance. Consider the story of Peter walking on water in Matthew 14:29-31—when Peter fixed his eyes on Jesus, he defied the natural elements; but as doubt crept in, he began to sink. This narrative serves as a poignant reminder that focusing on Christ enables us to transcend doubt and overcome obstacles, anchoring us in faith.

Anxiety, characterized by persistent worrying and a lack of peace, can ripple through our spiritual lives, creating disconnection from God's assurances. Philippians 4:6-7 (ESV) states, *"Do not be anxious about anything, but in everything by prayer and supplication with thanksgiving let your requests be made known to God. And the peace of God, which surpasses all understanding, will guard your hearts and your minds in Christ Jesus."* This verse offers a powerful antidote to anxiety, encouraging believers to present their requests to God through prayer and thanksgiving, promising that God's peace will guard their hearts and minds. By routinely casting our anxieties onto God, we create space for His peace to enter and settle within us, nurturing a state of spiritual calm.

Managing Distractions

To practically manage these distractions, begin by cultivating a regular practice of prayer and meditation. This provides a refuge where you can voice your fears and doubts to God, allowing His presence to deliver comfort and clarity. Engage in mindful breathing exercises or meditative practices centered on scripture. For instance, repeating Bible verses that emphasize God's sovereignty and love can help redirect your focus from internal chaos to divine tranquility.

Engaging with community is another powerful strategy. Sharing your struggles with fellow believers who can offer prayer, support, and accountability significantly diminishes the isolating effects of fear and doubt. Through communal bonds, you gain strength and wisdom, reminded that the Christian journey is a collective experience.

Additionally, purposeful journaling can provide an outlet for exploring and understanding emotional distractions. Write about your fears and anxieties, pairing these entries with scriptural responses. Document moments when God has been faithful in the past, using these accounts as anchors of truth when doubt begins to drift in. This process of reflection promotes a perspective shift from what is feared to what is assured through Christ.

When emotions threaten to overwhelm, turn to worship as a balm for the soul. Listening to or singing worship music can re-center your focus on God's goodness and faithfulness, uplifting your spirit and reinforcing His promises.

Ultimately, conquering emotional and mental distractions requires a steadfast commitment to maintaining a focus on Christ. It involves continual reliance on prayer, scripture, and community to renew the mind and calm the spirit. As these practices become ingrained in your routine, you build resilience against distractions, nurturing a deepened and unshakeable faith. Through the lens of a Christ-focused mindset, fear, doubt, and anxiety lose their hold, allowing you to walk confidently in God's purpose for your life.

Alex's Story

Alex, a dedicated teacher facing mounting pressures in his personal and professional life, often succumbed to fear and doubt, questioning his ability to positively impact his students. These feelings intensified during a challenging period when budget cuts threatened his school's resources, deepening his anxiety about supporting his students' needs. Yet, during this tense time, Alex decided to refocus on his faith, seeking strength beyond himself.

He began incorporating consistent prayer and scripture reading into his daily routine, finding solace in passages like Philippians 4:13: *"I can do all this through him who gives me strength."* This verse reminded him that through Christ, he possessed the resilience to face his fears. By centering his mindset on faith and relying on God's guidance, Alex experienced a profound transformation. His renewed focus on Christ enabled him to navigate challenges with a more peaceful and determined heart.

As Alex gradually shifted his perspective from self-reliance to divine reliance, he found new ways to inspire and support his students, despite limited resources. His story highlights how focusing on Christ can dissolve doubt and empower one to overcome daunting obstacles, leading to both personal growth and greater fulfillment in one's vocational calling. This narrative exemplifies the transformative power of a Christ-centered mindset in dispelling fear and cultivating perseverance in the face of adversity.

Throughout history, we see examples of focus amidst distractions. Consider Nehemiah, who led the rebuilding of Jerusalem's walls despite persistent threats and distractions. His story is a testament to unwavering commitment and the strength that comes from a focused mind guided by divine purpose.

Comparing Nehemiah's Focus with a Modern Example of Perseverance

The story of Nehemiah offers a timeless example of unwavering focus and perseverance as he led the effort to rebuild the walls of Jerusalem despite significant opposition. Nehemiah's narrative is not just a tale of construction; it vividly represents maintaining divine focus amidst distractions and adversity. In Nehemiah 6:3, when detractors tried to draw him away from his work, his reply was resolute: *"I am doing a great work, so that I cannot come down."* His steadfastness is a beacon for anyone facing trials while pursuing God-given missions.

Such focus finds a contemporary parallel in Nelson Mandela, a leader whose life exemplifies perseverance and dedication to a greater purpose. Like Nehemiah, Mandela faced formidable obstacles; he was imprisoned for 27 years for his fight against apartheid in South Africa. During this time, the temptation to give up was immense, yet Mandela remained focused on his vision of a free and equitable South Africa. He understood that his struggle was larger than any personal discomfort he endured and maintained his focus on the broader mission.

Mandela's perseverance was not marked by inaction; during his imprisonment, he actively engaged with resistance movements, wrote extensively, and forged relationships that would later be pivotal in dismantling apartheid. His ability to remain focused, even while isolated, parallels Nehemiah's contagious determination to rebuild amidst opposition and threat.

Both Nehemiah's and Mandela's stories highlight the importance of a clear, divinely inspired vision. Nehemiah's commitment to his task came from a deep understanding that he was fulfilling God's directive to restore Jerusalem. Similarly, Mandela's steadfast belief in racial equality and democracy fueled his resilience, impacting millions and transforming the socio-political landscape of his nation.

Nehemiah's story teaches us that when distractions arise, remaining anchored in one's purpose through prayer and reliance on God's strength is crucial. For Nehemiah, regular communion with God fortified him against doubt and fear, providing clarity and direction. This principle echoes in Mandela's practice of meditation and engagement with spiritual and political texts during his imprisonment; these kept him mentally and spiritually focused on his ultimate goals.

Practical Strategies

Practical strategies to emulate these historical figures include setting clear objectives aligned with divine purposes and cultivating a support network that believes in the mission. Just as Nehemiah empowered others to join in rebuilding and Mandela inspired a nation to envision a new collective future, building a community of faith and mutual support turns individual focus into a shared mission.

Additionally, maintaining a steadfast focus requires active discernment to distinguish between genuine opportunities and distractions. Nehemiah and Mandela both faced numerous diversions but persevered by saying "no" to paths that didn't align with their objectives. This discernment is essential today, as we must measure each opportunity against our core purpose and God's will for our lives.

Nehemiah's reliance on God for the restoration of Jerusalem's walls mirrors Nelson Mandela's commitment to ending apartheid in South Africa. Both leaders demonstrated remarkable resilience, vision, and determination, enabling them to maintain focus despite challenges.

Nehemiah exhibited unwavering faith by continually seeking God's guidance and strength through prayer. His resolute response to adversaries—"I am doing a great work, so that I cannot come down"—illustrates his intense focus on his divine mission.

Similarly, Mandela maintained a clear vision for freedom and equality, refusing to let imprisonment deter his purpose.

Key traits they both exhibited include the ability to inspire and mobilize others toward a unified goal. Nehemiah rallied the people of Jerusalem to rebuild despite opposition, while Mandela inspired a nation, even from prison, to pursue a vision of equality. Their stories show that anchoring oneself in a higher purpose and cultivating a supportive community can strengthen resolve against distractions and opposition.

Both leaders' dedication to their core missions, guided by a belief in a cause greater than themselves, exemplifies how faith and a clear vision can lead to transformative outcomes amid challenges. Their narratives encourage us to maintain clarity and dedication, drawing strength from our core values and beliefs to navigate and overcome even the most daunting obstacles.

Their lives demonstrate that when we anchor our goals in faith, embrace a supportive community, and align our daily actions with our mission, we can withstand and triumph over trials that seek to divert us from God's path. Through persistence and divine guidance, we not only achieve our objectives but also leave enduring legacies that inspire future generations.

Reducing Digital Distractions

To maintain focus amid distractions, we must first identify those that commonly arise. Digital distractions, such as constant notifications from devices, are prevalent. These interruptions can easily derail focus, drawing attention away from meaningful pursuits. To manage these distractions, consider setting specific times to check emails or social media. Use tools like focus apps to limit digital exposure during work or prayer times. Designating tech-free zones or hours can also help preserve mental clarity and spiritual awareness.

Here are three practical methods for reducing digital distractions:

1. Use Focus-Boosting Apps:

- Utilize apps like **Forest**, which encourages you to focus by planting virtual trees that grow while you stay off your phone. The incentive of a lush forest growing as you concentrate can be motivating.
- Another effective app is **Freedom**, which blocks distracting websites and apps across your devices, allowing you to schedule times when digital access is restricted.

2. Implement Time Management Techniques:

- Embrace the **Pomodoro Technique** by working in focused bursts of 25 minutes followed by a five-minute break. This method naturally limits time spent on distractions and enhances productivity. Use tools like **Tomato Timer** to keep track of these sessions.
- Set dedicated blocks for checking emails and social media, such as once in the morning and once in the afternoon. This habit helps avoid constant interruptions caused by notifications.

3. Create Device-Free Zones:

- Designate specific times and spaces as tech-free zones, such as during dinner or in your bedroom. This strategy fosters healthier habits by preserving areas and times for off-screen activities, promoting better focus and mental clarity.

Moreover, establishing clear, purpose-aligned priorities is crucial. Begin by reflecting on what truly matters. What are your most significant goals, spiritually and personally? Engage in setting daily or weekly plans that align with your larger purpose. Write these down and refer to them regularly, allowing them to guide your actions and decisions. Priorities help ensure that tasks are consistent with deeper values.

Incorporating exercises to sharpen focus can also be beneficial. Engage in quiet prayer, meditate on God's word, or practice focused breathing exercises to enhance clarity and focus. Journaling about your distractions and corresponding strategies can provide insights into recurring patterns, helping refine your focus strategies over time.

Biblical Guidance on Staying Focused on God's Path

In our pursuit of aligning with God's path, biblical guidance serves as a compass, helping us navigate life's distractions. In an increasingly distracted world, believers must exercise purposeful focus to remain steadfast in their spiritual journey. The following strategies, rooted in scripture, provide a framework for maintaining this focus.

Firstly, recognizing the need for focus begins with awareness of how easily distractions can divert our attention from God's purpose. Distractions come in various forms—whether attention-grabbing devices or deeper desires driven by the flesh. These distractions pull us from the path of spiritual growth. A key scriptural foundation is found in Philippians 3:14 (ESV): *"I press on toward the goal for the prize of the upward call of God in Christ Jesus,"* which reminds us to press toward the goal in Christ. Daily, we should seek to identify these distractions and consciously choose the narrow path, one less burdened by the world's noise.

Understanding the seasons of purpose, as Ecclesiastes 3:1 (ESV) states, *"For everything there is a season, and a time for every matter under heaven,"* helps us realize that each phase of life has a divine purpose. During different life stages, such as career changes or personal growth, God calls us to adapt while remaining aligned with our ultimate spiritual mission. This awareness allows us to embrace life's transitions as part of God's greater blueprint.

To remain focused, prioritizing God's wisdom is paramount. Feeding regularly on God's Word serves as sustenance for our spiritual journey, as Proverbs 4:20-22 suggests. When His wisdom guides our decisions, we find clarity amid confusion. Giving the first fruits of our time to God each morning establishes a foundation of focus and direction.

Resisting the urge to gratify sinful desires is also crucial. Romans 8:13 (ESV) states, *"For if you live according to the flesh you will die, but if by the Spirit you put to death the deeds of the body, you will live."* This encourages living by the Spirit rather than succumbing to the flesh. Begin each day by setting a spiritual focus, inviting the Holy Spirit to guide you away from temptations that vie for your attention.

Nadia Skipping Story

It reminded me of something that happened when our twins were still young.

We were out on a neighborhood walk as a family—nothing fancy, just a moment to stretch our legs and enjoy the evening air. Nadia, one of our daughters, was always the energetic, assertive one. That day, she was skipping ahead of the rest of us, full of joy and rhythm, swinging her little jacket in one hand like a jump rope.

At first, it was kind of cute. She was carefree and lighthearted, lost in her own world. But I noticed the way she was moving—and something in me just knew. The jacket was swinging too fast, her skipping was too unpredictable, and the concrete was too unforgiving.

So I called out gently, "Hey Nadia, stop swinging the jacket while you're skipping. You're going to fall."

Without slowing down, she looked back and replied with full six-year-old confidence, "No, I won't, Dad."

A few seconds later—thud.

The jacket wrapped around her leg mid-skip, and she went tumbling onto the pavement. There was silence, then a sharp inhale, and then the tears came. I jogged to her side and scooped her up. Her knee was scraped, but I could tell her pride had taken the harder hit.

That moment stayed with me—not just as a parent, but as a follower of Jesus.

Because I realized how often I had done the exact same thing.

God would warn me—through a whisper, a conviction, a word of wisdom from someone close—and I'd shrug it off. "No, I won't, God." I'd think I had it handled. I'd believe I knew the limits. And then I'd fall—sometimes hard. Not because God was absent, but because I had ignored His voice.

Nadia didn't fall because she was bad. She fell because she trusted her confidence more than my counsel.

And isn't that what pride really is? It's not always loud rebellion. Sometimes it's just quiet resistance—a belief that this time, we've got it covered. That we can skip a little faster, swing a little wider, and stay in control.

But Jesus doesn't speak to limit us—He speaks to lead us. Obedience doesn't always make immediate sense, but it always builds long-term security. Not just from pain, but from patterns that delay our purpose.

That day, Nadia learned to trust my voice just a little more. And I was reminded to trust God's voice *a lot* more.

Protecting Your Heart

The story of Nehemiah, who famously declared, *"I am doing a great work and cannot come down"* (Nehemiah 6:3), exemplifies steadfastness. Nehemiah refused to succumb to distractions, maintaining laser focus on his God-given mission. Emulating this example requires developing resilience against interruptions that threaten our spiritual path.

Protecting your heart, as advised in Proverbs 4:23, underscores the need to guard your core beliefs and maintain purity. A heart aligned with Christ remains focused, discerning not just between good and evil but between good and best—ensuring that our actions consistently reflect God's glory.

Lastly, placing full trust in the Lord, relying on His understanding rather than our own (Proverbs 3:5-6), allows us to navigate life's uncertainties with unwavering faith. Trusting God to direct our paths keeps us rooted, ensuring our focus aligns with His purpose.

Cultivate a Focused Spiritual Journey

By applying these biblical principles, we cultivate a focused spiritual journey, blocking out distractions to walk unwaveringly on God's path. Through purposeful prayer, reflection, and community support, we strengthen our capacity to stay aligned with God's will, reaping the eternal rewards of a purpose-driven life.

Having a faith-based accountability group or mentor can significantly help individuals stay focused by providing spiritual encouragement, guidance, and accountability. The presence of a group or individual who shares the same spiritual values offers a supportive environment where one can express doubts and receive feedback, fostering growth and persistence in faith.

An example of this is a person struggling to maintain regular scripture study and consistent prayer. By joining an accountability group, they are surrounded by others who encourage sharing progress and setbacks. This shared journey cultivates discipline, as participants are motivated by each other's successes and supported through challenges. Group meetings often include shared prayer, scripture discussions, and goal-setting, reinforcing personal spiritual disciplines and aligning them with communal faith practices.

Such a support system strengthens spiritual discipline by ensuring individuals stay committed to their goals, cultivate resilience, and find renewed motivation through community interactions. This structure mirrors how Nehemiah gathered support from Jerusalem's citizens, creating a unified effort to achieve God's vision.

Returning to our lighthouse analogy, just as the beacon cuts through darkness to guide ships safely, focus acts as a guiding light in life's storms. Nehemiah's story and modern examples like Tom's illustrate that true strength and direction come from steadfast focus and intentional living.

As this chapter concludes, consider the reflective question: "What are the most frequent distractions in my life, and how can I develop an actionable plan to enhance my focus?" Reflecting on this encourages you to identify and address distractions, paving the way for spiritual growth and clarity. Embrace tools and strategies that reinforce clarity and purpose in every aspect of life. The pursuit of focus is not merely a task but a spiritual discipline that underpins one's journey toward fulfilling God's purpose.

Rerouted Truth: *Focus is a spiritual weapon—when you guard it, you protect your assignment and stay aligned with God's plan.*

CHAPTER 8
Committing to Your Purpose

In the lush valleys beneath the towering mountains of ancient Israel, a shepherd boy named David dared to step into a role far greater than tending sheep. His heart, full of bold faith, led him to face a giant—not just in battle but in his commitment to a purpose that would crown him king. David's journey from the fields to the throne is a testament to recognizing one's divine purpose and making the daunting choice to commit fully to it, setting a powerful precedent for the faithful who follow.

As you navigate your own journey of faith, consider how David's unwavering commitment mirrors the challenges and decisions you might face today. Committing to your purpose involves focused actions and decisions that align your life with God's overarching plan, demanding sacrifice, foundation, and discernment. Reflect on Proverbs 16:3 (ESV), which states, *"Commit your work to the LORD, and your plans will be established."* This divine assurance highlights the importance of aligning your pursuits with God's will, reminding us that by emulating David's example through commitment and faith, our actions become anchored in a purpose larger than ourselves, readying us for the next chapter on how to remain committed to your true purpose.

Understanding that you are part of a larger divine plan means acknowledging the interconnectedness of all believers in God's mission. As 1 Corinthians 3:5-10 (ESV) illustrates, every believer contributes uniquely to the collective mission. This interconnectedness offers perspective on our efforts—they are parts of a grand tapestry designed by God.

From Interest to Investment

For a long time, I flirted with purpose. I talked about it, dreamed about it, even taught others to pursue it—but deep down, I hadn't fully committed. I had one foot in and one foot out. If something didn't work quickly, I pivoted. If a door didn't open on the first knock, I questioned whether I was supposed to be there at all.

But over time, God began to reveal that purpose doesn't respond to convenience. It responds to conviction. I had to confront the uncomfortable truth that I was more in love with the idea of purpose than the process it required. That realization hit me during a season when nothing was "working"—at least not on the surface. I wasn't getting recognition. I wasn't seeing results. And I was tempted to walk away.

That's when the Lord pressed something deep into my spirit: *"Are you only here for the rewards, or are you willing to be faithful even when it's hard?"* That question shook me. It exposed how often I had treated calling like a contract—expecting returns before I'd fully invested.

So I made a decision. I stopped asking what I could get from purpose and started asking what I could give. I stopped measuring success by speed or applause and began measuring it by obedience and consistency.

Committing to my purpose meant building when no one was watching. It meant writing words I wasn't sure anyone would read. It meant pouring into people who couldn't repay me. But it also meant peace. Because for the first time, I wasn't chasing something—I was being anchored by it.

And now, even when things get hard—and they still do—I don't question whether I'm called. I just recommit.

Quitting My Job to Start a Business

I remember the moment purpose stopped being theoretical for me.

I was in my early twenties, working at a respected law firm. It was the kind of job you hang on to—solid benefits, a clear path forward, and colleagues who actually liked each other. For a while, I really believed I'd be there for the long haul. My mentor had recently moved on, but I still felt grounded—like I belonged.

Until I didn't.

A situation came up—one of those workplace moments that seem small to outsiders but cut deep when you're the one on the receiving end. I felt overlooked. Dismissed. Treated unfairly in a way that shook my trust in the organization and even in myself. It was like the emotional rug got pulled out from under me, and everything I thought was secure suddenly felt conditional.

Anger rose up—but so did something else: clarity.

I'd always had an entrepreneurial streak. In college, I'd joke that I created Uber before Uber existed, selling seats in my car to other students who wanted a ride home to the D.C. area on weekends. It wasn't fancy, but it worked. So the idea of working for myself wasn't foreign—it had just been sitting dormant.

Until that moment.

I decided I was going to leave the firm. Not out of recklessness, but because something in me had shifted. I couldn't unsee the vision God was starting to show me—not just for business, but for autonomy, for impact, for ownership of my calling. It was part disappointment, part righteous frustration, and part divine stirring. And I knew I had to pay attention.

The decision didn't happen overnight. I still had to be wise, still had to plan. But internally, a line had been crossed. I was no longer content to clock in for someone else's dream. God was calling me to build something of my own.

Looking back now, I realize it wasn't really about the injustice—it was about the invitation. That experience was God's way of rerouting me toward the next chapter of my calling.

Sometimes we need disruption to wake us up. Sometimes purpose doesn't knock—it shoves. And sometimes, what looks like a setback is really just the shaking needed to move us forward in faith.

God used that moment—my disillusionment with a job I once loved—as the launching point for something much bigger. And I've learned that commitment doesn't always begin with comfort. Sometimes it begins with fire.

Understanding Commitment to Your Purpose

Discovering Your Purpose vs. Committing to It

Discovering one's purpose is akin to hearing the distant call of a lifelong adventure from atop a hill; it's the whisper of potential aligning with the soul's most harmonious tunes. It's the initial realization that there's a unique contribution you are poised to make in the world, akin to hearing your name across a crowded room. However, discovering your purpose is only the dawn. Just as an explorer might chart an unknown route on a map without setting foot on its path, you may know your purpose without actively embracing it.

Actively committing to your divine purpose is the setting out—boots to gravel, through rain and sun, driven not solely by novelty but by relentless resolve. Committing involves an understanding that transcends mere acceptance; it enfolds sacrifice and an unwavering focus on a larger design, mirroring the determination of biblical figures like David who did not merely recognize their calling but lived it daily through actions aligned with their beliefs and God's kingdom.

Commitment in Practice: An Analogy

Consider the purpose of a seed: its potential to grow into a towering tree is innate, an inherent part of its makeup when discovered. But for the seed to fulfill its purpose, it must be planted in fertile soil, watered, and given sunlight. This active nurturing is akin to commitment. Much like the seed requires favorable conditions to grow, committing to your divine purpose necessitates creating an environment of discipline, reflection, and consistent effort. Jesus Christ is the foundation for such commitment—His teachings are the nurturing soil from which your purpose can flourish.

Building Your Life on the Right Foundation

The Apostle Paul's analogy of builders and foundations in 1 Corinthians 3:10-15 illustrates this truth beautifully: only work built on the foundation of Jesus Christ is assured lasting significance. Consider how your daily spiritual practices—your prayer, service, and study—fortify this foundation. Reflect on whether your endeavors are cemented in Christ, ensuring they not only withstand scrutiny but also thrive with divine favor. Is your life akin to the wise builder who constructs upon rock, or the foolish who builds on sand?

Real-Life Application

Realizing your purpose without commitment is like a captain who acknowledges the existence of a treasure somewhere in the world but never sets sail, charting a mundane course instead. In the scriptural story of the widow's offering (Mark 12:41-44), we find potent imagery of pure commitment. Her small coin, given with total willingness and devoid of reservations, embodied more than just financial sacrifice—it represented an alignment of her entire life with God's will. In pursuit of your purpose, ponder what you might need to release. What comforts or securities might you sacrifice to align fully with God's plan?

Guidance and Mentorship

Wisdom and guidance are essential in sustaining commitment. Proverbs 15:21-22 (ESV): *"Folly is a joy to him who lacks sense, but a man of understanding walks straight ahead. Without counsel plans fail, but with many advisers they succeed,"* extols the virtues of counsel, encouraging a community of mentors who can help foster spiritual growth. As you navigate your path, reflect on the influences surrounding you. Seek out individuals who can guide you in maintaining your focus on divine intent.

The Role of Mental Renewal

Mental renewal is vital for maintaining a committed mindset, as Romans 12:2 instructs us to transform by renewing our minds. This ongoing process involves evaluating and realigning your thoughts and actions with divine purposes, making room for new insights and approaches. Strengthening your spiritual routines supports this transformation, ensuring your journey reflects God's will.

Vigilance Against Distractions

Finally, as Matthew 7:15-20 warns against distractions in the form of false prophets and misleading influences, stay vigilant. Reflect on your own life: what distractions might be pulling you off your divinely intended path? Devise strategies to stay true to your course, grounded in Christ's teachings, creating a buffer against any temptation to stray.

In conclusion, truly committing to your purpose demands more than an acknowledgment of existence; it requires action aligned firmly with God's plan—a continuous journey of faith, resilience, and dedication. Through this genuine commitment, your life can radiate divine purpose, creating a lasting impact that aligns with the grand tapestry woven by God.

Reflective Guide:
Seven Ways to Commit to God's Purpose

1. Your Work Must Be Bigger Than You: Reflect on how your current projects align with advancing God's kingdom, considering adjustments to enhance their divine purpose. Use this passage to ensure your daily tasks reflect a commitment to God's vision, turning work into a mission. Proverbs 16:3 (ESV) reminds us, *"Commit your work to the LORD, and your plans will be established."* Contemplate how your daily tasks align with advancing God's kingdom by serving others. Think about what adjustments could transform your work into a mission that reflects this divine alignment. You may write in your journal about efforts that can extend their reach and impact, pondering how these can grow to benefit the community around you.

2. Understand You Are Part of a Larger Plan: Reflect on sacrifices needed to achieve success in alignment with God's plan, inspired by the widow's offering. Determine what personal comforts you might surrender for deeper spiritual alignment and impact, using this scripture to prioritize divine desires over personal gain.

We are co-workers with God, contributing uniquely to His divine tapestry. Consider your contributions to your community or church. Reflect on questions like, "How do my spiritual and practical actions help build the larger body of Christ?" Consider joining or initiating collaborative projects that resonate with a shared missionary vision, understanding their broader, eternal impact.

3. Build on the Rock: Creating a strong foundation in Christ is essential for lasting purpose. In 1 Corinthians 3:10-15 (ESV),

Paul emphasizes building our endeavors on the enduring teachings of Christ. Review your spiritual practices, such as prayer and scripture engagement, and ask yourself, *"Is my life truly reflecting Christ's teachings?"* Consider enhancing your daily spiritual disciplines to reinforce this foundation, ensuring steadfastness through life's challenges.

1 Corinthians 3:5-10 (ESV): *"What then is Apollos? What is Paul? Servants through whom you believed, as the Lord assigned to each. I planted, Apollos watered, but God gave the growth. So neither he who plants nor he who waters is anything, but only God who gives the growth. He who plants and he who waters are one, and each will receive his wages according to his labor. For we are God's fellow workers. You are God's field, God's building. According to the grace of God given to me, like a skilled master builder I laid a foundation, and someone else is building upon it. Let each one take care how he builds upon it."*

4. The Price for Success Must Be Paid: Reflecting on the cost of commitment to a spiritual journey involves understanding and embracing the sacrifices that come with aligning one's life with divine purposes. Life presents numerous opportunities for decisions that reflect our priorities, and often, choosing a path rooted in spiritual alignment requires sacrifices that surpass material gains. The story of the widow's offering in Mark 12:41-44 (ESV) teaches us about giving beyond comfort, making choices that resonate with deeper spiritual significance.

5. Success Comes by Good Counsel: Rely on the wisdom gained through mentorship and accountability, as articulated in Proverbs, to strengthen decisions with input from spiritual mentors. Use these relationships to confirm and advance your spiritual mission. Proverbs 15:21-22 (ESV): *"Folly is a joy to him who lacks sense, but a man of understanding walks straight ahead. Without counsel plans fail, but with many advisers they succeed,"* advocates for deriving strength from wise advisers. Assess your current network: "Who provides spiritual wisdom and encouragement?" Plan to seek advice more frequently and deepen connections with spiritual mentors and communities that nurture growth.

6. Put New Knowledge in New Containers: Consider the transformation needed in thought patterns to align with God's purpose. Romans 12:2 (ESV) speaks to the renewal of the mind. Reflect on the changes needed in your attitudes and behaviors. Ask, "What aspects of my mindset need transformation to align better with my divine purpose?" Engage in scripture readings and meditative practices to cultivate a receptive, renewed mindset for God's guidance.

7. Beware of Smooth Talkers: Develop strategies for discerning truth and protecting your spiritual journey against deceptive influences. Reflect on influences that potentially mislead you from God's path, using this scripture to ensure your engagements are consistent with sincere biblical teachings. Matthew 7:15-20 (ESV) warns, *"Beware of false prophets, who come to you in sheep's clothing but inwardly are ravenous wolves. You will recognize them by their fruits. Are grapes gathered from thornbushes, or figs from thistles? So, every healthy tree bears good fruit, but the diseased tree bears bad fruit. A healthy tree cannot bear bad fruit, nor can a diseased tree bear good fruit. Every tree that does not bear good fruit is cut down and thrown into the fire. Thus you will recognize them by their fruits."* Consider, "What distractions need removal, and how can I protect my spiritual journey?" Develop strategies for discerning truth, ensuring your engagements and messages remain consistent with biblical teachings.

Career Decisions

Consider John, a dedicated professional offered a lucrative promotion that required relocating and working hours that significantly reduced his ability to engage in local church activities and community service. Despite the financial allure, John declined the offer and opted instead to invest time in mentoring youth through his local church. His choice to prioritize spiritual commitments over career advancement illustrated a common sacrifice faced by many striving to keep their work spiritually aligned.

Time Management

Rebecca, a young mother and church volunteer, felt overwhelmed by daily responsibilities and yearned for personal time. Between raising children and fulfilling volunteer commitments, she recognized the importance of carving out regular time for personal reflection and spiritual growth. As Rebecca examined her schedule, she recognized that sacrificing evening leisure TV would give her the time she needed to nourish her spirit. By managing her time wisely, Rebecca ensures that both her family and spiritual life benefit, reflecting an ongoing sacrifice of personal leisure for deeper spiritual nourishment.

Personal Relationships

For Anton, maintaining personal convictions sometimes puts him at odds with his peers. A pivotal moment arises when friends plan social gatherings that consistently conflict with his commitment to a weekly prayer group. Choosing to adhere to his prayer schedule, he consequently misses out on certain social events but discovers deeper friendships within his faith community. This sacrifice highlights the tension between social acceptance and spiritual commitment that many believers navigate, choosing pathways that reinforce their values over the allure of immediate social gratification.

Practicing spiritual commitment often requires sacrifices that, while challenging, lead to profound spiritual growth and fulfillment. By analyzing these examples, introspectively consider areas where God might be calling you to relinquish something in pursuit of a more authentic and fulfilling spiritual journey. This reflection may include setting aside time weekly for self-assessment or listing aspects of life that could be realigned to reinforce personal and communal faith objectives, prioritizing alignment with God's path over temporary comforts.

Committing to Your Purpose Spiritual Routine

Incorporate these reflective exercises into your spiritual routine to enrich your journey toward God's purpose. As you apply these principles, observe how your life increasingly aligns with and glorifies God's kingdom.

As you reflect on the journey outlined in Chapter 8, remember that each intentional commitment you make today shapes your path toward a life filled with divine anointing and purpose. Let David's unwavering dedication inspire you; he navigated challenges by grounding himself in faith, becoming a beacon of God's legacy. **Your commitments act as markers**, guiding you on a path to divine sustainability and fulfilling your spiritual mission.

Here is your call to action:
1. **Journal Daily:** Begin each day by documenting how your tasks align with your spiritual mission. Reflect on what you are willing to relinquish—whether comfort or conventional success—to pursue God's higher calling.
2. **Engage in Community:** Identify and join community service initiatives that resonate with your faith, reinforcing your interconnected role within God's divine tapestry.
3. **Seek Counsel:** Regularly consult with mentors who embody wisdom and devotion. Strengthen your spiritual framework with the insights they offer.
4. **Embrace Change:** Cultivate a mindset that welcomes divine transitions in your life as opportunities for profound growth and alignment with divine purpose.

The Faith-Driven Success Framework

As we transition into exploring "The Faith-Driven Success Framework," it's essential to build upon the insights gained from our previous discussions about aligning oneself with divine purpose. This section provides a structured framework that equips you with concrete spiritual strategies for living a life of intention and impact. By anchoring our commitments in scripture, we ground our journey in faith and draw strength and clarity from these eternal truths. The subsequent guide details five pivotal areas of focus, each interconnected with scripture, to help forge a path of faith-driven success that aligns harmoniously with God's will.

1. Awareness

- **Concept:** Reflect deeply to comprehend your true spiritual and earthly condition beyond surface appearances.
- **Scripture Reference:** Psalm 139:23-24 (ESV) – *"Search me, O God, and know my heart! Try me and know my thoughts! And see if there be any grievous way in me, and lead me in the way everlasting."*

2. Alignment

- **Concept:** Ensure your actions and goals harmonize with God's kingdom principles rather than conforming to secular expectations.
- **Scripture Reference:** Matthew 6:33 (ESV) – *"But seek first the kingdom of God and his righteousness, and all these things will be added to you."*

3. Assignment

- **Concept:** Discern your divine calling—whom you are meant to serve, driven by spiritual direction rather than societal pressures.
- **Scripture Reference:** Ephesians 2:10 (ESV) – *"For we are his workmanship, created in Christ Jesus for good works, which God prepared beforehand, that we should walk in them."*

4. Action

- **Concept:** Transform your faith into concrete actions that embody your divine purpose and serve God's plan.
- **Scripture Reference:** James 2:17 (ESV) – *"So also faith by itself, if it does not have works, is dead."*

5. Accountability

- **Concept:** Establish a faith community that encourages accountability and spiritual growth, reinforcing a life lived for God.
- **Scripture Reference:** Proverbs 27:17 (ESV) – *"Iron sharpens iron, and one man sharpens another."*

Living the Faith-Driven Success Framework

- **Self-Reflection Practice:** Continually engage in personal and spiritual assessments to ensure transparency about the state of your soul.
- **Align Your Life:** Regularly revisit and adjust life goals and actions to ensure alignment with God's kingdom values.
- **Clarify Your Mission:** Evaluate your gifts and passions to identify specific calling areas, relying on both personal insights and group discernment.
- **Faith in Action Plan:** Develop strategic plans that translate faith into action; establish routines and habits that foster resilience and initiative.

- **Community Engagement:** Build support within your faith community to reinforce accountability, facilitate sharing, and encourage mentorship.
- As you implement these practices, anticipate Chapter 9, where you will further explore the critical importance of living within God's purpose. Together, we will delve into understanding God's grand design and the impact of aligning your life with His intentions. Let these steps be your compass, guiding your commitment to action as you carve out a legacy aligned with divine intent. Prepare to embrace the transformative power of living a life fully integrated with the purpose God has designed for you.

Rerouted Truth: *Commitment to purpose means laying down comfort to pick up the cross you were meant to carry.*

CHAPTER 9
Why God's Purpose is Important

"What is the ultimate significance of living for God's purpose?" This penetrating question invites each of us to explore the depths of our spiritual journey, seeking understanding and embracing the richness that God's purpose brings to our lives. Engaging fully with God's purpose offers not just a path, but profound fulfillment, direction, and the promise of a life filled with peace and eternal significance.

Consider the transformation of Esther, a young Jewish woman whose life changed dramatically when she stepped into her divine calling. Elevated to the position of queen in a foreign land, Esther could have remained silent, protected by her royal status. But when her people faced annihilation, she made the bold choice to risk everything for the sake of her divine assignment. Her decision to speak up *"for such a time as this"* (Esther 4:14) demonstrates how embracing God's purpose often requires sacrifice, courage, and the willingness to confront fear.

Esther's shift from personal preservation to kingdom intervention exemplifies the power of aligning one's life with God's plan.

Her story reminds us that divine purpose is not reserved for ideal circumstances—it often emerges in moments of great tension and personal risk.

Living purposefully in line with God's will is the foundation of a meaningful life. Psalm 138:8 affirms, *"The Lord will fulfill His purpose for me; your steadfast love, O Lord, endures forever."* This verse emphasizes the assurance we receive from aligning with God's purpose—a life crafted with divine care and foresight, anchored in His enduring love.

Discovering the Weight of God's Purpose

For most of my life, I thought purpose was about finding what I was good at and doing it well. But the deeper I walked with God, the more I realized that my skills were only tools—His purpose was the real blueprint.

There was a moment during prayer when I sensed God asking me to release the plans I had meticulously crafted. Not because they were bad, but because they were mine—not His. That was hard. I had worked so hard to get to a place where things felt stable. Letting go felt like losing control.

But what I gained in exchange was clarity. When I stopped striving to build my own version of success and asked God to show me what He had in mind, I began to understand that His purpose always runs deeper than mine. His purpose wasn't just about what I did—it was about who I became while doing it.

The more I surrendered, the more peace I found. I stopped chasing validation and started seeking alignment. And with every step,

I began to see that God's purpose wasn't a destination—it was the path itself.

Even now, when things feel uncertain or slow, I remind myself: If I'm walking in His purpose, I'm already in the right place—even if it doesn't look like I imagined.

A Cautionary Contrast: Jonah's Misaligned Passion

While Moses's story shows the transformational power of aligning with God's purpose, Jonah serves as a cautionary example of what happens when passion lacks obedience. Jonah was a prophet with spiritual insight, but his strong will and nationalistic passion led him to resist God's assignment. Rather than embracing the call to preach repentance to Nineveh, he fled in the opposite direction—literally and spiritually.

Jonah's resistance wasn't rooted in fear of failure; it stemmed from a personal bias and a desire to control the outcome of God's mission. His passion for justice, though sincere, was disconnected from divine purpose. Even after reluctantly delivering God's message, Jonah resented the mercy shown to Nineveh. His story reminds us that zeal without alignment can lead to frustration, isolation, and spiritual stagnation.

Where Moses surrendered, Jonah resisted. Where Moses became a vessel of deliverance, Jonah became a warning of delay. Jonah's journey shows that being passionate—even spiritually gifted—is not the same as being purposeful. When we insist on our own outcomes, we risk forfeiting the peace and clarity that come from walking in step with God's will.

The Importance of God's Plan for Our Lives: Personal Applications

Understanding God's plan is crucial. Aligning with it enhances our spiritual growth and fulfillment. A life guided by divine purpose offers direction that transcends momentary challenges, leading us toward deeper, lasting joy. Our lives become part of God's greater tapestry, where His divine orchestration gives eternal weight to even the most ordinary acts of obedience.

But purpose is not always comfortable—sometimes, it collides with our preferences. What if God's purpose disrupts your plans? What if His calling asks you to release a dream, shift a career path, or forgive someone you'd rather forget? This kind of purpose tension is not a sign of confusion—it's often a signal that God is leading you beyond your comfort zone and into your growth zone.

Handling this tension requires spiritual maturity and a surrendered heart. It calls for trust when the road bends unexpectedly and obedience when the assignment feels unfamiliar. Rather than resisting disruption, ask God what He's forming in you through the redirection. Sometimes the very thing we fear losing is the thing God never intended to keep in our hands long-term.

Engaging in regular prayer, meditative reflection, and scriptural study helps us discern the difference between a personal preference and a divine calling. As we deepen our intimacy with God, we gain the courage to say yes—even when the direction feels unfamiliar—trusting that His purpose will always lead to His glory and our transformation.

When viewed through God's purpose, everyday choices transform into key moments of faith. Decisions regarding career, relationships, or service become opportunities to reflect God's love and wisdom in our actions. Psalm 138:8 affirms, "The Lord will fulfill His purpose for me; your steadfast love, O Lord, endures forever." This verse reinforces that even our most mundane decisions hold value within God's grand design, encouraging us to approach life with intentionality and trust in His enduring commitment to bring His purpose to completion in us.

Rooted in God's Purpose

Building a life rooted in God's purpose also involves community living, where believers uplift and support one another. Each individual's alignment with God's plan strengthens the broader faith community, creating a synergistic effect that empowers collective spiritual vitality. This integration mirrors the message of 1 Corinthians 12:12-14, depicting the church as a diverse yet unified body of believers, each part essential and valued. By engaging with fellow believers, we fortify our commitment not only to personal growth but also to enhancing our collective faith journey.

Practically speaking, embracing God's plan means recognizing and utilizing our unique talents. Consistent with the parable of the talents in Matthew 25:14-30, this involves stewarding our abilities wisely to multiply their impact for God's glory. Engaging in activities that utilize our God-given skills brings personal satisfaction and extends our reach, allowing us to contribute effectively to the world around us.

Seasons of waiting and action are integral to anyone's journey of purpose. Patience during uncertainty nurtures trust and dependence on God's timing, teaching us resilience and humility. Applying insights from Ecclesiastes 3:1, we recognize that life's seasons are divinely appointed, each playing a role in our growth and understanding. This awareness cultivates readiness, prepared to act when God opens doors or wait when He closes them.

Furthermore, staying attuned to God's plan demands regular spiritual assessment. Asking questions such as, "Am I following God's direction?" or "Have I been faithful in quiet obedience?" ensures alignment with His will. These reflections guard against distractions and reaffirm our commitment to His divine purpose, even when cultural pressures suggest otherwise.

In conclusion, embracing God's plan entails a holistic transformation that encompasses every aspect of our lives—personal goals, community involvement, and continuous spiritual growth. This commitment invites us to experience profound joy and fulfillment, rooted in the knowledge that we are living not just for ourselves, but for God's eternal purpose. By consistently applying these principles, believers can navigate their spiritual journeys with confidence and hope, assured that they are part of something infinitely greater than themselves.

Aligning with God's Purpose

Aligning with God's purpose brings tangible emotional benefits, including personal peace and joy. Finding one's role in God's greater narrative alleviates life's anxieties, as we trust in His divine timing and provision. The Apostle Paul eloquently states in Philippians 4:7 that this peace surpasses all understanding and guards our hearts and minds through Christ Jesus.

A modern testimony enriches our understanding of these concepts. Sarah, hindered by anxiety, felt unfulfilled despite material success. A transformative spiritual retreat prompted her to relinquish control and seek divine guidance. Recognizing her calling to support and uplift others, Sarah transformed her career perspective into a ministry of service. This alignment eased her anxieties and filled her life with joy and fulfillment previously unimaginable. All it took was aligning with God's purpose to give her a new perspective.

The importance of God's purpose is illustrated throughout scripture. Romans 8:28 reinforces this, affirming that *"in all things God works for the good of those who love Him, who have been called according to His purpose."* This reminds us that every life, when aligned with divine intent, weaves into God's greater plan, contributing to a tapestry of faith and service.

Evaluate Your Alignment with God's Purpose

To live in step with God's purpose, actively seek His guidance through prayer and scripture study, inviting Him to illuminate your path. Practice gratitude to remain focused on His blessings, mitigating distractions from worldly concerns. Engaging with a spiritual community and seeking wisdom from mentors can nurture your understanding and commitment to God's purpose.

Here are reflective questions designed to help evaluate your alignment with God's purpose in daily life, drawing on your passions, talents, and life experiences:

1. **What Passions Ignite Your Spirit?**
   Consider the activities or causes that invigorate you and reflect on how these passions align with God's calling. How can you channel this enthusiasm to serve His kingdom and contribute to the greater good?

2. **Are Your Talents Being Utilized for Divine Intent?**
   Evaluate whether you are leveraging your God-given skills in a way that aligns with your spiritual goals. Are there talents that remain dormant, and how might they be redirected to fulfill a higher purpose?

3. **How Do Your Experiences Inform Your Path?**
   Reflect on significant life experiences. How have these shaped your understanding of your divine purpose, and in what ways can they guide future decisions to align more closely with God's plan?

4. **What Adjustments Can You Make Today?**
   Examine your daily habits and choices. What small, consistent actions can you implement to ensure that your daily life reflects a commitment to spiritual growth and service?

5. **Who in Your Community Supports Your Spiritual Alignment?**
   Identify individuals or groups that foster your spiritual growth. How can you actively nurture these relationships, and how do they encourage you to live in accordance with God's design?

Engaging with these questions can reveal insights about your spiritual journey, helping solidify your commitment to living within God's purpose and emphasizing the profound impact of personal alignment on the broader faith community.

Addressing the Current Cultural Shift Away from God

A Cultural Drift from Divine Truth

In today's rapidly evolving society, individuals are increasingly turning away from traditional biblical truths and divine guidance. This cultural shift towards secularism is often marked by a focus on self-indulgence and moral relativity. Such trends create significant challenges for believers striving to align with God's purpose. As captured in 2 Timothy 3:2, *"For people will be lovers of themselves, lovers of money, proud, arrogant, abusive, disobedient to their parents, ungrateful, unholy,"* these words illustrate the many ways contemporary culture diverges from the divine path.

Maintaining Integrity in Faith

Understanding God's purpose is crucial for believers navigating a world where societal values frequently oppose spiritual teachings. The erosion of traditional morals and the rise of individualism foster an environment that dismisses absolute truths in favor of subjective morality. This shift prioritizes personal gain over communal well-being and fleeting pleasures over enduring truths. Believers are called to recognize this divergence and actively reaffirm their commitment to divine directives.

A Call to Reengage with Scripture

To counteract these cultural shifts, believers must deepen their engagement with Scripture, which provides the necessary discernment for distinguishing between transient worldly values and God's eternal principles. Regularly exploring biblical teachings equips individuals with the strength to remain steadfast amid pervasive secular influences. Moreover, building supportive communities that emphasize spiritual growth can serve as sanctuaries, encouraging mutual accountability and resilience against societal pressures.

Generational Implications

The cultural prioritization of self-gratification risks alienating future generations from foundational biblical truths. Today's believers bear the responsibility of imparting these principles, ensuring that God's purpose thrives across generations. Educating the younger ones in scriptural truths can preserve faith legacies, equipping them to uphold these values in an ever-changing world.

Spiritual Practices and Fortifications

Incorporating spiritual disciplines such as prayer, reflection, and worship is essential for anchoring believers amidst cultural storms. These practices cultivate a Christ-centered outlook, empowering individuals to engage critically yet faithfully with modern society. They affirm our primary aim: to honor God through our lives, upholding His truths despite societal divergence.

Embodied Hope and Divine Influence

As culture increasingly deviates from God's paths, the vital role of believers living purpose-driven lives becomes even more pronounced. Rather than succumbing to discouragement, recognition of this cultural shift should inspire believers to act as beacons of God's light, positively influencing the world. By aligning with divine purpose—consistent with scriptural teachings and regardless of societal trends—believers demonstrate the enduring significance of divine guidance and the transformative power of active faith. Through committed discernment and community engagement, believers can illuminate paths back to God's unchanging truth, serving as potent symbols of hope and divine love.

Expanding on How the Enemy Works Against Our Purpose

The importance of God's purpose in our lives is magnified when we recognize the enemy's relentless pursuit to disrupt and derail that plan. Scripture provides insight into the enemy's tactics, particularly in 1 Peter 5:8, where we are admonished to *"be sober-minded; be watchful. Your adversary the devil prowls around like a roaring lion, seeking someone to devour."* This vivid metaphor encapsulates the enemy's strategy: to distract, discourage, and ultimately destroy believers' alignment with God's divine purpose.

The enemy's primary objective is to create confusion and doubt, leading us away from spiritual fulfillment. By implanting seeds of fear and insecurity, the enemy seeks to obscure the clarity of God's voice, making His purpose seem distant or unreachable. During these moments of vulnerability, individuals are most susceptible to veering off their God-ordained path.

One of the enemy's most effective tactics is misdirection. He craftily introduces distractions that seem innocuous but are designed to pull us away from spiritual pursuits. Whether it's overcommitment to work, an obsession with material success, or engaging in behavior that diverts our attention from God, these distractions clutter our spiritual radar and dilute our effectiveness in pursuing God's mission.

Moreover, the enemy frequently uses discouragement as a tool to weaken our faith. Life's inevitable challenges—such as failure, loss, or unfulfilled dreams—can become breeding grounds for doubt about God's goodness and plans for us. In such times, it's crucial to cling to promises like those found in Jeremiah 29:11: *"For I know the plans I have for you, declares the Lord, plans for welfare and not for evil, to give you a future and a hope."* This assurance fortifies our resolve against the enemy's attempts to undermine our faith.

To combat the enemy's interference, immersing ourselves in God's Word and maintaining a robust prayer life is essential. The Scriptures equip us with wisdom and discernment, shielding us from deceptive influences. Through prayer, we align our hearts with God's, drawing strength and peace from His presence, empowering us to stand firm against the enemy's snares.

Community is another vital element in this spiritual battle. Surrounding ourselves with fellow believers provides encouragement, accountability, and support. In Ecclesiastes 4:12, we read that *"though one may be overpowered, two can defend themselves. A cord of three strands is not quickly broken."* This verse highlights the strength found in unity, reinforcing our defenses against the enemy's schemes.

Additionally, maintaining focus on God's promises and practicing gratitude can shift our perspective, lessening the impact of the enemy's lies. Keeping a gratitude journal or regularly reflecting on God's faithfulness in our lives reminds us of His unwavering presence, diluting the power of doubt and fear.

Ultimately, the enemy's attempts to disrupt God's plan in our lives underscore the significance of divine purpose. When we actively seek to understand and pursue God's will, we resist the enemy's distractions, recognizing them for what they truly are: attempts to prevent us from fulfilling our God-given potential. By remaining vigilant and grounded in our faith, we can thwart the enemy's plans, embracing a life that reflects God's glory and advances His kingdom. Through this alignment, we secure not only our spiritual growth but also our contribution to God's eternal plan.

Returning to our fundamental question, "What is the ultimate significance of living for God's purpose?" The clarity gained through exploration is profound. Living tethered to divine purpose transforms life from mere existence to something extraordinary, instilling everyday moments with lasting significance—a journey of service, joy, and eternal grace.

Self-Assessment for Recognizing Personal Purpose

Discovering and understanding your personal purpose is a journey that requires introspection, faith, and a willingness to align with God's divine plan for your life. This self-assessment is designed to guide you through reflection and discernment, helping you identify and embrace the unique calling God has for you.

1. Reflect on Your Joys and Passions:

Begin by considering activities and moments that bring you immense joy and satisfaction. Reflect on times when you've felt most alive and connected to something greater than yourself. What are you doing during these times, and how do these activities make you feel? Journaling about these experiences can uncover insights into your innate passions and strengths, offering clues to your God-given purpose.

2. Evaluate Your Skills and Talents:

Think about the skills and talents that come naturally to you. What do others frequently seek your help or advice on? These areas of natural proficiency often align with the gifts God has placed within you. Ask yourself, "How can I use these talents to serve others and glorify God?" This evaluation can illuminate ways to embed your abilities within a larger divine framework.

3. Consider Your Life Experiences:

Reflect on significant life experiences and challenges. What have you learned from them? How have they shaped you? Often, our past experiences, both joyful and challenging, prepare us for our unique purpose. These experiences can be stepping stones guiding you to a path that aligns closely with God's design for your life.

4. Identify Values That Drive You:

What values guide your decisions and actions? Consider writing down a list of your core values and assessing how they align with those of Christ. Values such as compassion, integrity, and service often point toward a life that seeks to follow God's heart. Understanding these values can clarify how you might enact your purpose in everyday life.

5. Pray for Divine Guidance:

Engage in regular prayer, actively seeking God's wisdom and clarity in understanding your purpose. Ask Him to reveal areas where

He wants you to grow or to provide opportunities that will lead you closer to His plan. As you pray, pay attention to recurring themes or confirmations you receive, as these often indicate direction.

6. Seek Confirmation in the Word:

Spend time in Scripture, searching for verses and stories that resonate with your spirit. God's Word serves as a lamp unto our feet, offering encouragement, direction, and affirmation. As you read, highlight the passages that speak to you and consider how they relate to your personal journey and purpose.

7. Engage with Community:

Discuss your discernment process with trusted friends, mentors, or spiritual leaders. Their insights can provide confirmation and guidance, helping to refine your understanding of your calling. Engaging with a community often reveals opportunities to express and fulfill your purpose through collective action.

8. Set Purposeful Goals:

Translate your reflections into action by establishing specific goals that align with your identified purpose. These may include small daily actions or long-term commitments to service or personal growth. Ensure that your goals are spiritually and practically aligned with your desired path, deepening your journey toward fulfilling God's plan for you.

By engaging in this self-assessment, you invite deep reflection and personal growth, fostering a greater understanding of the unique purpose God has set before you. As these elements unfold, remember that this journey is uniquely yours, and God walks with you every step, providing guidance and grace as you strive to live out His divine purpose.

Alignment with God's Purpose Action Steps

As our culture increasingly diverges from God's path, the importance of living with a purpose grounded in His teachings becomes even more critical. To strengthen your alignment with God's purpose, consider these actionable steps:

1. Deepen Your Engagement with Scripture: Dedicate time daily to reading and reflecting on biblical teachings. This practice provides the discernment needed to distinguish between worldly values and God's eternal principles. Consistent engagement with Scripture acts as a moral compass, guiding your decisions and actions in daily life.
2. Cultivate a Supportive Community: Surround yourself with fellow believers committed to spiritual growth. Participate in regular fellowship and discussions that nurture faith and encourage accountability. A strong community acts as a refuge against cultural pressures, reinforcing alignment with divine values through shared experiences and mutual support.
3. Embrace Spiritual Disciplines: Incorporate practices such as prayer, meditation, and worship into your routine. These disciplines foster a Christ-centered focus, anchoring you amidst society's shifting tides. They provide

spiritual fortification, helping you navigate life's complexities with grace and resilience.

As you reflect on these insights, prepare to explore "Chapter 10: Applying God's Wisdom in Leadership," where the focus shifts to harnessing divine wisdom to influence and lead in alignment with faith-based principles, fostering growth and positive societal impact.

Rerouted Truth: *God's purpose anchors your identity, fuels your impact, and ensures your legacy lasts beyond you.*

CHAPTER 10
Applying God's Wisdom in Leadership

The biblical narrative of Solomon serves as a beacon of leadership grounded in divine wisdom. When God appeared to him, Solomon didn't ask for wealth or power; instead, he sought wisdom to govern his people—a choice that defined his reign. This decision highlights a profound truth: true leadership stems from a commitment to values that transcend personal ambition, aligning with purpose and justice.

Leadership rooted in scripture embodies humility, wisdom, and integrity. Solomon's ability to balance humility with authority exemplifies the importance of prioritizing God's guidance over personal understanding. His reign illustrated a leadership style dedicated to fairness and community welfare—principles that remain vital today.

In modern contexts, leaders often face ethical dilemmas where biblical wisdom offers invaluable guidance. For instance, leaders must make decisions regarding environmental responsibility. Proverbs 22:1 reminds us that *"a good name is more desirable than great riches,"* emphasizing the significance of integrity over short-term gains. Leaders are encouraged to prioritize ethical stewardship of resources, reflecting long-term community and environmental welfare rather than immediate profit.

Shifting from Control to Calling

When I first stepped into leadership, I thought the role was about being the most capable person in the room. I carried the pressure to have all the answers, solve every issue, and lead with certainty. That mindset worked—until it didn't.

The deeper I went, the more I realized that what had gotten me started wasn't going to sustain me. I began to experience burnout—not because I didn't love the work, but because I was leading from human effort rather than divine wisdom.

It took a humbling season of frustration and fatigue for God to get my attention. I remember praying, *"Lord, I don't want to lead if it costs me peace."* His response wasn't audible, but it was clear: *"Then lead with Me."*

That moment marked a turning point. I began to invite God into every leadership decision—not just in emergencies but in the day-to-day. I started praying before meetings, seeking discernment before answering, and asking for wisdom rather than relying on charisma or experience.

Self-Delusion

After my business failed, I took a job in outside sales, working for a company that sold high-end residential security systems. It wasn't where I saw myself going professionally, but it was what God had placed in front of me at the time—and I needed the work.

My sales territory included all types of neighborhoods, from starter homes to multimillion-dollar estates. One of my regular responsibilities was following up with homeowners after a break-in—walking the property, assessing the vulnerabilities, and recommending solutions. On the surface, it was just another sales role. But as the weeks went by, something deeper started to take shape.

Almost every conversation followed the same script. Whether the homeowner was wealthy or middle class, Black or white, young professional or retired grandparent, they all said some version of the same phrase:

"I never thought it would happen to me."

I heard it so often, it began to feel rehearsed—like a line we all carry without realizing it. At first, I nodded empathetically and moved the conversation forward. But eventually, it hit me differently. This wasn't just a reaction to fear. It was a reflection of a deeper issue—what I now recognize as **a leadership blind spot.** A form of pride disguised as peace. A subtle assumption that **our preparedness protects us from pain.**

The irony? I had said those same words myself. Not in a living room with shattered glass, but in my own internal monologue when my business collapsed.

I thought I was too focused. Too strategic. Too spiritually aware for failure to touch me. I didn't say it out loud—but I believed I was immune.

I wasn't.

And just like those homeowners, I found myself stunned by a reality I didn't see coming. Because here's the truth: pain doesn't care about your position. Crisis doesn't respect your confidence. Leadership doesn't insulate us from hardship—it only intensifies the need for humility.

Jesus didn't say "if" the storm comes—He said **"when."** That's why He emphasized the difference between building on sand and building on rock. One looks stable until the pressure tests it. The other holds firm because of what it's anchored to.

That season taught me something leadership books rarely mention: you can protect the perimeter of your life and still be vulnerable in the core. You can install systems, strategies, and structures—and still miss the whisper of God warning, "Let me be your strength."

I've learned that wisdom in leadership begins not with knowledge, but with **surrender.** And often, it's not the external threats that pose the greatest risk—it's the illusion that we don't need covering because we've "got it handled."

Now, when I think back to those homeowners—or my own broken expectations—I don't just hear panic. I hear an invitation:

Lead with humility. Listen for truth. Don't assume you're untouchable.

Because the wise builder prepares **not to avoid storms**, but to stand through them—with Jesus as the anchor.

Leading with God's wisdom didn't make me perfect—it made me anchored. I didn't always have immediate solutions, but I had peace. I didn't chase outcomes the way I used to. I became more present, more discerning, and more focused on people than performance.

Over time, I also noticed that my leadership became more about stewardship than control. My question shifted from *"How do I grow this?"* to *"How do I honor God in this?"* That shift changed everything—from the culture I helped build to the decisions I made.

Enhancing Understanding of Applying God's Wisdom in Leadership through Brady and Woodward's Principles.

The leadership principles articulated by Chris Brady and Orrin Woodward emphasize foundational elements of character, tasks, and relationships. These principles resonate with the biblical view of leadership, where wisdom, integrity, and service intersect to create leaders who can inspire and guide effectively. Integrating these principles into a Christ-centered leadership framework enhances both personal and organizational growth, providing a robust approach to leading with purpose.

Character: The Cornerstone of Effective Leadership

In leadership, character is fundamental. It is the invisible force that drives ethical decision-making, inspires trust, and motivates followers. From a biblical perspective, this aligns with Proverbs 10:9: *"Whoever walks in integrity walks securely, but he who makes his ways crooked will be found out."* Leaders of strong character articulate a moral compass; they demonstrate consistency between words and actions, establishing credibility and setting standards for those they lead. Reflecting on one's ideologies and values ensures alignment with God's will, fostering environments of trust and transparency.

Tasks: Execution through Vision and Discipline

Effective leadership involves the seamless execution of responsibilities through clear vision, strategic planning, and disciplined action. Brady and Woodward stress the importance of task orientation rooted in clarity and effectiveness. For leaders, this means setting realistic goals, delegating appropriately, and maintaining focus on God's broader mission. Philippians 4:13 assures us that *"I can do all things through Christ who strengthens me,"* highlighting that reliance on divine strength equips leaders with the perseverance necessary to execute tasks, even in challenging circumstances.

Relationships: The Heart of Leadership Influence

Building and nurturing relationships are integral to effective leadership. Christ exemplified profound relational leadership through compassion, empathy, and service, developing leaders who are not only influential but transformative. According to Galatians 6:2, *"Bear one another's burdens, and so fulfill the law of Christ,"* leaders thrive on healthy relationships built on mutual respect and support. By cultivating rapport with their teams and engaging with stakeholders transparently, leaders create collaborative and empowered communities.

Integrating These Principles

Incorporating Brady and Woodward's principles requires intentional reflection and action. Start by assessing personal character—the core of your leadership style. Reflect on past decisions, identify areas for growth, and align your values with scriptural truths to guide ethical leadership. Next, concentrate on task execution. Develop comprehensive action plans that utilize both divine guidance and strategic methods to manage responsibilities effectively while prioritizing God's Kingdom as the ultimate goal.

Fostering meaningful relationships necessitates active listening, empathy, and consistent communication. Engage with team members and stakeholders authentically, modeling Christ-like behavior to strengthen bonds and inspire collaboration. Encouragement and mentorship play vital roles in reinforcing a culture of growth and collective success.

Ethical Leadership Challenges for Christian Leaders

Ethical leadership requires a delicate balance between achieving organizational goals and upholding core spiritual values. For Christian leaders, this often involves navigating complex situations where biblical teachings intersect with corporate demands. Here are several real-world challenges and practical insights for addressing them through biblical wisdom.

Navigating Business Ethics

Christian leaders frequently face dilemmas in maintaining transparency and integrity within the financial and operational aspects of a business. One common challenge is managing financial pressures that may lead to unethical accounting practices or cost-cutting measures that compromise product quality.

Example: A Christian CEO might feel tempted to exaggerate financial forecasts to attract investors. Here, biblical principles such as honesty and stewardship provide a framework for ethical decision-making. By prioritizing transparency and seeking God's guidance through prayer, leaders can uphold ethical standards while maintaining trust with stakeholders.

Balancing Corporate Expectations and Biblical Values

There is often tension between corporate growth targets and the need to uphold biblical values, such as compassion and service. Christian leaders may feel pressured to make decisions that improve short-term results but conflict with long-term ethical practices.

Example: A Christian manager might be asked to overlook unfair labor practices to boost production metrics. Biblical teachings emphasizing justice and the dignity of each individual guide leaders to address such issues directly. By advocating for fair treatment and working conditions, leaders not only uphold their spiritual values but also contribute to sustainable business practices.

Leading in Diverse Environments

Diversity in the workplace, including various religious beliefs, presents unique challenges for Christian leaders. They must respect diverse backgrounds while expressing their faith through actions rather than imposing beliefs.

Example: A Christian leader may need to support policies or initiatives that seem to contradict personal beliefs. Here, the biblical call to love and serve others inclusively becomes crucial. By respecting diverse perspectives and fostering a culture of understanding, leaders can create an environment that values all voices while personally adhering to their faith.

Practical Insights from Biblical Wisdom

Biblical wisdom offers several practical solutions to these challenges:

- **Prayer and Reflection:** Regular prayer and scriptural meditation help leaders seek divine guidance in decision-making, ensuring actions align with both faith and ethical standards.
- **Accountability Groups:** Engaging with accountability groups or mentors can provide support and diverse perspectives, assisting leaders in navigating complex ethical dilemmas.
- **Integrative Leadership Practices:** By incorporating both servant leadership and strategic planning, leaders can align organizational practices with biblical values, ensuring ethical integrity while achieving business success.

By leveraging biblical wisdom, Christian leaders can navigate ethical challenges with grace and integrity, ultimately fostering organizations that thrive on trust, respect, and shared values. This approach enhances personal leadership effectiveness and creates a legacy of ethical practices that resonate with broader societal expectations.

Embodying biblical leadership principles requires dedication, reflection, and commitment. By focusing on character, tasks, and relationships through the lens of Christ-centered leadership, leaders can navigate complexities with grace and assurance. When leaders apply these truths, they illuminate God's wisdom, effecting positive change within their spheres of influence and beyond.

Modern Examples of Applying God's Wisdom in Leadership

Why do contemporary role models reinforce these timeless biblical leadership principles? Modern leadership, infused with God's wisdom, stands as a beacon of integrity and purpose, showcasing the transformational power of spiritual values in action. By examining leaders who successfully integrate these values into their practices, we see the profound impact of spiritual insight in action, as it transcends time and deeply influences societal and organizational structures linked to followers' growth and transformation.

One compelling example is **Dan Cathy**, former CEO of Chick-fil-A. Under his stewardship, the company has gained renown not only for its business success but also for its commitment to Christian values. Cathy champions a leadership style rooted in servant leadership, emphasizing humility and service to both employees and customers. His approach is anchored in a dedication to Sunday closures, reflecting a commitment to rest and faith—principles drawn from biblical teachings. Cathy's leadership has fostered a company culture where employees feel valued and customers sense genuine care, exemplifying how aligning business practices with God's wisdom can yield both ethical and financially successful results.

Anne Beiler, founder of Auntie Anne's Pretzels, offers another illustration of applying God's wisdom in leadership. Her journey began from modest roots, driven by a vision to honor God through her business. Beiler's narrative highlights resilience and reliance on God's guidance in overcoming significant personal and professional challenges. She emphasizes integrity in all dealings, fostering a work environment that prioritizes values such as transparency and family. Her focus on building meaningful relationships within her franchise network has not only ensured sustained growth but also created a supportive community that reflects the principles of Christian fellowship.

Modern leadership also finds expression in **Rosalind Brewer**, CEO of Walgreens Boots Alliance. Her commitment to diversity, equity, and inclusion is informed by her faith. Brewer advocates for underrepresented voices and ensures that decision-making reflects the core Christian teaching of loving one's neighbor. Her initiatives have been pivotal in cultivating workplace cultures that thrive on inclusivity and equal opportunities, demonstrating how faith-driven principles can lead to innovation and progress in corporate environments.

Tim Keller, a respected pastor and author, provided another dimension of leadership through spiritual mentorship and intellectual engagement. As a leader of Redeemer Presbyterian Church in New York, Keller guided countless individuals in discerning God's purpose in urban life. His leadership, marked by humility and a commitment to theological depth, equipped others to apply biblical wisdom in addressing contemporary issues, blending faith with practical solutions in community outreach and cultural engagement.

These leaders illustrate how incorporating God's wisdom into leadership can transform both enterprises and communities. Through humility, integrity, and service, their impactful work serves as a testament to the power of leading with divine guidance. By prioritizing ethical principles and fostering inclusive cultures, they create environments where individuals are nurtured, and communities are strengthened.

For those aspiring to lead in a manner that reflects God's wisdom, these modern examples offer invaluable lessons. They demonstrate that true leadership is less about domination and more about elevating others through guidance and example. Embracing spiritual principles in leadership not only honors God but also fosters innovative and sustainable solutions that benefit society as a whole.

The Habit of Self-Reflection

Moving forward, leaders seeking to apply God's wisdom should cultivate a habit of self-reflection, continuously aligning their actions with biblical teachings. This involves practicing servant leadership, prioritizing community well-being, and maintaining integrity in all pursuits. Engaging in prayer and studying Scripture provides direction, ensuring that every decision is infused with divine insight. In doing so, leaders not only fulfill their roles effectively but also contribute to the advancement of God's kingdom on earth.

Applying God's wisdom in leadership involves cultivating a mindset aligned with divine principles. This begins with daily reflection on scriptures, reminding oneself of the eternal values that guide ethical decisions. Proverbs 3:13 praises those who "find wisdom" and gain understanding, reinforcing the necessity of aligning leadership practices with biblical teachings.

Prayer is central to inviting divine guidance in leadership decisions. This practice strengthens personal resolve and opens one's heart and mind to godly insights that shape trustworthy leadership. Engaging with the community and seeking counsel from spiritual mentors fortifies a leader's ethical framework, ensuring their decisions reflect service and responsibility.

Applying God's Wisdom in Leadership Across Life Roles

Leadership transcends formal positions and titles, reaching into every aspect of life where influence resides. Whether in parenting, ministry, or the workplace, applying God's wisdom in leadership manifests through a commitment to integrity, compassion, and purposeful service.

Parenting: Leadership in the Home

Leadership at home involves nurturing, guiding, and setting examples for children. Consider Proverbs 22:6, which offers timeless wisdom: *"Train up a child in the way he should go; even when he is old, he will not depart from it."* Parents are entrusted with the responsibility of leading their children toward spiritual and moral maturity—a journey requiring patience and a love grounded in biblical principles.

Creating a home where God's love is evident can involve regular family devotions, faith discussions, and embodying Christ-like behavior. Parents lead by modeling values such as honesty, empathy, and humility, aiming to raise children who not only understand God intellectually but also experience His presence personally and carry these teachings into their futures.

Ministry: Spiritual Leadership

In ministry, leading with God's wisdom involves shepherding a community with a servant's heart, much like Jesus did. Ephesians 4:11-13 (ESV) states, *"And he gave the apostles, the prophets, the evangelists, the shepherds and teachers, to equip the saints for the work of ministry, for building up the body of Christ, until we all attain to the unity of the faith and of the knowledge of the Son of God, to mature manhood, to the measure of the stature of the fullness of Christ."* This underscores the role of church leaders in equipping the saints for service and unity in faith. Here, spiritual leaders are called to facilitate growth, empowering each person to fulfill their God-given purposes.

Reliance on the Holy Spirit is essential for insight and guidance in ministry leadership. This role entails providing sound teaching, pastoral care, and shepherding with humility. It also involves recognizing unique gifts within the congregation and encouraging individuals to cultivate these talents for the edification of the Body of Christ. Leaders must remain receptive to growth and adapt their methods to address the evolving spiritual needs of their community.

Workplace: Leadership with Integrity

In professional settings, leadership founded on God's wisdom is crucial. Colossians 3:23-24 reminds us to *"work heartily, as for the Lord and not for men...for you are serving the Lord Christ."* This scripture highlights that the dedication and integrity brought to career tasks should first and foremost honor God.

Workplace leadership means fostering environments of respect, collaboration, and ethical practice. Leaders positively influence company culture by prioritizing transparency, fairness, and valuing everyone's contribution. They model productive conflict resolution, encourage team growth, and pursue excellence. When faced with challenges, turning to prayer and biblical principles can guide sound decision-making that aligns with divine teachings.

Building Interconnected Leadership Styles

Effective leadership recognizes that no universal style fits all contexts. Parenting, ministry, and workplace leadership each require distinct nuances yet are all underpinned by foundational *principles of God's* wisdom. Integrating these teachings, leaders create environments where spiritual values enhance policies, interactions, and growth processes.

This broader view of leadership necessitates ongoing personal development. Leaders must seek God's counsel continually, engage in lifelong learning, and actively contribute to community building. By fostering support networks and mentorship, they acknowledge leadership as both an individual calling and a communal journey.

In conclusion, applying God's wisdom across different areas of life fosters cohesive growth and strengthens communities. By leading with faith, compassion, and integrity, we inspire others toward immediate and eternal goals, enriching life and glorifying God through lasting influences that extend His teachings into the world. Balancing authority with humility, leaders prioritize service and engage teams with empathy, fostering alignment with a mission that serves the greater good.

Comparing Faith-Driven Leadership with Secular Leadership Models

Leadership, a cornerstone of organizational and personal success, can be approached through various models that reflect different values and principles. Faith-driven leadership and secular leadership present distinct frameworks, each with unique implications and methodologies. Understanding these differences enriches leadership practices, particularly when striving to integrate God's wisdom into everyday decisions.

Core Principles and Motivations

Faith-driven leadership is anchored in serving others through principles derived from biblical teachings, emphasizing values like integrity, compassion, and humility to glorify God. This model prioritizes ethical decision-making and fosters an environment where each person's intrinsic worth is recognized, cultivating a spirit of service and community that transcends mere transactions.

In contrast, secular leadership models typically prioritize outcomes such as efficiency, profit, and growth. Success is measured through tangible metrics like shareholder satisfaction and pursued through various frameworks, from transformational to transactional models. Ethical considerations in these approaches are often viewed through compliance or corporate social responsibility, rather than intrinsic spiritual motivation.

Approaches to Decision-Making

In faith-driven leadership, decision-making is a spiritual process involving prayer, scripture, and discernment to ensure alignment with divine purpose. Leaders assess the broader impact of their choices on community welfare and spiritual growth, embodying stewardship and accountability beyond organizational objectives.

Secular leadership emphasizes strategic planning, data analysis, and risk assessments. Decisions focus on maximizing performance and achieving predefined goals. While employee well-being and ethical practices are acknowledged, they often serve competitive advantage and profitability rather than a deeper spiritual or moral obligation.

Leadership Styles and Influence

Faith-driven leaders exemplify servant leadership, drawing inspiration from Jesus' example of serving others. This style creates a nurturing environment where team members are empowered, and the collective vision is fostered through compassion and mentorship.

Conversely, secular models may emphasize traditional hierarchical structures, exerting influence through charismatic or transactional leadership strategies. Here, authority often derives from positional power, motivating teams through vision or incentives to drive performance, which, while effective, often lacks the deep relational connection found in faith-driven approaches.

Impact on Organizational Culture

Organizations led by faith-driven principles cultivate cultures of inclusion, respect, and holistic growth. These environments create a sense of belonging and purpose, aligning personal values with organizational goals and viewing initiatives through a lens of service and communal benefit.

Secular organizations may prioritize innovation and competition, requiring adaptability to market dynamics. While this focus on efficiency and competitive advantage is essential for success, it can sometimes overshadow long-term value creation and ethical considerations unless explicitly integrated into the organizational culture.

Challenges and Critiques

A significant challenge for faith-driven leadership is aligning spiritual principles within diverse environments where beliefs may vary. Leaders must navigate maintaining spiritual integrity while being inclusive, ensuring that faith-based values enhance organizational life rather than alienate team members.

Secular models face the challenge of upholding ethical standards amidst pressures for immediate results. This includes prioritizing employee well-being and ethical considerations alongside aggressive market-driven goals, which can create tension within organizational priorities.

Integrative Possibilities

Blending elements from both leadership models can enhance organizational practice. Integrating the relational and ethical strengths of faith-driven leadership with the strategic focus of secular models enables leaders to cultivate an environment that respects individual values while achieving organizational success. This balance is crucial for personal growth and applying divine wisdom to navigate contemporary challenges.

Such integration highlights the transformative potential of infusing God's wisdom into modern leadership practices, inviting leaders to create environments rich in growth, purpose, and unity that resonate with both personal and organizational goals. This alignment allows for not just achieving success but also contributing to a greater societal good that transcends profit and performance.

Biblical Principles for Ethical Leadership

Leadership grounded in God's wisdom calls for adherence to ethical principles that reflect divine guidance and ensure integrity in every action. These biblical precepts align leaders with spiritual growth and foster environments characterized by justice, compassion, and truth. Here are key biblical principles for ethical leadership:

1. Love and Compassion

Leadership influenced by God demands a heart of love and compassion, as emphasized by Jesus in John 13:34-35: *"A new commandment I give to you, that you love one another: just as I have loved you, you also are to love one another. By this all people will know that you are my disciples, if you have love for one another."* Leaders must cultivate an atmosphere of genuine care, being empathetic to the needs and aspirations of others, thereby nurturing a community grounded in mutual respect and kindness.

2. Integrity and Honesty

Integrity is central to ethical leadership. Proverbs 11:3 outlines this clearly: *"The integrity of the upright guides them, but the crookedness of the treacherous destroys them."* Ethical leaders are expected to exhibit transparency in their actions and decisions, maintaining honesty even when it is costly. Upholding truth builds trust and secures a leader's credibility, encouraging others to align with both personal and communal objectives.

3. Humility

Biblical leadership embodies humility, as shown in Philippians 2:3: *"Do nothing from selfish ambition or conceit, but in humility count others more significant than yourselves."* Leaders should serve rather than seek to be served, placing the well-being of others before their own. This principle fosters a cooperative environment where team collaboration and community welfare are prioritized.

4. Justice and Fairness

Promoting justice is a biblical mandate for leaders, supported by Micah 6:8: *"He has told you, O man, what is good; and what does the Lord require of you but to do justice, and to love kindness, and to walk humbly with your God?"* This principle requires leaders to treat individuals equitably, making decisions that uphold fairness and righteousness, ensuring that actions benefit all rather than a select few.

5. Stewardship and Responsibility

Acknowledging that resources and talents are gifts from God, biblical leadership calls for prudent stewardship. 1 Peter 4:10 advises, *"As each has received a gift, use it to serve one another, as good stewards of God's varied grace."* Leaders are tasked with managing their resources wisely, cultivating growth and sustainability, and investing in their community's well-being.

6. Perseverance and Patience

Recognized in Galatians 6:9, perseverance is vital: *"And let us not grow weary of doing good, for in due season we will reap if we do not give up."* Leaders are encouraged to persist in their efforts, even amidst trials, trusting in God's timing. Patience allows leaders to make thoughtful decisions, maintaining focus on long-term outcomes over immediate gains.

7. Forgiveness and Reconciliation

An essential aspect of ethical leadership is the practice of forgiveness, as articulated in Ephesians 4:32: *"Be kind to one another, tenderhearted, forgiving one another, as God in Christ forgave you."* Leaders should create a framework for reconciliation, promoting healing in relationships, which strengthens unity and fosters a positive organizational climate.

By integrating these principles into their leadership style, leaders cultivate a culture reflective of God's kingdom, where ethical standards drive actions and decisions, and the transformative power of Christian values shapes every aspect of organizational life. Embracing these precepts expands a leader's influence, ensuring that their life's work exemplifies divine wisdom and serves as a testament to God's enduring love and truth.

Returning to Solomon's example, his wisdom-driven reign remains a reminder of leadership's ultimate goal: to govern with a heart aligned with divine intent. Solomon's legacy teaches us that wisdom and humility are indispensable in cultivating leadership that inspires and elevates others.

As you reflect on these insights, consider the path ahead in your leadership journey. Ask yourself: "Where do I see room for growth in my leadership?" and "How can I rely more on God's wisdom in my leadership decisions?" Let these questions guide you toward developing a style that harmonizes with biblical teachings while also meeting modern challenges.

Rerouted Truth: *Leadership isn't about control—it's about stewarding influence with wisdom, humility, and a heart aligned with God's will to serve.*

CHAPTER 11
Setting and Achieving Faith-Driven Goals

In the historical tapestry of faith, Nehemiah's story stands as a testament to the power of goals driven by divine purpose. Tasked with rebuilding the walls of Jerusalem amid adversity, Nehemiah exemplified how a faith-powered vision can turn monumental challenges into magnificent triumphs. His leadership was not solely about construction; it was a spiritual endeavor that united a community under God's direction, illustrating that goals anchored in faith transcend limitations.

The essence of setting and achieving faith-driven goals lies in their distinction from secular objectives. While secular goals often focus on personal gain or worldly success, faith-driven goals are deeply embedded in spiritual alignment with divine intent. These goals aim to manifest God's glory through personal achievements and community impact, connecting our daily actions with a broader divine narrative.

To embark on setting faith-driven objectives, start by discerning alignment with both personal callings and God's divine plan. Engaging in prayer and reflection is pivotal in this journey. As you converse with God through prayer, seek clarity on the desires He has planted in your heart, allowing these insights to shape your goals. Reflecting on Scripture provides further guidance; consider Proverbs 16:3 (ESV), *"Commit to the Lord whatever you do, and he will establish your plans,"* as a cornerstone.

When My Goals Became God's Goals

For years, I set goals like clockwork. Quarterly targets, annual milestones, vision boards—you name it, I did it. And for a while, that structure kept me motivated. But over time, I began to notice something unsettling: I was hitting goals, but not feeling fulfilled. I was checking boxes, but not growing spiritually.

That's when I started to ask harder questions: *Who gave me these goals? Are they rooted in faith or just ambition?* That inner shift began a journey I didn't expect—one that would move me from goal-chasing to Spirit-led planning.

It wasn't easy. I had to unlearn a lot. I used to think that faith-driven goals were just normal goals with a Scripture attached. But God began showing me that His goals required deeper trust, a slower pace, and often, unseen progress. He wasn't calling me to outcomes—He was calling me to obedience.

One night during prayer, I wrote down what I now call my "obedience goals"—things I sensed God asking me to commit to, even if I didn't know how they would turn out. Some of them scared me. Others felt too small to matter. But each one forced me to listen instead of lead.

Since then, I've watched God do more through my surrendered plans than I ever did through my strategic ones. Doors opened where I had stopped knocking. Ideas flowed where I had once been stuck. But more importantly, my relationship with God deepened. My goals became less about achievement and more about alignment.

I still plan, still write things down, but now I hold every goal loosely and every prayer tightly. Because my greatest progress has never been what I've accomplished—but how I've obeyed.

Finishing My Degree

One of the most pivotal goals I ever set wasn't about business, leadership, or even ministry—it was finishing my college degree.

When I first went to college straight out of high school, I had every intention of finishing in four years. But life didn't unfold the way I imagined. My parents were going through a divorce, and the emotional and financial impact of that season pulled the rug out from under me. After completing just two years, I had to step away.

It would be years before I returned to that unfinished chapter.

At the time, I didn't fully realize how deeply that incomplete goal lingered in the background of my life. But eventually, God began to press on my heart that it was time. Not because I needed a degree to prove anything to the world—but because He was doing something in me that required discipline, surrender, and completion.

So I enrolled in online classes while working a demanding job that required 50 to 60 hours a week—including frequent travel across the country. Balancing course deadlines and conference calls wasn't glamorous. I wrote papers in airports, took quizzes in hotel rooms, and studied late at night when my body begged for sleep.

Without the help of my wife, I never would've made it through.

It took me almost three years to cross the finish line. And I won't pretend it was easy. But I did it. And it changed me.

Now, I'm not suggesting college is for everyone. In fact, I believe in many cases, it's not necessary to fulfill the calling God has placed on someone's life. But for me—in *that* season—it was necessary. It was about obedience more than opportunity. It was about honoring something God had whispered long ago: "You have some unfinished business."

Looking back, finishing my degree wasn't about the diploma. It was about learning to keep going when the cost is high, and the applause is low. It was about honoring a commitment and walking it out to the end. And it taught me that goals—when given by God—are never just about achievement. They are tools of refinement. Instruments of formation.

That goal didn't just mark a milestone. It marked a shift in me.

Practical Goal-Setting Frameworks for Faith-Driven Goals

Setting goals that are actionable and achievable is crucial for aligning ambitions with faith-driven purposes. Inspired by scriptural wisdom, these frameworks guide believers in establishing goals that reflect personal aspirations while advancing God's kingdom. By integrating spiritual insights with practical strategies, these frameworks ensure that your efforts lead to meaningful and impactful outcomes.

1. Align Goals with Divine Purpose

Start by aligning your goals with your divine calling. Reflect deeply on 1 Corinthians 10:31, *"So whether you eat or drink or whatever you do, do it all for the glory of God."* This perspective anchors your goals in a higher purpose, ensuring that your pursuits honor God and serve others. Begin with prayer and meditation to discern God's guidance, asking for clarity on goals that align with His plans for your life.

2. Set SMART Goals

Utilizing the SMART criteria—Specific, Measurable, Achievable, Relevant, Time-bound—has long been a gold standard for goal-setting, ensuring focus and realistic planning. Adding an additional "S" for Spirit-led transforms this approach into a faith-driven method by ensuring that each goal aligns not only with personal ambitions but also with divine guidance. This nuanced addition redefines the entire process, guiding believers to pursue objectives underpinned by prayer and spiritual discernment.

For instance, a standard SMART goal might involve committing to volunteer a set number of hours at a local charity each month. By embedding a 'Spirit-led' approach, an individual begins by seeking prayerful insight, asking God to reveal where their contribution can have the most significant impact. Instead of merely fulfilling volunteer hours, the service reflects a deeper alignment with God's will, perhaps guiding them toward causes or communities they hadn't previously considered but feel spiritually called to support.

In this manner, the Spirit-led component not only instills spiritual depth but also ensures that every step taken is guided by a higher purpose, transforming personal achievement into a divine collaboration that echoes through personal growth and community benefit.

3. Create a Vision Board or Mind Map

Visualize your goals through a vision board or mind map. These tools provide a representation of your aspirations, reinforcing commitment and inspiration. Place images, scriptures, and quotes that resonate with your goals and God's promises, integrating them into your daily environment. This visual reinforcement keeps you focused and motivated, reminding you of the broader purpose behind each goal.

4. Break Goals into Manageable Steps

Deconstruct larger goals into smaller, manageable tasks. This method prevents overwhelm and provides a clear trajectory of progress. As Proverbs 16:9 reminds, *"In their hearts, humans plan their course, but the Lord establishes their steps."* Create a timeline with specific milestones, celebrating each achieved step as a testament to your faith and dedication.

5. Stay Accountable with a Support Network

Engage a network of supportive individuals who share your values and vision. This group provides encouragement, advice, and accountability. Whether through faith communities, small groups, or mentorship, these relationships strengthen resilience and maintain focus. Regularly update your network on your progress, inviting constructive feedback and prayers for continued strength and direction.

6. Reflect and Adjust Regularly

Reflect on your progress regularly, using this time for prayerful consideration of any necessary adjustments. Sometimes, goals need to evolve based on unfolding life circumstances or deeper insights from God. Be open to reshaping your objectives in alignment with ongoing spiritual discernment. This flexibility acknowledges that God's purpose for you may include surprising shifts and new opportunities.

7. Celebrate and Give Thanks

Celebrate milestones and express gratitude for each accomplishment. Acknowledge God's role in your achievements, praising Him for His support and guidance. As you reach each milestone, thank God for the journey thus far and seek His continued blessing for the path ahead. This practice not only honors God but also reinforces a thankful heart and inspires continued perseverance.

8. Document Insights and Learnings

Record your journey, insights, challenges, and triumphs in a journal. This documentation serves as a personal log of God's faithfulness and your growth, providing encouragement for future pursuits. Over time, these entries become a reflection of God's work in your life, showcasing the progression from intention to realization.

One inspiring example of these principles comes from a rural town. Facing economic decline and dwindling opportunities, the community members were determined to revitalize their town through faith-driven goals. They began by aligning their initiatives with a collective vision rooted in their faith, inspired by Isaiah 58:12 (ESV): *"Your people will rebuild the ancient ruins and will raise up the age-old foundations."*

They established a plan using SMART goals, aiming to restore their main street within five years. Creating a vision board filled with images and Scriptures brought their aspirations to life, fostering a shared sense of purpose. They broke down their ambitious project into manageable steps, focusing on one building at a time while ensuring each effort was accompanied by prayer and thanksgiving.

The community-maintained accountability through regular gatherings, where they shared progress and supported one another. When challenges arose, they embraced flexibility, allowing God to guide unexpected adjustments. Celebrating each restored building with a blessing ceremony, they gave thanks for every milestone achieved.

This collective journey not only revitalized their town but also strengthened the bonds within the community, showcasing a tangible expression of faith-driven goals transforming individual lives and the entire town. By living out these principles, they demonstrated the profound impact of aligning personal and communal goals with divine purpose.

Addressing Challenges in Achieving Faith-Driven Goals

Pursuing faith-driven goals is both a journey of spiritual growth and a practical endeavor. However, this pursuit often comes with its own set of challenges that can deter progress. Understanding these obstacles and equipping oneself with strategies to overcome them is crucial for any believer seeking to fulfill their divine purpose.

1. Navigating Doubt and Uncertainty

One of the primary challenges in achieving faith-driven goals is navigating doubt and uncertainty. This doubt often arises from a lack of immediate results, prompting questions about one's path and the feasibility of the established objectives. Spiritual attacks can also cultivate doubt, as Ephesians 6:12 (ESV) reminds us: *"For we do not wrestle against flesh and blood, but against the rulers, against the authorities, against the cosmic powers over this present darkness, against the spiritual forces of evil in the heavenly places."* To overcome this challenge, believers must anchor themselves in prayer and continually affirm God's promises. Engaging with Scripture that highlights God's past faithfulness can provide reassurance and direction, illuminating the path forward with divine clarity.

2. Balancing Secular Demands and Spiritual Aspirations

Another challenge is balancing life's demands with the pursuit of faith-driven goals. Modern life often compels us to prioritize secular achievements over spiritual ones, which can compromise the time and energy available for spiritual development. Such dissonance can dilute our focus and devotion to God's purpose. To address this, it is essential to establish clear priorities that align with one's spiritual values. Allocating specific times for spiritual engagement—whether through prayer, community service, or study—ensures that spiritual aspirations remain central in daily life, guiding secular activities rather than being sidelined.

3. Overcoming Resource Limitations

Resource constraints, whether related to time, finances, or support, can impede progress toward faith-based goals. Limited resources may lead to frustration and test one's faith. However, these moments challenge believers to trust in God's provision over their circumstances. According to Philippians 4:19, God will supply all our needs according to His riches in glory in Christ Jesus. This assurance encourages believers to rely on divine provision and seek creative solutions and alternative resources that align with God's timing and purpose.

4. Handling Opposition and Criticism

Pursuing a faith-motivated path can sometimes attract opposition or misunderstanding from others. Whether from the community, workplace peers, or even family, criticism can dishearten and distract from one's efforts. Recognizing that even Jesus faced opposition teaches believers resilience and the importance of focusing on divine approval rather than human validation. Building a supportive network of like-minded individuals can provide encouragement and reinforcement, helping navigate negativity while maintaining faith.

5. Maintaining Consistency and Perseverance

Persistence in the face of setbacks is another significant challenge. When progress seems minimal or goals appear out of reach, sustaining motivation can become difficult. Consistency in spiritual practices—prayer, study, and worship—fosters resilience and fortitude. Galatians 6:9 encourages believers not to grow weary of doing good, for in due time, they will reap a harvest if they do not give up. Keeping this promise in mind propels perseverance, reminding believers of the rewards that come from dedication and faithfulness.

By addressing these challenges with practical strategies anchored in faith, believers can navigate the complexities of life's journey toward achieving their faith-driven goals. Armed with spiritual resolve and practical wisdom, every challenge becomes an opportunity for growth and deeper alignment with God's purpose, ensuring a path marked by fulfillment and divine achievement.

A Modern Example

In practical terms, consider a modern church community determined to tackle homelessness. Inspired by faith and guided by a collective vision, they formulated a comprehensive plan involving partnerships, housing projects, and community services. Their efforts were not just about providing shelter but restoring hope and dignity—an embodiment of how faith-driven goals can create profound societal change.

Achieving these goals requires dedication and the cultivation of small daily practices that align with God's greater plan. Begin each day with focused prayer, asking for guidance and strength to pursue these goals. Embrace gratitude, allowing these practices to shift focus from personal obstacles to divine possibilities.

Templates for setting faith-driven goals can serve as valuable tools. Start by clearly defining your goal, ensuring it reflects a higher purpose. Break this goal into smaller, manageable steps, each aligned with a spiritual principle or Scripture. Establish regular reflections and checkpoints to assess progress, remaining open to adjustments guided by prayer and community feedback.

Step-by-Step Faith-Based Goal-Setting Guide

Setting and achieving faith-driven goals requires a structured approach that harmonizes spiritual insights with practical actions. This guide presents a coherent framework to assist believers in crafting goals that reflect their divine calling, ensuring alignment with both personal growth and service to God's kingdom.

1. Prayer and Reflection

- Initiate the goal-setting process with deep prayer and reflection to understand God's desires for your life. This foundational step aligns your ambitions with divine intent.

2. Define Motivations

- Clearly identify the 'why' behind each goal, ensuring motivations are rooted in spiritual values that enhance personal and collective growth.

3. SMART Goals with a Spiritual Dimension

- Adapt the SMART (Specific, Measurable, Achievable, Relevant, Time-bound) framework by adding a Spirit-led component, guiding each goal through prayer and divine wisdom.

4. Action Plan Development

- Construct a detailed action plan that breaks each goal into smaller, manageable tasks and timelines to maintain progress, inspiration, and celebrate milestones.

5. Visualization and Faith

- Use visualization tools like vision boards or mind maps infused with images and Scriptures that serve as daily reminders of your God-given path.

6. Accountability Network

- Cultivate relationships that foster encouragement and accountability. Engage with mentors and peers who share your vision and can support your journey.

7. Reflection and Adjustment

- Regularly reflect on progress, allowing for adjustments based on evolving insights and circumstances. Celebrate achieved milestones with gratitude, further fueling perseverance on your path.

Returning to the story of Nehemiah, his endeavor was more than a physical reconstruction of walls; it was a profound reaffirmation of faith and a redefinition of community identity. Faith-driven goals demonstrate their power not only by uplifting those who pursue them but also by inspiring observers to join the journey.

As we conclude this chapter, embrace the empowering call to integrate your ambitions with God's grand mission. Reflect deeply, pray earnestly, and establish immediate steps to pursue your faith-driven goals. Consider creating dedicated time for reflection and prayer to seek clarity on your values and aspirations. Write down specific actions that align with these newly clarified goals, ensuring they resonate with your spiritual journey.

Rerouted Truth: *Faith-driven goals are not about chasing results—they're about walking in obedience and letting God define the outcome.*

CHAPTER 12
Fostering Unity Across Communities

In the heart of a bustling town square, where tall buildings cast long shadows over cobblestone paths, a community stood shoulder to shoulder. Gathering to rebuild what was lost in a storm's fury, they formed a mosaic of hands wielding hammers and hearts bound by shared purpose. More than merely repairing structures, this powerful scene of collective effort represented a deeper truth—it highlighted the vital role that unity plays in propelling communities forward. As these individuals worked side by side, they encapsulated a fundamental lesson: unity is not just a solution for recovery but a proactive force that drives communities toward fulfilling collective aspirations. In the aftermath of the storm, it wasn't just buildings being rebuilt—it was hearts, united on a new course of collaboration through crisis.

This sense of togetherness underscores how unity weaves diverse lives into a single tapestry, enabling progress despite differences. When people unite with a common purpose, they create bonds that transcend cultural, ideological, and personal boundaries, echoing biblical teachings that urge us to love our neighbors as ourselves. In this unity, communities find the strength not only to rebuild but to forge stronger, more connected paths into the future.

Building bridges across these differences requires active listening and embracing inclusivity. Every individual's contribution is essential to the strength of the whole community. Historical movements like the Civil Rights Movement exemplify how powerful a force unity can be when driven by a common cause. These initiatives remind us that change is possible through collective will and shared purpose.

The unity evident in early Christian communities offers profound lessons for modern community-building efforts. According to Acts 4:32 (ESV), *"All the believers were one in heart and mind. No one claimed that any of their possessions was their own, but they shared everything they had."* This approach demonstrated a commitment to mutual support and shared goals, illustrating how pooled resources can significantly impact the community.

In today's world, these principles of unity and communal support remain relevant, providing a template for building stronger, more cohesive societies. Modern applications can include creating shared community resources, such as cooperatives and community gardens, where individuals contribute time and materials for the benefit of all.

Additionally, embracing a shared sense of purpose and collective responsibility can enhance social cohesion and resilience. Implementing inclusive community programs that address local needs, foster dialogue, and celebrate diversity mirrors the early Church's values—promoting harmony and collaboration across cultural and ideological divides. By applying these biblical principles, contemporary communities can strengthen their capacity to respond to challenges collectively and build a legacy of unity that benefits future generations.

True unity isn't about merging lanes by force—it's about letting God reroute us onto the same Kingdom highway.

Leading Toward Unity Without a Title

I've learned that you don't need a title to lead toward unity—you need intention, humility, and the willingness to go slow when everything around you wants to move fast. Unity doesn't begin with agreement; it begins with empathy. In every setting where I've been called to serve, I've seen how easy it is for division to grow—not because of malice, but because of misunderstanding.

One principle I've had to learn the hard way is this: unity doesn't mean uniformity. I used to think everyone needed to get on the same page before progress could happen. But over time, I discovered that real progress comes when we choose to honor one another, even when we disagree. It's about valuing people over preferences and relationships over results.

There were moments when tension surfaced—when different agendas clashed and expectations weren't met. I didn't always know what to say, but I knew the posture I needed to take: listen first, speak gently, pray always. When I focused on understanding instead of reacting, walls started coming down.

One practice that has become essential for me is asking this question before I engage in any partnership or decision: *"Am I showing up as a bridge or a barrier?"* That filter helps me slow down, ask better questions, and discern where God is working—even in perspectives that challenge mine.

What I've come to believe is this: fostering unity is sacred work. It's less about solving everything and more about being present, being patient, and being committed to peace—even when it's inconvenient.

Practical Steps for Fostering Unity Across Communities

Fostering unity within communities, especially under the divine guidance of scripture, requires purpose and dedication. Ephesians 4:3 beautifully captures this sentiment: "Make every effort to keep the unity of the Spirit through the bond of peace." This passage underscores the proactive nature of unity, encouraging believers to not only desire harmony but actively cultivate it. Here are practical steps to build and maintain community unity in alignment with this biblical principle:

1. Prioritize Active Listening

One fundamental step to fostering unity is cultivating an environment where everyone feels heard. This requires active listening—engaging with others without preconceived judgments and openheartedly considering their perspectives. In community settings, this might involve regular forums or town hall meetings where members voice concerns and seek solutions collaboratively. This practice not only reinforces respect and validation but also solidifies shared visions based on mutual understanding.

For example, a small neighborhood association held *community listening sessions* where residents could share concerns and suggestions without interruption. This practice greatly improved trust and cooperation, leading to effective solutions like a new neighborhood watch and enhanced public spaces.

2. Facilitate Inclusive Discussions

Unity thrives when everyone feels included and valued. To achieve this, encourage participation from people of all backgrounds, ensuring diverse voices are part of the conversation. This means creating spaces where varied experiences are acknowledged and respected, fostering a sense of belonging. When leaders promote inclusive discussions, they affirm each person's worth and contributions, strengthening the community. This approach reflects the biblical principle of unity illustrated in 1 Corinthians 12:12-14, which likens a community to the diverse yet interconnected parts of a body, each integral to the whole.

In a local high school, the administration started monthly *diversity* circles—platforms where students and teachers could discuss cultural differences openly. This initiative enhanced understanding and acceptance, integrating previously marginalized voices into school policy decisions.

3. Develop Clear Communication Channels

Establishing transparent and consistent communication channels is crucial for unity. Whether through newsletters, regular emails, or community apps, keeping everyone informed promotes trust and cohesion. Effective communication minimizes misunderstandings and ensures that everyone remains aligned with the community's goals and activities.

Transparent communication is the backbone of unity. In a midsize company, creating a company-wide *intranet* allowed for clear, consistent updates and reduced confusion. By regularly sharing progress and goals, employees felt more connected and motivated, improving overall morale and performance.

4. Create a Culture of Recognition and Appreciation

Acknowledging individual and collective achievements nurtures a positive environment where unity flourishes. By publicly celebrating contributions and milestones, communities strengthen relational bonds and encourage continued participation. This acts as a practical application of Romans 12:10, which urges believers to honor one another above themselves.

Recognizing achievements strengthens unity by making individuals feel valued. At a local charity, publicly acknowledging volunteers' contributions through monthly newsletters and small awards ceremonies boosted morale and increased volunteer engagement.

5. Implement Conflict Resolution Mechanisms

Conflicts are natural, but their resolution determines the health of community unity. Develop and implement effective conflict resolution strategies grounded in biblical principles of forgiveness and reconciliation. Encouraging open dialogue, mediation, and prayerful reflection can guide communities through disagreements, ensuring that issues are addressed constructively to preserve the spirit of unity.

Effective conflict resolution is key to maintaining unity. A rural church implemented *peace* circles, where individuals could voice grievances in a facilitated, non-judgmental setting. This approach helped resolve misunderstandings and promoted a spirit of forgiveness and reconciliation.

6. Foster Spiritual and Social Gatherings

Cultivate connections through spiritual and social gatherings that promote shared experiences and spiritual growth. Regular prayer meetings, worship sessions, and social events enable members to build stronger bonds beyond formal interactions, nurturing deeper relationships grounded in shared faith.

Spiritual and social events naturally build bonds. A city library hosts *monthly book club meetings* paired with potluck dinners, allowing residents to share insights over good food. This not only enhanced community connections but also fostered a culture of shared learning and enjoyment.

7. Encourage Servant Leadership

Promote a leadership style that prioritizes service and humility, encouraging leaders to set examples of integrity and compassion. As modeled by Christ, servant leaders focus on the needs of others, nurturing environments where unity is sustained through mutual respect and empathy.

Servant leadership prioritizes the needs of the group, as demonstrated by a nonprofit's executive director who spent time volunteering alongside her staff. This approach solidified her reputation as a committed leader, inspiring mutual respect and dedication from her team.

By applying these practical steps, communities can build and maintain unity that reflects God's purpose and love. Through active effort and engagement, believers can cultivate an environment rich in peace and understanding, aligning closely with the spiritual unity envisioned in Ephesians 4:3. This commitment to unity not only strengthens the communal fabric but also glorifies God by showcasing a living testament to His love and guidance.

Bridging Divides: Building Christ-Centered Unity Beyond Our Circles

In a divided culture, where suspicion, tribalism, and self-protection dominate both secular and spiritual spaces, fostering unity across communities is no longer a luxury—it's a mandate. If we claim to follow Christ, we cannot be content with unity that stops at the edges of our personal comfort. The cross compels us to go further, deeper, and wider.

We have illuminated a difficult but freeing truth: God's vision for unity is not confined to likeness—it is birthed in love, sustained through truth, and fulfilled in mission.

1. Unity Grows Through Proximity, Not Preference

The early Church wasn't built on preference—it was built on proximity. Acts 2 shows us Jews from every nation gathered, worshiping and hearing the Gospel in their own languages. Cultural, ethnic, and linguistic differences were not obstacles to unity—they were platforms for the Holy Spirit to showcase His glory.

In contrast, today's Christian communities often retreat into what's comfortable. But unity that only exists among the like-minded is not unity—it's uniformity. True unity invites us to the unfamiliar table, where we must learn new rhythms, listen deeply, and resist the urge to dominate. The Spirit still speaks in many tongues—will we listen?

2. Honest Conversations Break the Spirit of Division

One of the most transformative teachings from the study came from Paul's confrontation with Peter in Galatians 2. Peter, though once a bridge-builder, withdrew from eating with Gentiles when faced with pressure. Paul didn't overlook the shift—he addressed it boldly and lovingly.

This moment reminds us that division grows in silence. When believers avoid hard conversations about race, class, theology, or offense, we may preserve superficial peace but forfeit redemptive growth. Godly unity doesn't demand we agree on everything—but it does require we speak truth, seek clarity, and commit to the work of reconciliation. Healing begins where honesty lives.

3. Unity Is Evangelistic

In John 17, Jesus prayed not for our sameness, but our oneness. Why? So that the world would believe in Him. Our unity isn't just for our benefit—it's a witness. When believers unite across generational, cultural, and denominational lines, they reveal the supernatural nature of the Gospel.

Disunity tells the world that Christ's love has limits. Unity, however, declares that His love is boundless, strong enough to hold what culture would tear apart. When we walk in unity, we model Heaven's reality—a family redeemed by grace, gathered by the cross, and sustained by the Spirit.

4. The Ministry of Reconciliation Is Not Passive

2 Corinthians 5:18 calls us ministers of reconciliation. That role requires intention. We can't "hope" unity into being. We must pursue it.

Reconciliation demands proximity and posture. It asks us to enter wounded spaces, risk discomfort, and initiate conversations even when we feel unqualified. It's not about fixing others—it's about reflecting Christ. When we walk toward those who've been marginalized or misunderstood, we reflect the Good Shepherd who left the ninety-nine to find the one. Unity requires that we go—first, humbly, and consistently.

5. Love Must Outpace Agreement

We don't need to see eye to eye to walk hand in hand. Unity built on agreement alone will collapse the moment conflict arises. But unity built on love—the kind of love described in 1 Corinthians 13, the kind that "bears all things, believes all things, hopes all things, endures all things"—can withstand tension without fracturing.

Jesus didn't demand agreement before offering love. He loved the Samaritan woman, the Roman centurion, the leper, the tax collector. That kind of love confounded religious systems and invited transformation. It still does today. If we want to build bridges, we must love beyond our limits.

6. Create Space for Mutual Learning and Transformation

The Gospel is not Western. It is not urban or rural, Black or white, charismatic or traditional. It is the Gospel of the Kingdom, and every tribe and tongue has a revelation to offer.

When we enter diverse communities, we do not arrive as experts—we arrive as learners. Humility is the currency of Kingdom unity. If we posture ourselves to receive as much as we give, we'll discover the Spirit moving in unfamiliar places and through unfamiliar people. God's fullness is revealed not in isolation, but in shared, Spirit-led transformation.

7. Unity Demands Spiritual Maturity

Bridging divides is not for the spiritually immature. It requires depth, discernment, and devotion to Christ above self. Too often, division is perpetuated not by theology or culture, but by wounded egos, immature expectations, and an inability to endure discomfort for the sake of the Gospel.

In Hebrews 5:12–14, the writer rebukes believers for remaining on milk when they should be eating solid food—"trained by constant practice to distinguish good from evil." Unity across communities takes that kind of maturity. It demands that we not be easily offended, not carried by emotion, and not dependent on always being "right." Instead, we are called to be rooted in truth, submitted to the Spirit, and willing to bear one another's burdens even when it feels inconvenient or messy.

Maturity also means we learn to discern what hills are worth dying on. Not every disagreement is doctrinal. Not every style is sinful.

Spiritually mature believers know how to stay grounded in conviction while remaining gracious in community. They build bridges without compromising the foundation of Christ.

As we grow in spiritual maturity, our capacity to lead, love, and listen across dividing lines increases. And as we mature in Christ, we begin to value unity not as a project—but as a person. Jesus is our unity, and the more we reflect Him, the more we reflect His heart for reconciliation.

Living the Prayer of Jesus

Jesus prayed, "that they may all be one, just as You, Father, are in Me and I in You... so that the world may believe that You sent Me" (John 17:21, ESV). This is more than a poetic ideal — it's a divine strategy for awakening the world to God's love.

Fostering Christ-centered unity across communities isn't a side mission. It is the mission. It demands spiritual maturity, humility, courage, and relentless love. It means engaging across discomfort, embracing differences with grace, and refusing to allow offense or fear to dictate our reach.

When we actively pursue unity in the face of chaos, we become answers to Jesus' prayer. We become signs of the Kingdom breaking through the noise. We stop being merely members of churches and become ambassadors of Heaven — bridge-builders, truth-speakers, and peacemakers who model a Gospel that reconciles the impossible.

If we truly desire revival, we cannot bypass unity. If we desire healing, we cannot ignore reconciliation. And if we long for the fullness of God to be revealed in our generation, we must be willing to walk together — even when the road gets narrow.

Overcoming Divisions Within Communities

Overcoming divisions within communities requires a proactive and compassionate approach guided by faith-driven principles. The task is challenging yet essential for building a harmonious environment that reflects God's love and unity. Here is a guide, rooted in scriptural wisdom, to help communities bridge divides and foster unity.

1. Acknowledge and Understand Differences

The first step in overcoming divisions is acknowledging existing differences. Recognizing that diversity in culture, opinions, and beliefs can enrich community experiences is crucial. Embrace these differences as opportunities for growth and learning, allowing them to highlight unique perspectives and ideas. Ephesians 4:2-3 encourages believers to always be humble and gentle, bearing with one another in love, which serves as a foundation for harmonious coexistence.

2. Promote Open Dialogue and Communication

Establishing platforms for open dialogue where community members can share their thoughts and experiences is essential. This includes organizing forums, workshops, and discussion groups focused on mutual understanding and respect. Active listening and empathetic communication help dispel misconceptions and build trust. Galatians 6:2 urges believers to bear one another's burdens, fostering a culture of empathy and shared responsibility.

3. Foster Forgiveness and Reconciliation

Encouraging forgiveness and reconciliation as pivotal elements in resolving conflicts can bridge gaps within communities. This involves practices such as mediation sessions and promoting peacebuilding activities that encourage healing and understanding. As Colossians 3:13 advises, *"Bear with each other and forgive one another if any of you has a grievance against someone. Forgive as the Lord forgave you."*

4. Build a Culture of Respect and Inclusion

Creating a community where respect and inclusion are core values ensures everyone feels valued and integrated. This can be achieved by implementing policies and practices that discourage discrimination while promoting acceptance. Educational workshops and awareness campaigns are effective tools for cultivating respect for diversity. Romans 12:10 encourages fostering brotherly love and prioritizing others' needs, which is central to building respectful relationships.

5. Pray for Unity and Guidance

Prayer is a powerful tool for seeking divine guidance in resolving divisions. Encourage the community to come together in prayer, asking God to heal rifts and bring about unity. Praying for wisdom, patience, and love strengthens community bonds and aligns efforts with God's will. Matthew 18:19-20 reminds us of the power of collective prayer: *"Again I say to you, if two of you agree on earth about anything they ask, it will be done for them by my Father in heaven."*

6. Celebrate Unity and Shared Achievements

Finally, celebrating milestones and achievements born from collaborative efforts reinforces unity. Recognizing and honoring these successes through communal events, acknowledgments, or storytelling galvanizes the community, reminding everyone of the powerful outcomes possible when united. Highlighting such achievements encourages continued cooperation and fosters a legacy of collaboration that future generations can build upon.

By integrating these steps, communities can overcome divisions and foster environments rich in unity and compassion. These efforts build stronger, more cohesive communities that reflect God's love and purpose, demonstrating the transformative power of faith-driven unity in action. Through persistent and intentional application of these principles, division diminishes, making way for a harmonious and supportive community experience.

Activities to Promote Unity in Local and Online Communities

Building unity across local and online communities requires focused activities designed to foster engagement, understanding, and collective purpose. Here is a list of initiatives that can be tailored to fit different environments, encouraging harmony and collaboration among diverse groups.

Local Community Activities:

1. **Community Service Projects:**
   Organize regular service projects such as neighborhood cleanups, food drives, and recycling programs. These activities not

only serve the community but also unite individuals around a common cause, reinforcing teamwork and shared values.

2. **Cultural and Diversity Events:**
   Host multicultural festivals or potluck dinners where community members can share their heritage through food, music, and art. Such events celebrate diversity and encourage openness, fostering mutual respect and appreciation for different backgrounds and traditions.

3. **Workshops and Educational Programs:**
   Develop workshops focused on skill-sharing or personal development, such as financial literacy classes or gardening tutorials. These programs provide opportunities for learning and interaction, building bridges among participants through shared interests and goals.

4. **Interfaith Dialogues and Prayer Gatherings:**
   Facilitate interfaith dialogues and joint prayer gatherings that promote understanding and spiritual solidarity among different religious groups. These events encourage faith-based unity and a collective pursuit of peace and goodwill.

5. **Sports and Recreational Activities:**
   Organize sports leagues, games, or fitness classes that encourage physical activity and friendly competition. Such events enhance community spirit and help build relationships through teamwork and shared interests.

Online Community Activities:

6. **Virtual Discussion Forums and Study Groups:**
   Create virtual platforms for members to engage in meaningful discussions and collaborate on topics of mutual interest,

ranging from book clubs to current events analyses. These forums provide a safe space for expression and foster community dialogue.

7. **Online Workshops and Webinars:**
Host educational webinars to gather individuals around themes of growth, peace, and creativity. These online sessions can include expert talks or collaborative projects that unite individuals toward common learning pursuits.

8. **Social Media Challenges and Campaigns:**
Initiate social media campaigns that celebrate unity through challenges that encourage participation, aimed at promoting goodwill and shared achievements. A simple photo challenge dedicated to acts of kindness or gratitude can significantly enhance a sense of belonging and positivity.

9. **Virtual Community Service Initiatives:**
Engage in online volunteering events such as virtual tutoring or tele-mentoring to reach broader audiences and provide support beyond geographic limitations. Such initiatives foster a sense of global solidarity and empower individuals to make a difference from anywhere.

10. **Collaborative Art and Storytelling Projects:**
Promote unity through creative projects where community members contribute to collective art installations, murals, or storytelling compilations. These projects allow for personal perspectives to be highlighted, creating a tapestry of shared experiences and insights.

By incorporating these diverse activities, communities—both local and online—can cultivate the unity envisioned in Ephesians 4:3, fostering environments abundant in peace and collaboration.

These initiatives not only strengthen ties among members but also ensure that unity continues to deepen across every platform through purpose-driven engagement and mutual respect.

A contemporary example reveals a small town struck by floods, where various faith communities banded together to rebuild homes and lives. Their response involved not only resources but also empathy and faith, forming a movement that restored infrastructure and renewed hope and resilience. This united effort was far more powerful than any could have achieved alone, epitomizing the scriptural call to unity.

Reflecting on the town square community, their unity not only rebuilt structures but also rejuvenated their collective spirit and purpose. Embrace unity to drive community progress and service. Channel collective aspirations into reality by reflecting God's love in your actions.

The Power of Testimonies in Unity

Sharing testimonies serves a dual purpose in faith communities: they inspire and connect, reinforcing the speaker's understanding of their purpose while offering listeners motivation and renewal of faith. These narratives are powerful tools, deeply embedded in the Christian tradition. Examining scriptural examples reveals that Jesus often used parables to convey profound truths, capturing the imagination and hearts of those who listened. His storytelling was not just informative but transformative, urging listeners to see beyond the surface and connect with deeper spiritual truths.

I used to hesitate when it came to sharing my story. Not because I didn't believe in what God had done—but because I thought it had to be polished, profound, or packaged just right to make a difference. I didn't realize that the raw and unfinished parts of my journey were often what people needed to hear most.

What changed me was the moment someone came up after I'd shared my testimony and said, *"I thought I was the only one. You helped me see that God's not finished with me either."* That moment sealed it for me. I knew I had to keep telling the truth—not the filtered version, but the honest one. The version that included the struggle, the doubt, the setbacks, and the slow healing.

I also began to notice how much strength I gained just by hearing other people's stories. Whether it was a five-minute encouragement after church or a vulnerable confession in a small group, each testimony reminded me that purpose is never isolated. It's always connected.

Now, I look for opportunities to testify—not for attention, but for breakthrough. Because every time I speak of what God has done, something shifts in me and in the people listening. It's like lighting a match that sparks hope where darkness had settled in.

I've come to believe this: your testimony may not be the loudest voice in the room, but it might be the one someone's soul was waiting to hear. And that's enough reason to keep telling mine. This helps foster unity across communities.

Rerouted Truth: *Unity isn't optional in God's kingdom—it's the divine soil where revival, restoration, and real purpose take root.*

CHAPTER 13
Embracing a Life of Service

"Imagine a world where every dawn heralds countless acts of kindness and compassion—a world bound not by transactional motives but by the genuine desire to serve. In such a world, acts of service transcend grand gestures, embedding themselves into the fabric of everyday life. Here, faith finds expression in the simplest of tasks, where service and spirituality meld seamlessly into one. This vision is not merely a utopian dream but a profound invitation to turn our divine purpose into tangible actions. Through faith, we sculpt this world, carving out spaces filled with love and understanding.

Mother Teresa's life remains a testament to the profound impact of faith-driven service. Born Agnes Gonxha Bojaxhiu in 1910, she felt a calling to help humanity from a young age. Moving from Macedonia to join the Sisters of Loreto in Ireland at 18, and then to India, she was deeply moved by the suffering in Calcutta's slums. This led her to establish the Missionaries of Charity in 1950, dedicated to serving those society shuns—like the homeless and unloved.

Her philosophy centered on the intrinsic value of every individual, echoing her belief that the greatest poverty is the feeling of being unwanted. Mother Teresa's approach was not just about providing aid but about affirming each person's dignity with empathy and love. Her mantra, "Do small things with great love," underscores her legacy of using everyday acts as expressions of deep faith and compassion, demonstrating that enormous change often starts small. Her path wasn't linear—it was a divine detour that rerouted her life into a legacy of compassion, proving purpose often hides in humble places. Her story continues to inspire many to lead by serving, fueled by passion and an unwavering spirit of kindness.

Throughout her life, Mother Teresa encountered challenges and criticisms, yet her commitment never wavered. Her resilience and faith-based leadership in the face of adversity demonstrated the importance of perseverance and reliance on divine strength. Her work earned her the Nobel Peace Prize in 1979, although she humbly attributed her achievements to God's will.

Mother Teresa's legacy is enshrined in numerous homes for the destitute and dying around the globe, where her teachings and practices continue to thrive. Beyond institutional memory, her legacy survives through countless individuals inspired to walk similar compassionate paths, motivated by her example to integrate service into their lives.

By living her life as a testament to the principles of humility, faith, and unwavering dedication to love, she continues to inspire generations to serve others selflessly. She illustrates how one life can be illuminated by purpose. Her legacy serves as a timeless reminder that true greatness is found in serving others with a heart full of love, a lesson that remains significant for all who seek to embrace a life of service.

Scripture offers profound insights into the nature of service. As articulated in Galatians 5:13, *"Serve one another humbly in love,"* service is portrayed as an act of love that is fundamental to Christian living. This verse reminds us that service is not only a moral duty but also a spiritual celebration of our connection to God and humanity.

The impacts of service are evident in contemporary examples, such as a church's outreach program that revitalized a local neighborhood. By facilitating food banks, mentoring programs, and family support services, the church not only addressed physical needs but also rekindled hope and fostered a stronger community. These acts exemplified the principle that serving others nurtures spiritual growth and societal transformation.

Living a life of service doesn't require grand gestures; it includes small, everyday actions that enrich lives. A practical approach is to seek opportunities within daily activities to help, such as offering a listening ear to a friend, volunteering at local shelters, or simply extending kindness to strangers. Each act, no matter how small, contributes to a culture of service.

What Service Has Taught Me

I've come to believe that service isn't something you do to feel better—it's something you do because you've been transformed. True service flows from compassion, not obligation. It's less about what I offer and more about who I'm becoming as I offer it.

In every act of service I've engaged in, I've learned that showing up consistently matters more than showing up perfectly. I've seen how small gestures—when offered with sincerity—can open hearts, build bridges, and quietly minister to people in ways words cannot.

One of the deepest lessons I've internalized is that service must be rooted in humility. It's not about rescuing others; it's about being present with them. I've learned to listen more, judge less, and ask God to show me where the real need is—not just the visible one.

Service has also shaped my perspective on leadership. It reminded me that the most impactful leaders aren't the loudest—they're the ones who are willing to get low, to be available, to carry unseen weight. I've had to ask myself regularly, *"Am I serving from a place of surrender or from a need to be seen?"* That question has kept my heart in check.

Ultimately, a life of service isn't built on grand gestures—it's built on daily decisions to put others before yourself, to obey God's nudge, and to love in ways that may never be acknowledged. And that, I've found, is where joy lives.

Incorporating Small, Everyday Acts of Service

Service lies at the heart of a purpose-driven life, presenting countless opportunities to effect positive change, deepen spiritual fulfillment, and forge meaningful connections. Integrating small acts of service into daily routines enhances personal growth and embodies God's love and compassion in practical ways. Here are several examples of how service can be woven into everyday living, fostering a lifestyle rich in kindness and empathy.

1. Share Words of Encouragement

One of the simplest yet most impactful acts of service is offering encouragement. This can take the form of a kind note left on a colleague's desk, an appreciative text to a friend, or words of affirmation during a conversation. Such gestures uplift spirits, boost confidence, and spread positivity.

2. Practice Active Listening

Engage fully with those around you by practicing active listening. Give your full attention when someone speaks, respond empathetically, and affirm their feelings. This act of service shows respect and validation, significantly impacting those who might feel unheard or overlooked.

3. Volunteer Your Time

Offer your time to local community projects or support groups. Whether helping at a food bank, assisting in a shelter, or participating in a community clean-up, these efforts contribute to societal well-being and create a sense of communal solidarity.

4. Lend a Helping Hand

Look for opportunities to assist others with tasks or challenges, both big and small. Help a neighbor with groceries, offer to babysit for a friend needing a break, or assist an elderly person with yard work. Such acts ease others' burdens and demonstrate compassionate living.

5. Express Gratitude

Take a moment to thank those who serve or support you in any capacity. Expressing gratitude to service staff, healthcare workers, teachers, or colleagues can brighten their day and reinforce the value of their contributions.

6. Pay It Forward

Engage in random acts of kindness to express gratitude. This might include buying coffee for the person behind you in line, leaving coins in a vending machine, or surprising a friend with a small gift. These unanticipated acts of generosity inspire others to do the same.

7. Build Community Connections

Foster community connections by organizing or participating in neighborhood gatherings or social events. Introductory meetings, potlucks, or holiday celebrations promote unity and provide a welcoming atmosphere where lasting friendships and support networks can flourish.

8. Spread Joy with a Smile

Never underestimate the power of a smile or a polite greeting. A warm smile can be infectious, spreading joy and easing tension in daily interactions. It costs nothing but can make a world of difference in someone else's day.

By incorporating these small acts of service, believers can weave the principles of a life of service into their daily routines, turning each day into an opportunity for a positive impact. These seemingly minor actions accumulate to create significant influences, enhancing individual spiritual journeys and enriching the community at large. Through consistent engagement in service, believers become tangible expressions of God's love, illuminating the essence of a purpose-driven life committed to serving others.

Integrating service into busy lives involves being deliberate about creating opportunities to help others. Consider setting aside regular times each week or month dedicated to serving, aligning your schedule with community events, or even combining family activities with service—such as participating in community clean-ups or preparing care packages.

Challenges of Serving and How to Stay Motivated

Engaging in a life of service offers immense rewards but also presents unique challenges. These hurdles can be both external and internal, testing the resolve of those committed to serving others. Recognizing and addressing these challenges is essential for maintaining motivation and effectiveness in service work.

Challenges in a Life of Service

1. Emotional Exhaustion:

Continuous exposure to the needs and struggles of others can lead to compassion fatigue, a state of emotional exhaustion where caregivers become desensitized or overwhelmed by service demands. This can diminish the quality of care provided and drain personal energy reserves, reducing overall effectiveness.

2. Resource Limitations:

Limited resources—whether time, finances, or manpower—can significantly hinder the ability to serve effectively. These constraints often lead to frustration and impact the scope of assistance that can be provided, causing stress and discouragement.

3. Balancing Personal and Service Commitments:

Maintaining balance between personal responsibilities and obligations to serve can be challenging. Everyday demands, such as work or family commitments, can conflict with the desire to dedicate time and energy to service work, potentially creating guilt or burnout.

4. Facing Unappreciation and Criticism:

Service work can sometimes be met with unappreciation or criticism, undermining motivation. Those engaged in service might feel undervalued when their efforts go unrecognized, dampening enthusiasm and dedication.

5. Exposure to Suffering:

Constant exposure to suffering and hardship can have psychological impacts, such as distress or vicarious trauma. This exposure challenges resilience, especially when change seems slow or intangible.

Embarking on a journey of service undoubtedly brings profound satisfaction and purpose, yet it is equally riddled with challenges that test our conviction. While hurdles like emotional exhaustion, resource limitations, and constant exposure to suffering are inevitable, they need not be insurmountable barriers. Instead, they can serve as catalysts for growth and opportunities for refining our approach. By recognizing these challenges as integral components of the service landscape, we can intentionally develop strategies to navigate them.

This proactive stance not only helps maintain a resilient service orientation but also lays the foundation for sustained motivation and effectiveness. With the right tools and mindset, one can transform these obstacles from roadblocks into stepping stones, ensuring that service remains rewarding amidst adversity. Keeping this perspective, we now turn to practical strategies for staying motivated and engaged in the face of these inevitable trials.

Staying Motivated in the Face of Challenges

1. Reaffirming Purpose:

Regularly remind yourself of the deeper purpose behind your service, focusing on the positive impact it has on others and its alignment with your core values. Journaling personal reflections can reinforce motivation, reminding you why you embarked on this path of service.

2. Setting Boundaries and Practicing Self-Care:

Establish clear boundaries to maintain personal well-being while serving others. Self-care practices such as regular rest, engaging in hobbies, and seeking spiritual nourishment help recharge and prevent burnout. By acknowledging personal limits, you promote sustainability in service.

3. Connecting with a Supportive Community:

Engaging with a community of like-minded individuals provides a network of support and encouragement. Sharing experiences and challenges with peers fosters camaraderie and offers practical advice for overcoming barriers. Such connections reinvigorate passion and reinforce commitment to shared goals.

4. Celebrating Small Successes:

Recognize and celebrate small victories and positive feedback received during service. This practice provides motivation and confirms that every effort, regardless of size, makes a difference. Celebrations can be personal or communal, ensuring that achievements are honored and shared.

5. Regular Reflection and Prayer:

Incorporate regular reflection and prayer into your daily routine to seek guidance and replenish spiritual strength. This practice nurtures a deeper connection with God, renewing your sense of purpose and providing clarity amid trials.

6. Being Open to Adaptation:

Flexibility enables you to adjust to changing circumstances and challenges in service work. Embrace new methods and approaches that address emerging needs while efficiently utilizing available resources. An open heart fosters growth and innovation within service roles.

7. Focusing on Long-Term Impact:

Maintaining perspective on the long-term impact of your service can help prevent discouragement from temporary setbacks. Reflect on the broader significance of your efforts within the context of societal and spiritual improvement, reinforcing your vision to persevere with hope.

By embodying these strategies, individuals are better equipped to navigate challenges in service work, ensuring continued engagement and fulfillment. Prioritizing motivation and compassion makes the path of service a rewarding journey of empowerment, resilience, and transformative impact on both servers and those they assist. This dedication aligns with a purposeful life, infusing everyday actions with meaningful intent and divine connection.

Revisiting the question of how the world would look if everyone embraced service, we find the answer in the incremental yet powerful change service brings to communities and individual lives. Service strengthens communal bonds, crosses divides, and reflects our divine mission to love and serve. It transforms both us and those we serve, creating ripples that extend far beyond our individual actions.

30-Day Service Challenge: Inspiring Acts to Cultivate Kindness and Community

Embrace the transformative power of small acts of kindness over the next 30 days. Each day's challenge offers an opportunity to express compassion and connect more deeply with your community, reflecting Mother Teresa's wisdom that great change often begins with small, deliberate actions.

Throughout this challenge, each day becomes an opportunity to act on your faith and serve others, embodying kindness and compassion. Remember that every small act of service contributes to a broader tapestry of love and community. Let this challenge mark the beginning of a lifelong commitment to serving others with purpose and joy.

Week 1: Building Connection and Understanding

Day 1: Reconnect with a Loved One

Reach out to someone you haven't spoken to recently. Offer warm words and genuine interest in their well-being, rekindling ties that may have dimmed over time.

Day 2: Smile with Intention

Make a conscious effort to smile at everyone you meet today. This simple gesture can be a powerful catalyst for joy, demonstrating the warmth of kindness.

Day 3: Express Gratitude Publicly

Identify an unsung hero in your life—a teacher, mentor, or peer—and express your appreciation, highlighting their positive impact on your journey.

Day 4: Share a Meal

Invite someone to join you for lunch or dinner, creating space for dialogue and mutual understanding through shared food and conversation.

Day 5: Practice Deep Listening

Give someone your undivided attention today. Listen without interruption or judgment to understand their perspective and share in their experiences.

Day 6: Join a Community Event

Participate in a local event designed to bring people together. Your presence can enhance communal ties and foster stronger neighborhood connections.

Day 7: Offer Kindness to a Stranger

Let small gestures, like offering your place in line or helping someone with their bags, demonstrate empathy and consideration for others.

Week 2: Acts of Kindness and Generosity

Day 8: Pay it Forward

Surprise someone by covering the cost of their coffee or meal, illustrating spontaneous generosity and spreading goodwill.

Day 9: Write an Anonymous Encouragement

Leave a note of encouragement for someone you don't know personally. Allow your words to uplift and bring hope to their day.

Day 10: Share Your Expertise

Offer your skills or knowledge by organizing a free workshop or class to help others grow, fostering community and personal advancement.

Day 11: Contribute to the Environment

Plant a tree or flowers in your local area, contributing to a healthier environment and beautifying spaces for all to enjoy.

Day 12: Donate Necessities

Select items to donate to a local shelter or community in need—a simple act with profound implications for those who receive your generosity.

Day 13: Extend an Invitation

Invite someone new into your circle or community activity, widening your embrace and making others feel valued and included.

Day 14: Volunteer Your Time

Dedicate part of your weekend to volunteering at a charity, embodying service through active participation in uplifting others.

Week 3: Engaging with the Community

Day 15: Mentor Someone

Offer guidance and support to someone younger or new to your field. Share your experience to help them navigate their journey with confidence.

Day 16: Assemble Care Packages

Gather essentials and comfort items to create care packages for those in need, bringing relief and kindness to others.

Day 17: Support a Neighbor

Assist a neighbor with chores or errands, especially if they are elderly or have restricted mobility, reinforcing community support.

Day 18: Organize a Book Swap

Host or participate in a book exchange, allowing new stories and ideas to circulate within your community, fostering knowledge and entertainment.

Day 19: Host a Community Gathering

Facilitate a virtual or in-person get-together to connect with others and brainstorm ways to improve your collective environment.

Day 20: Amplify Local Businesses

Write a positive review for a local business, supporting their work and encouraging others to explore what they offer.

Day 21: Acknowledge Sacrifice

Send a heartfelt letter or care package to someone serving the community, such as a healthcare worker or soldier, expressing gratitude for their contribution.

Week 4: Reflecting and Committing to Growth

Day 22: Dedicate Time to Prayer or Meditation

Reflect on your recent service experiences, offering gratitude for the lives touched and seeking further opportunities to serve.

Day 23: Pause for Personal Reflection

Consider how these acts of kindness have affected your perspective and sense of purpose. Document changes and commitments to continue serving others.

Day 24: Inspire Others to Serve

Encourage friends or family to embark on their own service journey by sharing your experiences and inviting them to join in future endeavors.

Day 25: Improve Your Surroundings

Take part in a neighborhood clean-up initiative, contributing to environmental well-being and fostering pride in your local area.

Day 26: Share Nourishment

Prepare a homemade meal or baked goods to deliver to someone, emphasizing care and community through the gift of nourishment.

Day 27: Reconnect with Someone New

Revisit someone you connected with during the challenge. Strengthen this new relationship by exploring shared interests and common goals.

Day 28: Recognize Recent Influences

Express gratitude to three people who have been positive forces in your recent life, acknowledging their influence on your journey.

Day 29: Assess Personal Growth

Examine your journey over these 28 days—consider how you've grown spiritually and emotionally and decide how you will incorporate service into your daily life.

Day 30: Plan a Long-Term Service Project

Create a plan for sustaining service efforts beyond this challenge. Commit to participating in or leading an initiative that aligns with your ongoing purpose to serve.

Engage in these challenges not as tasks to complete but as heart-led steps toward forging a world where service is both frequent and fulfilling, manifesting love in action.

As you reflect on the insights gathered from this chapter, let them propel you into immediate action. Imagine embarking on a journey where each step enriches not only your life but also the lives of those around you. Service is not merely an act—it's a transformative process that deepens your spiritual journey and amplifies your purpose. Begin integrating small acts of service into your daily routine now. Whether it's a warm smile or a helping hand, these gestures ripple outward, creating waves of compassion.

Commit to cultivating a long-term habit of service. Use each day's challenges as stepping stones; reflect on their impact and consider how these acts align with your divine calling.

Rerouted Truth: *When you serve others with love, you unlock the supernatural pathway to a purpose that outlives you.*

CHAPTER 14

Overcoming Burnout in a Purpose-Driven Life

Pastor Samuel gazed out over his community from the solitude of his study. He felt the heavy weight of exhaustion creep over him. Despite diligently following his divine calling, burnout had begun to dim the vibrant light that once guided his every step. This narrative reflects the often-unseen pressures inherent in faith-driven pursuits, illustrating the critical need for self-care and boundary-setting to ensure that the pursuit of purpose remains fulfilling rather than a path to exhaustion.

The journey of purpose is not immune to burnout, a condition that erodes physical, emotional, and spiritual vitality. Understanding spiritual burnout involves recognizing the signs—persistent fatigue, a cynical outlook, and decreasing performance—each chipping away at one's spiritual vigor and enthusiasm for purpose-driven pursuits.

When Purpose Wasn't Enough to Keep Me Going

I didn't see burnout coming. I was doing everything I believed I was called to do—serving, building, leading, showing up with passion and vision. On the outside, things looked strong. But on the inside, I was running on fumes. I had confused drive with endurance, output with obedience. I had been speeding down a road of performance, unaware that God was rerouting me toward rest and renewal.

The irony was, I was fully immersed in purpose—but I had neglected the pace of grace. I rarely rested. I rarely paused. I assumed the weight of everything around me, as if it were all up to me. Slowly, the joy I once had began to dull. I lost creativity, struggled to focus, and honestly, I didn't want to pray—I just wanted relief.

The turning point came when I finally admitted to myself that I was tired—not just physically, but spiritually and emotionally drained. I confessed it in prayer, not with shame, but with desperation. And that's when I sensed God whisper something I wasn't expecting: *"You were never meant to carry it all."*

That broke me—in the best way. I began to rebuild from there. I took intentional time to rest, not as a reward but as a rhythm. I started journaling not just to reflect but to release. I restructured my schedule to prioritize spiritual replenishment, not just productivity. And most importantly, I let go of the silent pressure to prove my worth through constant performance.

Burnout taught me something I couldn't learn in success: how to be still. And in that stillness, God reminded me that I'm not valuable because of what I do—I'm valuable because of who I am in Him.

Understanding Spiritual Burnout and Recognizing the Warning Signs

In the quest for a purpose-driven life, the risk of encountering spiritual burnout is significant, particularly for those deeply committed to their faith. Spiritual burnout differs from general burnout in that it primarily affects one's spiritual vitality and relationship with God. Understanding its nuances and recognizing the warning signs is crucial for maintaining a balanced and fulfilling spiritual journey.

What is Spiritual Burnout?

Spiritual burnout diverges from general burnout due to its profound impact on one's faith journey and sense of divine connection. Unlike the broader experience of burnout, which affects personal and professional aspects with symptoms of exhaustion and stress, spiritual burnout specifically targets one's spiritual vitality. This form of exhaustion arises primarily from prolonged periods of intense religious devotion and service without necessary acts of spiritual replenishment.

For those deeply engaged in ministry or faith-related activities—like Pastor Samuel—spiritual burnout drains their capacity to feel connected to God, leaving them with a sense of spiritual dryness or stagnation. It disrupts their sense of purpose, turning acts of worship and ministry from sources of joy and affirmation into burdensome obligations. This disconnect can create feelings of isolation from God and an emotional void, making it difficult to recognize the blessings and fulfillment that faith once provided. Addressing the root causes is crucial—not only to restore personal spiritual fervor but also to rejuvenate one's ministry and broader faith community engagement.

Recognizing the Warning Signs

Awareness of spiritual burnout's warning signs is essential for timely intervention and recovery. These signs may include:

1. **Persistent Fatigue:**
   Unlike ordinary tiredness, this fatigue is pervasive and impacts spiritual activities, making even simple acts of devotion feel burdensome. Reading the Scriptures might feel more draining than uplifting, or praying may become a chore rather than a source of solace.

2. **Loss of Passion:**
   A once deep-seated passion for spiritual practices diminishes, leading to a lack of enthusiasm for activities that were previously fulfilling, such as attending worship services or participating in ministry.

3. **Emotional Exhaustion:**
   Spiritual burnout often results in emotional depletion, making it challenging to maintain optimism and fostering an overarching sense of despair. This emotional cloud can suppress joy and obscure the recognition of blessings.

4. **Cynicism and Detachment:**
   An increased tendency toward negativity and a critical outlook on religious or communal activities can develop, leading to feelings of being an outsider within one's faith community.

Acts of service or worship may seem superficial or lacking depth.

5. **Feeling Disconnected from God:**
   A hallmark of spiritual burnout is a perceived distance from God, where prayer feels unanswered and Scriptures no longer resonate as they once did. This disconnect can intensify feelings of isolation and spiritual loneliness.

Recognizing the warning signs of spiritual burnout is a crucial step toward nurturing a balanced and fulfilling spiritual life. However, identifying these signs alone is not enough. To truly address burnout holistically, it is essential to delve deeper into the underlying causes that contribute to these feelings of depletion and disconnection. Understanding what triggers spiritual exhaustion allows us to craft a strategy encompassing both prevention and healing.

By examining factors such as overcommitment, unrealistic expectations, insufficient rest, and neglecting personal spiritual needs, we can develop a comprehensive approach to restoring spiritual vitality. This holistic understanding not only empowers us to tackle burnout symptoms effectively but also encourages sustainable practices that nourish our spiritual lives over the long term.

Contributing Factors

Understanding what contributes to spiritual burnout is critical for both prevention and healing. Factors can include:

- **Overcommitment:**
  Consistently taking on more spiritual responsibilities than is healthy can erode one's spiritual foundation. Without balance, even meaningful service can become a burden rather than a joy.

- **Unrealistic Expectations:**
  Holding oneself to perfectionist standards in spiritual practices may lead to disappointment and self-criticism, particularly when perceived efforts don't translate into visible outcomes.

- **Lack of Rest:**
  As Jesus modeled in His ministry, periods of retreat and reflection are vital. A constant push without rest denies the soul opportunities for renewal, leading to fatigue and weariness.

- **Ignoring Self-Care:**
  Neglecting personal spiritual needs in favor of serving others can rapidly drain spiritual reserves. Regular self-care practices, such as daily prayer or personal reflection time, are essential to avoiding burnout.

Moving Beyond Burnout

Recognizing the warning signs of spiritual burnout is the first step toward recovery. By implementing structured routines that prioritize rest, self-care, and balanced commitments, individuals like Pastor Samuel can rediscover their spiritual passion and deepen their connection with God. Embracing the biblical precedent for rest and renewal not only serves one's spiritual life but enhances the ability to serve others effectively, illustrating the importance of a balanced approach to living a purpose-driven life.

Biblical foundations highlight the necessity of rest and renewal. Jesus exemplified this balance by withdrawing to secluded places for prayer, underscoring the importance of reflection and spiritual rejuvenation. These moments of retreat emphasize a divine mandate for rest as an essential component of life. Furthermore, the Sabbath, as a divinely instituted time for renewal, emphasizes the balance between work and restful rejuvenation.

Setting healthy boundaries is crucial for enduring purposeful living. Prioritize your time to include periods of rest and reflection; these are vital not only for preventing burnout but also for maintaining clarity and focus. Practical steps include integrating regular practices such as prayer, meditation, and a dedicated Sabbath to restore spiritual energy. These intentional pauses enable a rejuvenation of purpose and prevent the spiritual depletion caused by constant activity.

Biblical Examples of Rest and Renewal

Embracing rest and renewal is vital for sustaining spiritual vitality, as demonstrated profoundly by biblical figures. Jesus often withdrew from crowds to find solitude and pray, illustrating the necessity of reflection and spiritual rejuvenation. In Mark 1:35, Jesus rises early to seek a quiet place for prayer, highlighting the importance of intentional retreat for maintaining a flourishing ministry.

Similarly, the concept of Sabbath, as established in Genesis 2:2-3, depicts rest as a divine mandate, underscoring the balance between work and spiritual refreshment. Observing Sabbath principles cultivates a dedicated space for renewal and connection with God, essential for holistic well-being.

Elijah's experience further exemplifies this need for spiritual recharging. In 1 Kings 19, after intense ministry and conflict, Elijah retreats to Horeb. It is in the quiet presence of God that he finds renewal and strength to continue his mission's call.

These narratives affirm that rest is not a sign of weakness but a crucial component of spiritual endurance and growth. By integrating these practices, believers can maintain a balanced lifestyle that honors God's framework for rest, preventing burnout while nurturing a life filled with purpose and divine alignment.

Practical Strategies for Maintaining Balance in a Purpose-Driven Life

Establish Clear Priorities

- **Action:** Identify your core values and align your time and resources accordingly.
- **Result:** Stay focused and avoid distractions, ensuring that your actions reflect broader spiritual goals.

Schedule Regular Rest Periods

- **Action:** Plan consistent breaks and observe a weekly Sabbath to rejuvenate.
- **Result:** Reinvigorate your spirit and body, enhancing clarity and inspiration for your divine purpose.

Commit to Spiritual Practices

- **Action:** Incorporate daily activities such as prayer, meditation, and scripture study into your routine.
- **Result:** Anchor your day spiritually, maintaining a strong connection to God's guidance.

Set Realistic Goals

- **Action:** Break objectives into achievable milestones to prevent burnout.
- **Result:** Allow steady progress and celebrate small victories to sustain motivation and focus.

Foster Healthy Relationships

- **Action:** Cultivate supportive relationships that encourage personal and spiritual growth.
- **Result:** Build a network of mutual support, enhancing perspective and balance amid challenges.

Delegate Responsibilities

- **Action:** Share tasks with trustworthy team members or peers to prevent overload.
- **Result:** Lighten your workload while fostering a collaborative, growth-oriented environment.

Embrace Flexibility

- **Action:** Adapt plans as needed to handle life's unpredictability without stress.

- **Result:** Achieve resilience and creativity, maintaining harmony across all facets of life.

By incorporating these strategies, individuals can cultivate a balanced lifestyle that supports a vibrant, purpose-driven existence. These practices nourish spiritual, physical, and emotional health, ensuring sustained growth and effectiveness in service to God's kingdom. Through intentional application, believers can navigate life with clarity, peace, and fulfillment, realizing their potential while honoring God's divine purpose.

Reflecting on Jesus' practices of renewal, let these enduring lessons inspire you to sustain a life aligned with purpose. Like Pastor Samuel, who transformed exhaustion into renewed vigor through rest and spiritual reflection, use these insights as a guide to maintain your equilibrium on this journey.

As we close this chapter, I invite you to look inward and identify signs of burnout in your life. Consider how you can make one small change today—a single step toward integrating restful practices or setting healthier boundaries. This intentional action can spark the reinvigoration of your passion and strengthen your pursuit of purpose.

Embrace this moment as an opportunity for growth, knowing that your well-being is integral to fulfilling your divine calling. Let this commitment be the first of many, leading to a vibrant, balanced life.

Rerouted Truth: *Burnout is not a badge of honor—it's a signal to rest in the One who never called you to carry purpose alone.*

CHAPTER 15
Measuring Impact and Success

"Success might not be what you think." This counterintuitive statement invites a reevaluation of conventional success metrics. In a world that often measures success through wealth and status, redefining it through purpose and service provides a richer, more meaningful yardstick. When aligned with faith, success encapsulates not only achievements but also alignment with God's plans and the positive impact on those around us.

Joanna, a devoted schoolteacher, exemplifies the kind of impact that resonates quietly yet profoundly within her small town. Known not for receiving public accolades but for her unwavering commitment to her students, Joanna's influence transcended traditional markers of success. She understood that her role was not limited to imparting knowledge but also to molding future generations. Her success lies in the countless lives she touched, guiding them toward brighter paths unknown to her. By instilling values of integrity and perseverance, Joanna's legacy is marked by the positive transformation she imparted to her students, illustrating that genuine impact often unfolds quietly and without immediate recognition.

Traditionally, success is quantified by external validations—positions, financial success, accolades. In contrast, spiritual success is characterized by inner fulfillment and measurable positive impacts on others. It involves a shift from metrics of accumulation to those that value purpose-driven life changes.

Redefining What Counts

There was a time in my life when I measured impact almost exclusively by scale—how many people showed up, how many downloads, how many reposts, or revenue milestones. I was chasing metrics that made me feel successful, but deep down I knew they weren't the whole story.

What changed everything for me was a quiet conversation with someone who said, "You probably don't remember what you said at that event, but it kept me from walking away from my faith." That hit me harder than any applause or online feedback ever had.

In that moment, I realized I had been tracking the wrong data. God wasn't measuring me by platforms—He was measuring me by obedience and faithfulness. I realized I had been following a cultural GPS, but heaven had a different route marked out—one that prized quiet faithfulness over public praise. He wasn't asking, *"How much have you built?"* but rather, *"How deeply have you loved? How consistently have you served?"*

Since then, I've started asking different questions to evaluate my impact:

- Did I obey what God asked of me today?

- Was I fully present with the people in front of me?
- Did I point others to Him—or to myself?

I've learned that quiet faithfulness over time leaves a deeper legacy than loud moments of recognition. Now, when I look back over a week, I don't just assess results—I look for fruit: peace, clarity, love, transformation. Those are the metrics that matter most to me now.

Real-World Examples of Measuring Spiritual Impact

Measuring spiritual impact in communities involves both qualitative and quantitative assessments, addressing the intangible yet profound effects of spiritual activities and initiatives. Here, we explore real-world examples that illustrate how spiritual impact is effectively measured, ensuring that spiritual goals align with community needs and divine purpose.

Evaluation of Community-Based Programs

One effective approach to measuring spiritual impact is evaluating community-based programs designed to promote spiritual growth and engagement. Churches and religious organizations worldwide have leveraged this model to assess the effectiveness of spiritual initiatives. Through surveys, testimonies, and attendance tracking, these institutions gather data reflecting the influence and reach of their programs. For instance, a church involved in community outreach might assess spiritual impact by noting increased participation in services, testimonies of life transformations, and enhanced community engagement.

Regular Reflection and Testimony Sharing

Spiritual growth assessments often involve regular reflection gatherings where members share personal stories of transformation and spiritual progression. These testimonies provide qualitative data on how individual lives are altered through consistent engagement with spiritual practices. Organizations like AA (Alcoholics Anonymous), which incorporate spiritual principles in recovery, often measure success through personal testimonies that reflect transformation and personal victories over addiction.

Longitudinal Studies of Spiritual Practices

Longitudinal studies track spiritual practices over extended periods, revealing insights into enduring spiritual effects. Faith-based groups often conduct these studies, following participants in discipleship or mentoring programs for several years. These studies observe transformations in spiritual lives, family relations, and community engagement, providing a comprehensive view of the lasting influence of spiritual disciplines within the community.

Community Surveys and Feedback

Surveys focused on spiritual and emotional wellness offer quantitative insights that complement qualitative assessments. These community surveys often explore how spiritual activities enhance mental health, social connections, and overall life satisfaction. Gathering feedback is key to identifying areas for improvement while celebrating successes. For example, a faith-based group might annually survey members to grasp the effects of spiritual teachings and activities on their lives, measuring metrics like peace, hope, and life purpose, ensuring that community efforts align with members' spiritual needs and well-being.

Analyzing Volunteer Engagement and Service Impact

Volunteering is a cornerstone of many faith-driven initiatives. By measuring volunteer engagement levels and the direct impact of service projects, organizations can assess spiritual health and vibrancy. Tracking volunteer hours, project outcomes, and feedback from those served helps evaluate the effectiveness of spiritual service work in fostering individual growth and community transformation.

Collaboration with Local Agencies and Councils

Partnerships with local government or social service agencies can provide valuable data and perspectives on spiritual impact within communities. Collaborative efforts often involve joint initiatives addressing social issues with a spiritual component, such as community healing events or faith-driven educational programs. Evaluating these collaborations illustrates how spiritual endeavors complement broader societal goals, highlighting areas where spiritual impact aligns with communal benefits.

Conclusion: A Comprehensive Approach

Measuring spiritual impact involves a blend of creative strategies and traditional tools. Through qualitative testimonies, quantitative surveys, and longitudinal studies, communities can assess how spiritual practices influence individual development and collective growth. As these real-world examples demonstrate, thoughtful measurement of spiritual impact not only affirms the value of spiritual pursuits but also refines and enhances future initiatives, ensuring a continually evolving and impactful spiritual journey.

Reflection serves as a tool for assessing these nontraditional forms of success. Regularly ask yourself essential questions: What drives your definition of success—personal ambition or divine purpose? Are your goals reflective of personal advancement or the broader betterment of society? Incorporate these reflections into a journal or meditation practice to realign personal plans with spiritual values.

Understanding spiritual impact within a community through various quantitative and qualitative methods provides a comprehensive view of collective growth and challenges. These community-focused assessments highlight the broader shifts and achievements accomplished through spiritual initiatives, demonstrating how community goals align with divine purposes. As we examine the successful implementation of community-based programs and collaborative efforts, we discover a pivotal intersection that naturally leads to an exploration of personal spiritual tracking.

Just as community programs utilize measurement tools to refine their approaches and outcomes, individuals can also benefit from self-assessment techniques. Transitioning from external measurements to personal reflection is a logical next step, allowing for deeper engagement with one's spiritual journey. The insights garnered from community dynamics serve as a backdrop against which personal growth can be measured and understood. This alignment fosters a deeper connection between individual purpose and community upliftment, ensuring that personal spiritual practices resonate internally and contribute to collective well-being.

Embracing structured methods of personal spiritual tracking echoes the robust evaluations seen in community initiatives. By implementing routine self-reflection, community feedback, and adaptive goal-setting, individuals can elevate their spiritual journeys, ensuring they remain attuned to both personal and community spiritual objectives.

Structured Method for Tracking Spiritual and Personal Growth

Assessing spiritual and personal growth can seem abstract, but a structured method provides clarity and direction. This approach integrates self-reflection, goal-setting, and community feedback to offer comprehensive insights into one's spiritual journey.

1. Establish Core Values and Goals

Begin by identifying core values that define your spiritual and personal aspirations. Consider the principles that guide your decisions and actions, such as compassion, integrity, and faith. Reflect on how these values align with your beliefs and spiritual objectives. Once established, set clear goals that reflect these values, ensuring they are specific, measurable, and aligned with divine purpose.

2. Create a Regular Reflection Schedule

Incorporate regular intervals of reflection to assess progress. Allocate time weekly or monthly to evaluate personal growth and spiritual alignment with your goals. This reflection enables you to recognize areas of advancement and identify aspects needing attention. Consider journaling your thoughts and insights to track changes over time and maintain a tangible record of your spiritual evolution.

3. Implement Self-Assessment Tools

Utilize self-assessment tools to measure spiritual and personal development effectively. These tools might include questionnaires that evaluate your devotional practices, emotional intelligence, or spiritual disciplines. Incorporate questions that prompt introspection on your relationship with God, your community engagement, and the consistency of your spiritual practices.

4. Engage in Community Feedback

Incorporate feedback from trusted peers, mentors, or spiritual leaders to gain external perspectives on your growth. Constructive feedback can provide fresh insights into your spiritual journey, helping to identify blind spots or reinforce positive developments. Participating in small groups or spiritual mentorship fosters accountability and support, enhancing personal growth through shared wisdom.

5. Regularly Review and Adjust Goals

As you assess your growth, be prepared to adjust your goals. Life's circumstances and personal insights may necessitate changes in direction or focus. Revisit your goals and values periodically to ensure they remain relevant and achievable. Flexibility allows for adaptive growth aligned with the evolving stages of your spiritual journey.

6. Celebrate Milestones and Achievements

Recognizing and celebrating milestones reinforces positive momentum and motivation. Whether achieving a personal breakthrough in faith, reaching a community service goal, or deepening your understanding of scripture, these achievements serve as testimonies of God's faithfulness and your dedication. Use these moments as reminders of progress and encouragement.

7. Integrate Prayer and Meditation

Central to this method is the integration of prayer and meditation as foundational practices. These disciplines center your reflections and assessments in God's wisdom, offering peace and clarity. Regular prayer and meditation cultivate a spiritual mindset that fosters continuous growth and a deepening connection with your faith journey.

By applying this structured method, you can effectively track your spiritual and personal growth, ensuring a deliberate and purposeful journey aligned with God's plan. This approach promotes sustained progress, enriched understanding, and a life that reflects your spiritual aspirations and commitments.

Success emphasizes how our seemingly mundane contributions can cultivate lasting change. These actions may not always attract popular recognition, but they are the undercurrent that strengthens communities and bolsters faith.

Adopt this perspective by creating a personal reflection guide. Outline your achievements not only in professional terms but also through your contributions to others' lives and spiritual growth. Engage with community feedback to understand the visible and invisible impacts of your work and adjust accordingly.

Self-Assessment Tool for Evaluating Purpose-Driven Success

This tool is designed to guide deep reflection on aligning actions with personal and spiritual goals. Regular evaluations can steer your journey toward a well-defined purpose rooted in divine guidance.

Purpose Clarity and Alignment

- **Reflective Prompts:**
    - What deep-seated values drive my sense of purpose today?
    - How do my daily actions connect with this larger purpose?
    - Where might I sense a disconnect between my aspirations and my current path?

Engage with these prompts to uncover motivations that tether you to your higher calling. As you journal, let insights emerge that chart your spiritual evolution.

Goal Setting and Achievement

- **Reflective Prompts:**
    - Which specific goals resonate with my core values, and how am I progressing toward them?
    - Reflect on a recent goal accomplishment—what path led to this success, and what did it reveal?
    - How might shifts in my life call for a reassessment of my goals and strategies?

Continually aligning goals ensures they serve your divine purpose and remain achievable and relevant.

Personal Growth and Challenges

- **Reflective Prompts:**
  - How has my personal and spiritual growth unfolded over the past months?
  - Consider the challenges faced—how have they shaped my path and understanding?
  - How has my faith empowered me amid life's trials?

Assessing growth through adversity highlights strengths and areas ripe for development, emphasizing faith's guiding role.

Community Engagement and Impact

- **Reflective Prompts:**
  - In what ways has my community involvement echoed my personal purpose?
  - What direct impacts do my engagements foster?
  - How do my actions reflect a meaningful commitment to serving others?

Community engagement illustrates how personal purpose translates into broader societal benefits.

Spiritual Practices and Discipline

- **Reflective Prompts:**
  - How consistent are my spiritual practices, and how do they shape my connection to God?

- What role do these practices play in deepening my sense of purpose?
- Are there aspects of my spiritual discipline that need refreshing or reinvigoration?

Maintaining discipline in spiritual practices strengthens the foundation of a purpose-driven life.

Feedback and Accountability

- **Reflective Prompts:**
  - Who are my trusted guides, and how do they enhance my understanding of purpose?
  - How do external insights align or contrast with my self-perception?
  - What feedback has affirmed or challenged my path, prompting reflection or action?

Incorporating feedback provides a holistic view of success, blending personal insights with external validation.

Celebrating Successes and Learning from Failures

- **Reflective Prompts:**
  - How do I celebrate victories that align with my purpose, fueling motivation?
  - What lessons do failures teach, and how will they influence my future efforts?

Celebrating triumphs fosters positivity, while analyzing setbacks ensures resilient, informed growth.

By engaging with these questions, you'll navigate your path more effectively, empowered by clarity and a divine understanding of success.

Implementing this self-assessment tool allows individuals to evaluate their purpose-driven success thoroughly, ensuring that life's endeavors align with their highest spiritual and personal aspirations. Continuous evaluation equips believers to live purposefully, guided by clarity and a deeper understanding of success.

As you conclude this chapter, let this newfound understanding of success inspire a fresh exploration of your unique calling. Reflect deeply on what success means to you—not just in terms of personal advancement, but also in measuring your spiritual impact on others. Consider how your actions align with God-given purposes and how they create positive change in your life and the lives of those around you.

Take a moment to evaluate your current path: Are your efforts resonating with your true purpose? How might you adjust your goals to better reflect a life driven by spiritual fulfillment? By delving into these questions, you can embark on a more intentional journey toward aligning your success with a deeper, more meaningful impact.

Rerouted Truth: *Real success isn't measured by what you build but by how faithfully you steward what God gave you to carry.*

CHAPTER 16

Embarking on Your Purposeful Journey

In the hushed tranquility of her corner office, Monica sat quietly, the gentle hum of city life filtering through the window. The familiar scent of fresh coffee mingled with the leather of her chair, yet it did little to comfort her. As she gazed at the skyline, the towering structures mirrored the constraints she felt within—immense yet stifled. The incessant buzz of notifications on her phone served only to agitate the soft whisper of her heart, urging her toward something greater.

In that moment, Monica realized that despite her corporate accolades, the true summit she sought lay beyond recognition and human praise. During this poignant reflection, she chose to step away and journey toward a vision of hope and change. Leaving behind the predictability of her desk, she embraced her inner calling, driven by a resolve as steady as the mountains she loved to hike. This leap of faith was not merely a career change but a profound realignment of her spirit with her purpose.

Discovering one's purpose involves a harmonious blend of introspection and divine guidance. This journey commences with listening—paying attention to the inner inclinations that guide our souls. Engaging in prayerful reflection assists in this discernment, offering a spiritual compass to navigate life's terrain. This echoes the example of Paul the Apostle, whose missionary expeditions exemplified a life infused with divine purpose, illustrating how such guidance fuels life's adventures.

Overcoming initial fears and uncertainties is crucial. Monica battled the fear of relinquishing financial security. Yet, by trusting that her chosen path was divinely sanctioned, she found assurance and embraced the transition. The lesson here is one of deep trust—faith that pursuing one's true calling leads to provision and growth beyond immediate understanding.

Aligning a career with spiritual ambitions entails deliberate focus and action. Begin by assessing how current pursuits dovetail with your calling. Steps to integrate purpose into one's career might include volunteering in relevant areas, considering career shifts, or embedding purpose-driven projects within your existing platform.

The Fear Before the First Step

When I first sensed God calling me into a deeper purpose, I hesitated. Not because I didn't want it—but because I didn't feel ready for it. There were questions I couldn't answer, responsibilities I didn't want to drop, and a fear I hadn't faced yet: *What if I step out and it doesn't work?*

I wrestled with that fear longer than I care to admit. I kept busy doing good things, but deep down, I was avoiding the one thing God was asking me to fully trust Him with—my next step.

It wasn't until I admitted my hesitation that God met me with reassurance, not rebuke. Through prayer, journaling, and quiet surrender, I began to understand that courage isn't the absence of fear—it's obedience in the face of it.

And so I moved forward, not because I had it all figured out, but because I finally believed God was with me in the unknown. Each small act of courage became a building block in my journey: making the call, sending the email, showing up even when I felt uncertain. None of it was flashy, but all of it was sacred.

Looking back now, I see that the real breakthrough wasn't the platform or the project—it was the moment I decided to stop waiting for perfect conditions and start trusting God's voice more than my own doubt. Sometimes the journey begins where your map ends—when God reroutes you into an unexpected path packed with purpose.

When Obedience Looks Like Hesitation

There have been a number of moments in my life where I knew—without a doubt—that God was leading and guiding me toward something directly tied to my purpose. And in those moments, I wish I could tell you I leapt with bold faith. But more often than not, I paused. I hesitated. And to be honest, I'm still hesitating on a few things that I know deep in my spirit God is prompting me to move into.

Sometimes it's hard to tell—is it me dragging my feet, or is it that the season simply hasn't arrived yet? That question has wrestled with me in the quiet. I've turned it over in prayer, asked God for confirmation, and still found myself standing in the tension between the now and the not yet.

When I get stuck in that place, I come back to one Scripture over and over again: *"Be anxious for nothing, but in everything by prayer and supplication with thanksgiving let your requests be made known to God"* (Philippians 4:6). That verse anchors me. It quiets the noise. It reminds me that clarity doesn't always come before movement—and that obedience sometimes means trusting the peace, not the plan.

There's a sobering reality I've had to face: there are seasons in life where you have to burn the boats. Where moving forward means letting go of the ability to return to what's comfortable, familiar, and safe. I've felt that tug. I've known, in my heart, that certain relationships, roles, and even rhythms of life were no longer where I was supposed to be. But because my heart was still attached—because I had built something there, not in lust but in love—it made the burning that much harder.

Make no mistake about it: when you're being rerouted, there will come a time when you'll have to eliminate the option to go back. You'll have to release your grip on Plan B in order to walk into God's Plan A. It won't always feel brave. It might feel like heartbreak. But that's often the doorway to breakthrough.

That's why a strong relationship with our Creator matters so much. Without intimacy with God—without the guidance of the Holy Spirit in prayer and quiet meditation—it's nearly impossible to discern the difference between fear and timing, between waiting and wavering. But when we stay rooted in Him, even our hesitation becomes holy. Even our pause becomes preparation.

I'm still learning to move when He says move—even if I don't feel ready. I'm learning that sometimes, burning the boats is the very act that sets your purpose ablaze.

Overcoming Initial Fear and Resistance in Your Purposeful Journey

Beginning a purposeful journey inevitably brings encounters with fear and resistance. These feelings are natural responses to stepping into unknown territories or contemplating significant life changes. However, overcoming these initial challenges is essential for embracing a life aligned with divine purpose. Here are practical strategies to help you navigate and conquer the fear and resistance that may arise as you embark on this path:

1. **Acknowledge and Confront Your Fears**
   The first step in overcoming fear is acknowledging its presence. Fear often stems from the uncertainty of uncharted paths and the possibility of failure. Reflect on the specific fears you face—whether it's fear of inadequacy, judgment, or the unknown. By defining these fears, you can begin to understand and address them rather than allowing them to remain vague and paralyzing.

2. **Reframe Fear as a Catalyst for Growth**
   Reframing fear as an opportunity for growth changes your perspective. Instead of viewing fear as a barrier, see it as a signal that you are on the brink of transformation. Fear indicates that you are stepping outside of your comfort zone—a necessary step for growth and deeper alignment with your purpose. Remember 2 Timothy 1:7, which emphasizes that *"God gave us a spirit not of fear but of power, love, and self-control."*

3. **Draw on Faith and Scriptural Guidance**
   Faith provides a strong foundation for overcoming fear. Delve into the Bible to find stories and passages that inspire

courage and faithfulness, such as the account of David facing Goliath or Jesus calming the storm. These narratives serve as powerful reminders that God equips His people to face challenges with strength and faith.

4. **Set Realistic Expectations and Goals**
Setting achievable expectations alleviates the pressure that can accompany new ventures. Break down larger goals into manageable steps, allowing for gradual progress and reducing feelings of overwhelm. Celebrate small successes along the way to reinforce a positive mindset and maintain motivation.

5. **Seek Support and Community**
Surrounding yourself with a supportive community revitalizes courage and provides accountability. Share your goals with friends, mentors, or a faith community willing to offer guidance, encouragement, and prayer. Knowing that others are rooting for your success makes facing resistance less daunting.

6. **Practice Gratitude and Self-Reflection**
In moments of doubt, gratitude and self-reflection can bring clarity and peace. Take time to pause, breathe, and center your thoughts. Reflect on past instances where you successfully overcame challenges, reinforcing your capacity for resilience and adaptability.

7. **Develop a Strong Personal Affirmation Practice**
Affirmations are powerful tools for building confidence and counteracting negative thoughts. Create a list of affirmations rooted in personal strengths and divine promises. Repeat these affirmations daily to instill a mindset of faith and readiness to embrace newfound opportunities.

8. **Keep a Journal of Your Journey**
   Documenting your journey in a journal can serve as both a reflective tool and a motivational resource. Record experiences, emotions, prayers, and insights gained along the way. Over time, reviewing your entries will reveal growth patterns, victories over fear, and divine interventions, further encouraging perseverance.

By implementing these strategies, you transform fear from a block to a bridge leading to greater purpose and fulfillment. As you proceed, anticipatory fears give way to divine confidence, empowering you to pursue your God-given path with enthusiasm and courage. Embrace your journey, knowing that within every step lies the potential for profound insight and transformation.

The journey from overcoming fear to creating impactful change is a natural progression that starts within and projects outward. As internal barriers are conquered, the resulting clarity and confidence naturally lead to external action. Consider Joanna, a community volunteer who began her journey by organizing local clean-up events. Her initiative blossomed into a full-fledged environmental advocacy group, transforming small, focused efforts into significant, cumulative impact.

Monica's own story of transformation underscores the adventurous and gratifying nature of purpose-led endeavors. Her establishment of a non-profit to fight poverty showcases how embracing this calling not only fulfills personal spiritual needs but also generates widespread community effects.

As you reflect on beginning your purposeful journey, embrace the adventure and uncertainty it guarantees. The role of faith becomes central, acting as a stabilizing force amidst doubt. Draw support from mentors and faith communities to reinforce resilience and guide your steps.

Step-by-Step Method for Transitioning into a Purpose-Driven Life

Transitioning into a purpose-driven life is a journey of alignment and intention. Here's a concise, actionable method to guide you:

1. **Clarify Your Vision and Purpose**
   Seek understanding through **prayer and reflection**. Consider past experiences and innate talents to define your purpose. For example, if you've always found joy in teaching, your purpose might involve education. Compose a vision statement inspired by scripture, like Jeremiah 29:11 (ESV): *"For I know the plans I have for you, declares the LORD, plans for welfare and not for evil, to give you a future and a hope,"* to ground your aspirations.

2. **Set Specific, Purpose-Driven Goals**
   Once clarity is achieved, break down your vision into **SMART goals**. For instance, if your purpose involves community service, set a goal to start a local outreach program. Ensure each objective is linked to a spiritual aim that serves both personal growth and your community.

3. **Cultivate Daily Spiritual Practices**
   Integrate **spiritual disciplines** into your routine, such as daily prayer and meditation. These practices anchor your day, providing guidance and resilience, much like a gardener tends to their plants for a flourishing life.

4. **Create a Structured Plan**
   Develop a step-by-step action plan with timelines. Break goals into smaller, manageable steps, such as scheduling weekly meetings for your outreach program. Regular reviews keep your progress aligned with your spiritual objectives.

5. **Seek Guidance and Mentorship**
   Connect with **mentors or spiritual guides** who offer wisdom and insight. As with a seasoned traveler providing a map, their mentorship can illuminate paths you hadn't considered and offer encouragement in challenging times.

6. **Embrace Change and Flexibility**
   Be open to **adaptation**. Life can be unpredictable, but flexibility enables you to pivot gracefully when necessary, viewing changes as opportunities rather than setbacks.

7. **Measure Progress and Reflect Regularly**
   Set aside time to **reflect** on your journey. Journals are effective for documenting progress, learning from challenges, and celebrating milestones, fostering a cycle of growth and gratitude.

8. **Engage in Community Service**
   Participating in community service projects not only helps others but also reinforces your sense of purpose. For example, volunteering at a local shelter can provide personal fulfillment while creating a positive impact.

9. **Maintain Resilience and Perseverance**
   Cultivate a mindset of perseverance, fueled by your faith. Remember, as 2 Timothy 1:7 notes, you are empowered by a spirit of strength and discipline for the journey ahead.

By following these steps, you'll discover that transitioning into a purpose-driven life is not just a series of actions but a fulfilling lifestyle that aligns you more closely with your spiritual calling. Each step bolsters your faith and confidence, transforming aspirations into your lived reality.

Finding Mentors and Supportive Communities

Embarking on a purpose-driven path is enriched by guidance and community support. Here's a streamlined approach:

1. **Identify Mentor Qualities:** Seek mentors with integrity, wisdom, and spiritual depth who challenge you to grow and align with your values.
2. **Leverage Networks:** Connect through faith communities and professional groups, approaching leaders with respect and clarity regarding how their guidance can benefit you.
3. **Utilize Platforms:** Use platforms like LinkedIn and spiritual forums to connect with mentors and peers committed to personal growth.
4. **Join Faith-Based Groups:** Actively participate in faith-based workshops to meet potential mentors and like-minded individuals.
5. **Attend Events:** Conferences offer prime opportunities to encounter mentors who resonate with your spiritual and personal journey.

6. **Set Expectations:** Clearly define goals and expectations within mentoring relationships to ensure mutual understanding and support.
7. **Build Community:** Engage in supportive groups that provide encouragement and accountability, fostering a sense of belonging and shared purpose.

By cultivating these connections, you create a nurturing environment for growth, equipped to support and celebrate each step of your journey.

Exercises to Help Create an Action Plan

Embarking on a purposeful journey requires a clear and structured action plan that aligns with your spiritual and personal objectives. Here are exercises designed to guide you in creating a tailored action plan, facilitating a transition into a purposeful life that resonates with your divine calling:

Exercise 1: Vision Casting

- Begin by quieting your mind through prayer or meditation, seeking clarity from God about your life's vision and purpose.
- Write a detailed description of where you envision yourself in five to ten years. Reflect on spiritual, personal, and professional dimensions.
- Consider how this vision aligns with biblical principles and God's promises. Use scriptures that resonate with

you as anchors for this vision, ensuring it aligns with God's will.

Exercise 2: Goal Identification

- Break down your overarching vision into key goals. Identify specific areas you desire to focus on, such as career, relationships, health, and spiritual growth.
- For each area, set SMART goals — Specific, Measurable, Achievable, Relevant, and Time-bound. Ensure each goal reflects both personal aspirations and divine purpose.
- Document your goals, considering how each contributes to your long-term spiritual and personal growth.

Exercise 3: Creating a Life Map

- Use a large sheet of paper or a digital tool to create a life map. Chart out the milestones and key steps needed to achieve your goals.
- Plot these milestones along a timeline, providing visual clarity and structure to your endeavors.
- Consider potential obstacles and devise strategies for overcoming them, drawing from spiritual wisdom and past experiences to inform solutions.

Exercise 4: Daily Practices and Habits

- Reflect on daily habits that align with your purpose and goals. Consider which current habits support or hinder your progress.
- Develop a daily routine that incorporates spiritual practices, such as prayer, meditation, or scripture study, as foundational elements of your day.
- Identify new habits that nurture your growth and align with your goals, integrating them into your daily life incrementally.

Exercise 5: Seeking Support and Accountability

- Identify potential mentors, peers, or communities that can provide support, guidance, and accountability.
- Write down the qualities you seek in an accountability partner and potential candidates who fit these criteria.
- Plan regular check-ins with these individuals, using their feedback to adjust your action plan and foster continuous growth.

Exercise 6: Reflective Journaling

- Set aside time each week for reflective journaling to assess your progress, reflect on insights gained, and realign with your purpose.
- Use prompts such as "What have I learned this week?" or "How have I served God's purpose in my actions?"

- Document challenges faced and strategies used to overcome them, fostering a habit of reflection that reinforces learning and resilience.

Exercise 7: Celebrating Milestones

- Recognize and celebrate achievements, no matter how small, that align with your purpose and goals.
- Plan regular celebrations—personal or with your support network—acknowledging progress as encouragement for continued perseverance.
- Reflect on these achievements, considering how they reinforce your commitment to a purposeful journey and remind you of God's faithfulness.

By engaging with these exercises, you can construct a comprehensive action plan that serves as a roadmap for your purposeful journey. This process encourages clarity, commitment, and growth, aligning personal aspirations with divine intent. By following this plan with faithfulness and dedication, each step brings you closer to a life of meaningful purpose and spiritual fulfillment.

Rerouted Truth: *You don't need all the answers to start—you just need enough faith to take the next obedient step.*

CHAPTER 17

Embracing Change as Part of Purpose

Embracing this journey signifies spiritual maturation and growth, an essential facet of fulfilling divine purpose. Accepting and embracing life's transitions is critical for discerning and realizing this purpose, embodying growth rather than fear or resistance.

How Shifts in Calling Are a Normal Part of Spiritual Growth

Spiritual growth is often accompanied by changes in one's calling, as subtle and significant directional shifts occur over time. These shifts are not anomalies but intrinsic elements of a dynamic faith journey, reflecting deeper alignment with God's evolving plans. Understanding the fluidity of calling as a natural part of spiritual maturation allows believers to embrace these changes with trust and openness, recognizing them as integral to their spiritual development.

Throughout biblical history, many figures experienced changes in their callings that were integral to their growth and contribution to God's narrative. These examples serve as guiding lights, illuminating the path for modern believers as they navigate life's transitions.

When Change Was the Only Way Forward

There have been seasons in my life when change wasn't optional—it was necessary. I didn't ask for it. I didn't always want it. But I came to realize that if I was going to walk in purpose, I had to stop resisting what God was using to refine me.

One of the biggest shifts came when I had to release a role I had poured my identity into. It wasn't just a job—it was part of my story, my routine, my sense of worth. But God was nudging me into a new space, and everything familiar started to lose its grip. I tried to hold on, but the harder I clung, the more restless I became.

Letting go felt like loss at first. But once I surrendered, I saw it for what it really was: realignment. God wasn't stripping me—He was preparing me. The space He cleared made room for something more aligned, more fruitful, and honestly, more freeing than I expected.

That season taught me to stop fearing change and start welcoming it as part of my discipleship. Change wasn't punishment—it was permission to grow.

Now when things begin to shift, I ask: *Is this God moving me forward?* And more often than not, the answer has been yes.

When the Drift is Invisible

There's a quiet pressure we face every single day—the kind we don't always notice until we've moved too far. It's the pressure of our flesh. The pull of the world. The slow erosion of spiritual discipline and direction. I've come to know it well. It's called spiritual drift, and it rarely announces itself. It sneaks in gently, subtly, like a wave moving you inch by inch without your consent.

I learned this lesson long before I could name it.

Every summer when I was a kid, my family took a trip to the beach. One year stands out more than any other. I was about ten years old. As soon as our feet hit the sand, my brother and I ran toward the water while my parents set up the blanket and umbrella—the home base for our day in the sun. We played in the ocean for nearly two hours. Splashing. Laughing. Pushing each other underwater. The time flew.

But when we finally came out to grab something to eat, I couldn't find our umbrella. I looked around and nothing looked familiar. I started to panic. For a few moments, I was convinced we were lost. Everything around me looked the same, and yet... different. It wasn't until I looked far down the shoreline that I saw it—our bright, multicolored umbrella—almost 100 yards away.

The ocean hadn't pulled me under. It had pulled me down. Quietly. Gradually. While I was busy having fun, it moved me away from the place I needed to return to.

That's what spiritual drift looks like.

It begins with subtle compromises—skipping prayer here, ignoring conviction there, exchanging solitude with God for the noise of life. You don't notice it at first. But slowly, your soul starts moving. Not because God moved, but because you stopped looking for Him. Drift happens when direction is no longer intentional. And eventually, when life gets hard—when you're hungry for hope or thirsty for peace—you try to come back to God... only to realize you don't recognize where you are anymore.

The absence of spiritual alignment creates distance. Like a branch pulling away from the Vine, you lose the very connection that feeds you. It's easy to start relying on your feelings instead of the truth, reacting to life rather than responding to God. That's when disunity sets in. Not just with God, but with others. With yourself.

But here's what I've learned: course correction doesn't require shame. It requires humility.

You don't fix spiritual drift by trying harder. You fix it by surrendering faster. Galatians 5:25 says, *"Since we live by the Spirit, let us keep in step with the Spirit."* That's not a call to perfection—it's a call to alignment. To sync your steps with the One who knows exactly where home is.

That beach day taught me more than any Sunday school lesson could. Life will always have waves. The world will always have currents. And your flesh will always try to drag you further than you meant to go. But if you know where home is—if you know how to spot the umbrella—you can get back. You can refocus. You can realign.

And more importantly, you can stand firm in seasons of redirection because you'll know the difference between movement from God and drift away from Him.

Biblical Examples of Calling Shifts

The story of Moses provides an insightful example of a transformative shift in divine calling. Initially, Moses lived a life of privilege in Pharaoh's palace, seemingly far removed from the plight of the Hebrew people. However, after a dramatic encounter with God through the burning bush (Exodus 3), Moses' life purpose shifted dramatically from murderer to outcast, from prince to liberator of Israel. This pivotal change not only marked a new path for his life but also catalyzed significant spiritual growth, preparing Moses to lead with wisdom and courage.

Similarly, the prophet Daniel experienced a remarkable shift in his role throughout his life. Taken into Babylonian captivity as a young man, Daniel adapted his skills and convictions to serve in King Nebuchadnezzar's court, evolving from a captive to a trusted advisor (Daniel 1-2). His unwavering faith amid changing callings reflects the necessity of adaptability and steadfastness in God's service. Daniel's example encourages believers to recognize that shifts in calling often open new avenues for influence and impact.

As we reflect on historical narratives like those of Moses and Daniel, we find profound templates for navigating modern spiritual growth. Moses' transformation from a prince to a liberator showcases the potential for pivotal shifts that reveal new paths and foster personal development. Likewise, Daniel's adaptability in the face of changing roles exemplifies the importance of steadfast faith and flexibility, also considering David's transition from shepherd to king. These stories are not merely ancient tales but mirrors for our own journeys, offering guidance on how divine shifts can manifest in our lives today.

Building on this historical wisdom, how can we apply these insights to our personal journeys? Recognizing a shift in divine calling often begins with an internal restlessness that prompts reflection on our current path. As believers, discerning these pivotal moments involves not only introspection and prayer but also seeking counsel from trusted mentors. Grounded in Romans 12:2, we learn that transformation is integral to spiritual maturation. By embracing change as a divine process rather than a disruption, we open ourselves to growth and align our lives more closely with divine purpose.

Recognizing and Embracing Calling Shifts

Identifying the signs of a calling shift can be subtle, often beginning with an internal restlessness or an emerging vision for a different path. These divine nudges invite believers to reflect on their current roles and consider new directions. Prayer and seeking God's guidance through scripture are essential in discerning these shifts, as is open dialogue with trusted friends or spiritual mentors.

Embracing change as a hallmark of spiritual growth requires a faith-based perspective, viewing transitions not as failures or losses but as milestones in God's unfolding plan. Romans 12:2 reminds believers to be "transformed by the renewing of your mind," a process that necessitates openness to the new and a willingness to part with the old. By accepting change as part of the divine process, believers can grow from each season, allowing their journeys to be marked by purpose and divine alignment.

Taking Practical Steps Toward New Callings

- **Seek God's Confirmation through Prayer and Scripture:** As potential changes emerge, engaging in prayerful dialogue with God helps clarify and confirm His direction. Scriptures may provide reinforcement, pointing to paths He urges believers to take.
- **Reflect on New Opportunities and Skills:** Changes in calling often require new skills or adaptations. Reflecting on and developing these skills positions individuals to take full advantage of new roles. Whether through formal learning or personal growth, these periods of preparation foster readiness for fresh callings.
- **Engage in Community Support and Mentorship:** Sharing desires and potential shifts with a supportive community offers insight and encouragement. Mentors and spiritual advisers can provide guidance, enriching the transition process with wisdom from their experiences.
- **Remain Open to the Spirit's Leading:** Above all, maintaining openness to the Holy Spirit ensures that believers remain responsive to divine prompts and guidance. Flexibility in plans and goals allows for adjustment and alignment with God's ever-expanding purpose.

Embracing calling shifts as a natural aspect of spiritual growth encourages believers to view changes as opportunities for deepened faith and broader impact. With prayerfulness and openness to divine guidance, transitions become gateways to a more profound alignment with God's will, enriching both personal journeys and their broader contributions to God's kingdom.

Biblical Example of Paul Who Experienced Changing Paths

Change often heralds spiritual growth, marking progress and a deeper alignment with God's will. Such transformations are vividly illustrated through the biblical narrative of Paul, whose story is a testament to the power of divine purpose in radically altering life's trajectory.

Paul, initially known as Saul, was a staunch Pharisee committed to upholding Jewish laws. His zeal manifested in the persecution of early Christians, whom he viewed as a threat to tradition. This fervor was sanctioned by religious authorities, making him a formidable figure against believers. However, Saul's life took a transformative turn on the road to Damascus (Acts 9). During this journey, he encountered a divine revelation—a blinding light and the voice of Jesus challenging his persecution. This supernatural experience led to both physical blindness and a spiritual awakening.

Following divine instruction, Saul was led to Damascus, where Ananias, a disciple, restored his sight, symbolizing a renewal of vision and purpose. This marked the inception of his new identity as Paul, a dedicated apostle of Christ. His transformation underscores how even deeply entrenched beliefs can be altered by divine intervention, redirecting life toward fulfilling God's higher purpose.

Paul's story provides pivotal insights for contemporary spiritual journeys:

1. **Openness to Change:** His readiness to embrace a new mission highlights the essential nature of being open to God's redirection, even when it challenges long-held beliefs.
2. **Faith in Transformation:** Paul's trust in God's vision, despite his past actions, teaches the importance of faith in divine plans to repurpose experiences for future roles.
3. **Commitment to Purpose:** His immediate dedication to preaching underscores the courage required to pursue new paths, often involving unknown challenges.
4. **Impact on Community:** Paul's transformation transcended personal change, significantly shaping early Christianity. His letters continue to inspire, exemplifying the far-reaching effects personal transformations can have on communities and history.

Paul's narrative encourages us to emulate his courage and openness to life's changes, trusting that divine purposes often yield unexpected but transformative shifts.

Biblical Example of Ruth Who Experienced Changing Paths

The story of Ruth offers a profound example of how shifting paths are central to embracing divine purpose and spiritual growth. Her journey illustrates unwavering faith and the transformative power of loyalty and commitment in the face of life's uncertainties.

Ruth, a Moabite woman, faced a significant life change after the deaths of her husband and father-in-law. This tragic event marked the beginning of a transformative journey for Ruth, prompting a decisive turn in her life's direction. Despite the opportunity to return to her own family and culture, Ruth chose to stay with Naomi, her mother-in-law, declaring with heartfelt loyalty, *"Where you go, I will go; where you lodge, I will lodge; your people shall be my people, and your God my God"* (Ruth 1:16). This pivotal decision set Ruth on a path of faith that would lead her into the heart of Israel's story.

Ruth's journey from Moab to Bethlehem was not just a physical move but also a spiritual and cultural transformation. By aligning herself with Naomi and the God of Israel, Ruth embraced a new cultural identity and faith that ultimately connected her to God's greater design. This decision exemplifies how embracing new directions can lead to personal and spiritual enrichment.

Her faithfulness and diligent work in the fields of Boaz, a relative of Naomi, demonstrate her commitment to her new path, blending hard work with trust in God's provision. Boaz recognized Ruth's loyalty and diligence, which made her stand out in the community. Through her marriage to Boaz and her inclusion in the lineage of David—and ultimately Jesus—Ruth's story underscores the transformative impact of embracing God-directed changes.

Ruth's journey provides several lessons about adapting to new roles and callings:

1. **Commitment to God's People:** By choosing Naomi's path, Ruth demonstrated a profound commitment not only to Naomi but also to God's people. This integration with Israel reflects the unity and inclusivity characteristic of God's kingdom, where faith transcends cultural boundaries.
2. **Trust in God's Provision:** Ruth's faith amid change showcases unwavering trust in God's provision. Her willingness to step into unfamiliar roles reassured her that God's plans were still at work, even amid uncertainties.
3. **Impact of Faithfulness on Divine Purpose:** Her story illustrates that faithfulness in small, everyday acts can lead to significant roles in God's plan. Ruth's ordinary acts of loyalty and perseverance culminated in an extraordinary legacy.
4. **Embracing New Identities:** Ruth's willingness to adopt a new cultural and spiritual identity exemplifies the transformative potential of embracing God-driven changes. Her story teaches believers that adaptation and acceptance can lead to spiritual maturity and integration into God's covenant people.

Ruth's life is a testament to the power of change embraced through faith. Her journey from widowhood to a pivotal matriarch in biblical history inspires those navigating life's transitions. It serves as a reminder that shifts, guided by faith and trust in God's providence, enhance our spiritual journey, aligning us more closely with His overarching purpose. Ruth's willingness to leave the familiar reveals a deeper truth: divine purpose often demands a complete reroute, not just a detour.

Adopting a growth mindset allows us to view change as an opportunity rather than a setback. Cultivating faith means trusting that God's plan unfolds with each transition, especially when the path appears uncertain. Embrace these shifts as divine appointments for growth, fostering resilience and spiritual acuity.

Joshua's Story

Joshua's journey from a corporate environment to human rights advocacy is a profound narrative of growth and discovery. In his corporate career, Joshua enjoyed financial stability and a clear trajectory, yet beneath this apparent success lay a persistent sense of unrest. His work increasingly felt disconnected from his values, prompting internal conflict about his purpose.

Driven by a desire for meaningful work, Joshua began exploring opportunities that aligned more closely with his passion for justice and equality. This transition was gradual, marked by doubt and fear of the unknown. Conversations with mentors and introspective reflection played pivotal roles in his decision to change course. A key turning point came when an opportunity to volunteer with a human rights organization arose—an experience that deeply resonated with him and reignited his commitment to serving others.

Embracing this new path required Joshua to step out of his comfort zone and confront uncertainty head-on. The challenges were manifold, from the financial instability of advocacy work to the emotional toll of confronting human suffering. However,

Joshua's faith and conviction in God's guidance strengthened his resolve. He viewed these challenges not as setbacks but as integral steps in a divinely directed journey.

Through persistence and dedication, Joshua found renewed purpose and vigor. Aligning his career with his faith provided a sense of fulfillment previously elusive in his corporate role. His story exemplifies the transformative power of embracing divine reroutings, serving as a blueprint for those seeking deeper meaning in their lives. Joshua's path underscores the potential for profound personal and professional reinvention when one's life aligns with their calling.

Embracing change involves practical steps: view change as an invitation to maturity rather than a threat; establish spiritual disciplines like prayer and meditation to find peace amid transitions; maintain a supportive community that encourages exploration of new paths. Action motivates growth and sustains a transformative journey that amplifies faith and purpose.

Practical Mindset Shifts for Embracing Change with Faith and Resilience

Navigating change with faith and resilience involves adopting new perspectives that allow believers to view transitions as opportunities for growth rather than obstacles. Here are mindset shifts that can help foster a positive embrace of change, reinforcing trust in God's plan:

1. **Embrace Change as a Divine Opportunity**
   Start by redefining change as an opportunity ordained by God rather than a threat to the status quo. This shift transforms how change is perceived—seeing it as God's way of

guiding you to greater understanding and purpose. Recognize that God's plans are intricately designed for growth and fulfill His promises, as highlighted in Isaiah 46:10: *"My purpose will stand, and I will do all that I please."* This verse reminds us that God's direction is intentional, steady, and always aimed at fulfilling His greater vision for our lives.

2. **Develop a Growth Mindset**
   Adopt a growth mindset, focusing on the potential for learning and development in every new situation. Instead of fearing failure or uncertainty, view each change as a learning curve contributing to spiritual maturity. Reflect on James 1:2–4, which urges, *"Consider it pure joy, my brothers and sisters, whenever you face trials of many kinds, because you know that the testing of your faith produces perseverance. Let perseverance finish its work so that you may be mature and complete, not lacking anything."* This perspective anchors us in hope and purpose, even when the road feels unclear.

3. **Cultivate Resilience through Scripture**
   Immerse yourself in Scripture to gain strength and resilience. The Bible is rich with stories and teachings that offer encouragement and wisdom for handling transitions. Reflecting on transformative narratives, such as the journeys of Joseph or Paul, can embolden you to trust in God's transformative power and continual presence.

4. **Practice Gratitude**
   Gratitude anchors the soul in positivity, keeping you focused on blessings regardless of circumstances. Practicing gratitude involves acknowledging God's gifts, big or small, and celebrating progress in your journey. Techniques like meditating

on the Word help ground you in the present moment, preventing stress about the uncertain future and fostering peace.

5. **Seek Community Support**
Engage with a faith community that fosters sharing and support. Surrounding yourself with individuals who provide perspective, counsel, and encouragement is vital during times of change. Hebrews 10:24-25 advises believers not to forsake meeting together but to inspire one another, reinforcing the significance of fellowship in sustaining faith through transitions.

6. **Prioritize Prayer and Reflection**
Prayer is a powerful tool for navigating change, providing clarity and connection with God. Prioritize consistent prayer to seek God's wisdom and guidance, ensuring your decisions and actions align with His will. Reflection allows you to consider past transitions and recognize God's faithfulness, reinforcing confidence in His ultimate plan.

7. **Embrace Adaptive Flexibility**
Accept that flexibility is essential when embracing change. Plans and paths may shift, but maintaining an open heart receptive to God's adjustments through the Spirit enables seamless transitions. Flexibility allows for adaptation without losing sight of overarching goals, ensuring responsiveness to the Holy Spirit's leading.

These mindset shifts offer a framework for facing change with faith and resilience, viewing each transition as an integral part of a divinely ordained journey. With an emphasis on learning, gratitude, and trust in God's plan, believers can embrace change as a fundamental element of growth and spiritual fulfillment. By integrating these perspectives, transitions can be approached with courage and optimism, reinforcing a purposeful walk in alignment with God's will.

As we conclude this chapter, let us reflect on the profound stories of transformation experienced by Paul and Ruth. These narratives remind us that life's transitions are not random disruptions but harmonious elements of God's grand design, advancing our personal growth and deepening our sense of purpose.

Pause for a moment to consider your own journey. What transformations have you faced, and how might they guide you toward greater alignment with your divine calling? Life's unexpected turns can indeed be challenging, yet they serve as pivotal points inviting us to embrace change with courage and faith. As you navigate your path, know that each shift brings you closer to your true purpose.

Rerouted Truth: *God often uses unwanted change as the very doorway to the assignment you never knew you needed.*

CHAPTER 18

Navigating Challenges on the Path

In the heart of a desperate urban landscape, where hope often seems overshadowed by hardship, Robert stood on the brink of a remarkable transformation. His resolve to establish a community shelter amidst significant societal apathy and bureaucratic bottlenecks reveals a profound truth: true growth emerges from overcoming adversity.

Your journey toward purpose is not a straight path. Challenges such as fear of failure, societal resistance, and personal doubts are common. Yet, these are not mere hurdles; they are the forging tools that build resilience and deepen your commitment to the journey ahead. You will discover that each obstacle you encounter provides a unique opportunity to grow stronger, ensuring that each step forward is not just part of a journey but a transformative experience in itself.

When the Path Got Hard

There have been moments in my journey where I seriously questioned if I was on the right path. Not because I lacked calling—

but because the resistance was real. Just when things would start to move forward, it felt like the ground beneath me shifted—delayed opportunities, strained relationships, financial strain, even doubt that crept in like a shadow that lingered no matter how much light I tried to let in.

What made it harder was that I was trying to honor God. I wasn't running from Him—I was running with Him. But somehow, that didn't exempt me from the weight.

One night, in total frustration, I cried out in prayer, *"God, if this is what purpose looks like, why does it feel like pressure?"* And gently, but clearly, I sensed this response: *"Because you're trying to carry it alone."*

That moment shifted everything.

I began laying down the idea that I had to be strong all the time. I let God into the parts of the journey I was trying to manage in silence. I got honest with my mentors. I started resting more intentionally, praying less about outcomes and more about strength. Slowly, things didn't necessarily get easier—but I got steadier.

Now, when challenges come—and they still do—I don't immediately assume I've done something wrong. I ask, "What is God developing in me here?" He hasn't always changed my circumstances, but He has changed me through them. Instead of quick fixes, He's built endurance. Instead of escape routes, He's taught me surrender. And in that surrender, I've had to confront deeper temptations—like the urge to do it all myself, the pull toward bitterness when things don't go my way, or the instinct to isolate when I feel misunderstood. True surrender isn't just laying down our plans—it's resisting the habits that try to protect us from pain but also keep us from growth. It's choosing God's presence over our pride, again and again.

Scriptural References for Encouragement While Navigating Challenges

In the pursuit of purpose, scripture offers a reservoir of strength and guidance, encouraging believers to remain steadfast in the face of challenges. Here are key scriptural references that provide reassurance, helping to navigate the path with faith and courage:

1. **Philippians 4:13** – *"I can do all things through Christ who strengthens me."*

This verse serves as a powerful reminder of the divine strength available to believers, ensuring that no challenge is insurmountable with Christ's empowerment. It encourages resilience and perseverance through difficulties, reinforcing the belief that personal limitations can be overcome through divine strength.

2. **Isaiah 40:31** – *"But they who wait for the Lord shall renew their strength; they shall mount up with wings like eagles; they shall run and not be weary; they shall walk and not faint."*

Isaiah emphasizes the reward of patience and trust in God's timing. This promise assures believers that resting in God's presence brings renewal, enabling continuous progress even when the way is arduous. It reaffirms that God's support provides the endurance needed to persist through trials.

3. **Romans 8:28** – *"And we know that for those who love God all things work together for good, for those who are called according to his purpose."*

   In moments of uncertainty, this verse reassures believers of God's sovereignty and the assurance that all circumstances contribute to His greater good. Trusting in this promise fosters peace and confidence, knowing that even setbacks are woven into a divine tapestry of purpose.

4. **James 1:2-4** – *"Count it all joy, my brothers, when you meet trials of various kinds, for you know that the testing of your faith produces steadfastness. And let steadfastness have its full effect, that you may be perfect and complete, lacking in nothing."*

   In every pothole and detour, God recalibrates the route—not to delay us, but to develop us.

   James' words encourage a shift in perception, viewing challenges as opportunities for growth and completion in faith. This passage highlights the refining process trials bring, producing maturity and resilience essential for fulfilling divine purpose.

5. **1 Peter 5:7** – *"Casting all your anxieties on him, because he cares for you."*

   This verse offers solace, reminding believers to entrust their worries to God. It underscores God's loving care and willingness to bear burdens, providing peace and relief from anxiety.

6. **Joshua 1:9** – *"Have I not commanded you? Be strong and courageous. Do not be frightened, and do not be dismayed, for the Lord your God is with you wherever you go."*

   Joshua's charge instills confidence through the assurance of God's constant presence. This passage calls for courage and steadfastness, affirming that believers are never alone in their journey.

By meditating on these scriptures, individuals embarking on their purposeful journey can remain rooted in faith, drawing encouragement and unwavering hope despite the challenges they encounter. Such promises act not only as sources of strength but also as reminders of God's faithful support and guidance along the way.

To effectively navigate these adversities, begin by anchoring yourself in contemplative prayer and meditation, seeking clarity and strength from divine guidance. Develop strategies that embrace both flexibility and perseverance. Acknowledge setbacks not as barriers but as lessons steering your journey. Engaging with mentors and support networks grounds you spiritually and provides perspective during trials.

Community and mentorship play pivotal roles during these trials. Surround yourself with a supportive network that reinforces your spiritual base, offering encouragement and wisdom when doubt creeps in. Mentors who have traversed similar paths can provide insight and strength, showing that challenges are part of a shared journey towards purpose.

Practical Strategies for Overcoming Setbacks

Navigating the inevitable setbacks encountered along a purposeful journey requires resilience, faith, and adaptable strategies. Addressing these challenges effectively involves a blend of personal reflection, strategic problem-solving, and spiritual strength. Here are practical methods to overcome setbacks and continue progressing toward your purpose:

1. Reframe Challenges as Learning Opportunities
Begin by shifting your mindset to view setbacks not as failures but as valuable learning opportunities. This reframe enables you to analyze what went wrong, identify lessons, and apply them moving forward. Remember that challenges often provide insight into areas needing improvement, guiding future strategies with clarity and focus.

2. Engage in Reflective Practices
Regular reflection is essential for processing setbacks. Set aside time for prayer, meditation, or journaling to gauge past experiences, emotions, and responses. Through this practice, you can uncover underlying issues, gain new perspectives, and determine more effective paths forward. Documenting these reflections also creates a resource for future reference when facing similar challenges.

3. Develop a Flexible Action Plan
Flexibility within your action plan is crucial for accommodating unexpected setbacks without derailing your progress. Break down your goals into smaller, manageable steps that allow for adjustments along the way. Ensure your plan has room for alternative

routes, adapting to changes while still moving forward. Being open to redirection reflects trust in God's timing and wisdom, as Proverbs 19:21 reminds us, *"Many are the plans in a person's heart, but it is the Lord's purpose that prevails."*

4. Strengthen Your Support Network
Surround yourself with a supportive community that offers encouragement, accountability, and wisdom. Engage with mentors, peers, or faith groups who understand your journey and provide constructive feedback. Sharing setbacks with trusted individuals fosters a sense of belonging, helping to dispel feelings of isolation and reinforcing resilience through collective support.

5. Focus on Emotional and Spiritual Resilience
Building emotional and spiritual resilience is key to enduring and overcoming setbacks. Practice self-care by maintaining a healthy balance in your life—emotionally, spiritually, and physically. Prioritize activities that enrich your spirit, such as engaging with scripture, participating in worship, or spending time in nature. Strengthening this foundation ensures stability and grace under pressure.

6. Cultivate a Growth Mindset
Adopting a growth mindset encourages perseverance and adaptability, viewing challenges as catalysts for personal and spiritual growth. Emphasize continuous learning and flexibility, allowing setbacks to refine your skills and deepen your faith. This mindset fosters courage and determination, transforming setbacks into stepping stones rather than roadblocks.

7. Rely on Prayer and Trust in Divine Guidance
In times of difficulty, leaning into prayer fosters a deeper connection with God, offering peace and direction. Pray for wisdom,

patience, and insight, trusting that God equips you with the strength needed to overcome obstacles. Faith in God's sovereignty and purpose assures you that setbacks are part of a greater plan that ultimately leads to fulfillment.

By implementing these strategies, you can effectively process setbacks as integral components of your journey, fortifying your resolve and commitment to living a purpose-driven life. Embrace challenges with patience and faith, understanding that they shape and prepare you for the fulfillment of God's divine purpose, even when the path ahead seems uncertain.

Reflect on the life of Nelson Mandela, whose steadfast dedication to justice and equality endured through years of imprisonment. His work demonstrates the power of purpose to transcend obstacles, showing us how resilience can ignite social transformation and personal growth.

Faith-Based Problem-Solving Framework

Successfully navigating challenges along your spiritual journey involves employing a structured, faith-based approach to problem-solving. This framework integrates spiritual practices with practical steps, ensuring that solutions align with divine guidance and enhance personal growth. Here is a step-by-step process to tackle challenges effectively:

1. Prayerful Discernment
Begin any problem-solving process with prayer, seeking divine wisdom and clarity. Ask God to illuminate the situation, providing insight into the root causes and potential solutions. Incorporate scriptures that emphasize divine guidance, such as Proverbs 3:5-6: *"Trust in the Lord with all your heart and lean not on your*

own understanding; in all your ways submit to him, and he will make your paths straight."

2. Reflect and Define the Issue

Take time to clearly define and understand the challenge at hand. Assess the scope of the problem and its impact on your spiritual path. Write down observations and insights to ensure a comprehensive understanding of the situation. Tracing the spiritual pattern creates a foundation for effective problem-solving by highlighting the true nature of the challenge.

3. Gather Information and Seek Wisdom

Collect relevant information that can inform potential solutions. This might include seeking wisdom from scripture, spiritual literature, or advice from mentors and spiritual advisors. Proverbs 15:22 reinforces the value of counsel in decision-making: *"Plans fail for lack of counsel, but with many advisers, they succeed."*

4. Identify Possible Solutions

When identifying potential solutions, consider both spiritual convictions and practicalities. For example, Anna, a dedicated teacher, faced challenges integrating her faith with her professional life in a secular education system. She felt a profound calling to create a supportive environment for students struggling with self-esteem and identity issues.

During her brainstorming session, she listed both faith-based and practical strategies. Spiritually, she considered initiating a student-led mentorship program rooted in biblical principles of compassion and service. Practically, she explored logistics such as creating partnerships with local community leaders and securing parental approval to implement these programs within the school.

By blending her commitment to faith with tangible, actionable steps, Anna developed a robust plan that aligned with her spiritual beliefs while meeting the operational criteria of the education system. This balanced approach not only resonated within her profession but also brought a refreshing dynamic to her pursuit of transformative education.

5. Evaluate and Prioritize Solutions

Evaluate each potential solution against criteria such as feasibility, alignment with spiritual goals, and potential impact. Utilize the wisdom gained through prayer and counsel to prioritize solutions that reflect God's will. Ask yourself, "Does this solution promote personal and spiritual growth in line with divine purposes?"

6. Take Action with Faith

Commit to implementing the chosen solution with boldness and trust in God's provision. Taking action requires a faithful step forward, even amidst uncertainty. Draw strength from Philippians 4:13: *"I can do all things through Christ who strengthens me,"* reinforcing your commitment to pursue solutions driven by faith.

7. Monitor Progress and Adapt

Regularly assess the progress of the implemented solution, remaining open to adjustments as new insights or challenges arise. Stay attuned to God's leading, adapting strategies as needed to remain in harmony with His guidance. Monitoring ensures that you remain proactive, preventing small issues from becoming major setbacks.

8. Reflect and Give Thanks

After resolving the issue, take time to reflect on the outcomes and lessons learned. Offer thanksgiving to God for His provision and guidance throughout the process. Psalms 107:1 encourages gratitude: *"Give thanks to the Lord, for he is good; his love endures forever."* Thankfulness promotes humility and reinforces the importance of divine partnership in problem-solving.

By applying this faith-based problem-solving framework, you harness both spiritual and practical resources to navigate challenges effectively. This approach not only addresses immediate issues but also strengthens your ability to face future challenges with confidence, fostering a journey that remains closely aligned with God's purpose. Embrace this process as a spiritual discipline, ensuring that you are equipped to meet life's challenges with resilience and grace.

Reflection Exercises on Handling Disappointments with Faith

Acknowledging that disappointment is part of life's journey, these exercises integrate scriptural wisdom and personal insight to convert setbacks into opportunities for growth.

1. **Identify and Acknowledge Emotions**
- **Exercise:** Reflect on a recent disappointment, allowing all emotions to surface without judgment.
- **Scriptural Anchor:** Psalms 42:11 encourages hope in God during times of emotional struggle.
- **Outcome:** Accepting emotions is the first step toward healing and movement.

2. **Seek God's Perspective**
- **Exercise:** Journal about your disappointment, inviting God's wisdom to reveal lessons and broader perspectives.
- **Scriptural Anchor:** Romans 8:28 reassures that all things work for good for those who love God.
- **Outcome:** Reframing fosters reassurance and a sense of purpose in adversity.

3. **Reflect on Past Victories**
- **Exercise:** List past challenges overcome, noting divine interventions and patterns of resilience.
- **Scriptural Anchor:** 1 Samuel 7:12 serves as a reminder of God's continual help.
- **Outcome:** Identifying past victories fortifies confidence in God's ongoing support.

4. **Practice Gratitude**
- **Exercise:** Write daily gratitude entries for a week, focusing on life's abundant joys beyond current challenges.
- **Scriptural Anchor:** 1 Thessalonians 5:18 guides thanksgiving in all situations.
- **Outcome:** Gratitude shifts focus to positivity and strengthens faith, counterbalancing disappointment.

5. **Formulate a Faith-Driven Action Plan**
- **Exercise:** Utilize previous insights to craft a plan of faith-aligned actions with achievable goals.

- **Scriptural Anchor:** Proverbs 16:9 reminds that while humans plan their steps, God establishes them.
- **Outcome:** Moving forward with a faith-informed plan turns setbacks into catalysts for spiritual and personal advancement.

These exercises transform disappointments into valuable moments of reflection and spiritual development, reinforcing that God's plans encompass all life experiences.

Every purpose-driven path will, at some point, pass through valleys of resistance, fatigue, and uncertainty. These moments are not signs that you've missed your way—they are evidence that you're stepping into something meaningful. The weight you feel doesn't always mean you're doing something wrong; sometimes, it simply means you're carrying something important.

Pressure isn't proof of failure—it's often preparation. God uses these difficult places to teach you surrender, to build your resilience, and to shape your character. So when the path gets hard, don't retreat. Lean in. Ask what God is developing in you. Trust that He's not just leading you somewhere—He's forming something in you along the way. Your calling isn't confirmed by ease, but by your commitment to keep moving forward, even when the way is steep.

Rerouted Truth: *Your obstacles are not detours—they are divine pressure points shaping you for impact greater than comfort can offer.*

CHAPTER 19
Purpose-Driven Relationships

At the heart of purpose-driven relationships lies a robust framework of mutual support, where partners hold each other accountable, encouraging the pursuit of God-given purposes with integrity and courage. Examples like the biblical friendship of Jonathan and David enrich this exploration, showcasing how spiritual and loyal partnerships can sustain individuals through life's trials. This chapter sets the stage for understanding how relationships rooted in faith become catalysts for growth, facilitating a journey enriched with shared ideals and continuous personal development.

Learning to Build with Purpose

I've come to realize that not all relationships are meant to go where God is taking me. That was a hard truth to accept. I used to believe that loyalty meant keeping everyone close, no matter the cost. But as God began to clarify my purpose, He also began to shift my relationships.

Some of the hardest moments were recognizing that certain connections—though once meaningful—no longer aligned with the man I was becoming. It didn't mean I stopped caring; it meant I had to make peace with letting go. I had to trust that honoring God sometimes meant walking alone for a while until He brought the right people into the next chapter.

At the same time, I learned to be more intentional with the relationships that did matter. I stopped being passive with friendships that nurtured my growth. I reached out more, prayed with people more, and opened myself up to deeper accountability.

Whether in friendships, mentorships, or partnerships, I've learned to ask a simple question: *"Is this relationship sharpening me toward purpose or pulling me from it?"* That one filter has saved me from confusion and positioned me for clarity more times than I can count.

Purpose-driven relationships are rarely perfect—but they're always anchored in truth, trust, and growth. And I thank God for teaching me that alignment matters just as much as affection.

Conflict Resolution in Purpose-Driven Partnerships

Navigating challenges in purpose-driven relationships requires mastering conflict resolution while focusing on shared goals and spiritual alignment. Conflicts can arise in friendships, family, or professional partnerships due to differing perspectives and expectations. Addressing these issues within a faith-based context demands patience, understanding, and a commitment to preserving unity.

1. Recognize and Acknowledge Conflict

Begin by acknowledging the existence of conflict and its impact on the relationship. Ignoring the issue or pretending it doesn't exist only worsens the situation. Respectfully acknowledge the tensions without placing blame, creating a foundation for open dialogue.

2. Engage in Open and Honest Communication

Effective conflict resolution begins with communication. Foster an environment where everyone feels safe to express their thoughts and feelings. Practice active listening, which involves understanding others' perspectives without interrupting or judging. Valuing each voice fosters mutual respect and empathy.

3. Reflect on Shared Purpose

Return to the shared purpose and values that unite the partnership. Reflecting on these commonalities reminds both parties of the bigger picture and the goals that brought them together. This shared commitment can motivate finding resolutions that benefit the relationship as a whole.

4. Pray and Seek Divine Guidance

Incorporate prayer into the conflict resolution process. Praying together or individually invites divine wisdom and peace, allowing for cooler heads and softer hearts. Scriptures like James 1:5 guide this practice, reassuring believers that God provides wisdom to those who ask.

5. Explore Options and Compromise

Encourage brainstorming multiple potential solutions that accommodate both parties' needs. Exploring diverse options allows for creative problem-solving and demonstrates a willingness to compromise. Aim for solutions that reflect the partnership's purpose and values, ensuring alignment with shared objectives.

6. Reach an Agreement

Once potential solutions are outlined, collaboratively decide on the best course of action. Strive for an agreement that upholds integrity and sustains harmony within the partnership. Securing alignment ensures both parties are committed to moving forward with mutual understanding and support.

7. Follow Up and Maintain Communication

After resolution, continue engaging in open dialogue and regular check-ins. This practice reinforces commitment to the relationship, allows for necessary adjustments, and ensures any residual tensions are addressed. Maintaining communication solidifies trust and fortifies the partnership against future conflicts.

Having navigated conflict resolution successfully, where open communication proves vital for reinforcing trust and mutual growth, it is now essential to focus on the broader viewpoint—relationship evaluation. This shift from resolving immediate conflicts to assessing long-term relational health highlights the ongoing commitment required for nurturing meaningful connections. Our ability to confront and manage conflict gracefully sets the stage for a critical examination of how these relationships align with our spiritual and personal objectives.

As we evaluate relationships, reflect on how they support your spiritual aspirations. Consider their role in inspiring, challenging, and aligning with your goals. By doing so, you ensure that each relationship not only withstands conflicts but also contributes to your long-term growth and spiritual journey. This reflective process is crucial for nurturing purposeful partnerships that support mutual development and shared aspirations.

Self-Assessment Checklist for Evaluating Relationships

To effectively assess your current relationships and their alignment with your spiritual goals, use the following checklist. This will help you determine if a relationship supports or detracts from your spiritual journey:

Relationship Evaluation Criteria

- **Inspiration:**
    - Does this relationship inspire you to pursue your God-given purpose?
    - Does it motivate you to grow spiritually and personally?

- **Challenge:**
    - Does this relationship challenge you to improve and hold you accountable?
    - Does it encourage you to adopt a broader outlook in your spiritual journey?

- **Alignment with Spiritual Goals:**
    - Is this relationship aligned with your faith and spiritual objectives?
    - Does it bring you closer to what you believe God's purpose is for you?

- **Mutual Support and Growth:**
  - Is this relationship characterized by mutual encouragement and support?
  - Do both parties help each other grow and succeed in spiritual and personal endeavors?

Reflective Questions

After evaluating each relationship using the checklist, ask yourself:

- Overall, does this relationship bring me closer to God's purpose for my life?
- How does this relationship contribute to my spiritual progress, and are there areas needing improvement?

Action Steps

- Engage in regular reflections, revisiting these criteria to ensure relationships remain supportive and aligned with your values and goals.
- Consider discussing these reflections with your partner to foster open communication and collaborative growth.

By regularly assessing your relationships against these criteria, you can nurture stronger, more purposeful connections that support your long-term spiritual and personal growth.

Tips for Fostering Healthy, Faith-Based Partnerships

Cultivating relationships anchored in faith and purpose involves intentional actions and a commitment to nurturing mutual growth and understanding. Here are key tips to help foster healthy, faith-based partnerships:

1. Root the Relationship in Shared Values
Establish a strong foundation by identifying and aligning on shared values and spiritual beliefs. Discuss what aspects of faith are most important to each partner and how these can guide interactions and joint decisions. This shared understanding provides stability and consistency, ensuring the partnership is guided by common principles.

2. Prioritize Open and Honest Communication
Maintain open lines of communication where both parties feel safe to express their thoughts and emotions. Emphasize honesty and transparency to facilitate understanding and eliminate misunderstandings. Regularly check in with each other, discussing both joys and challenges, and how faith can guide you through them.

3. Practice Active Empathy and Support
Show empathy by truly listening to each other's experiences and challenges, offering a supportive and non-judgmental space. Being present reinforces the bond of faith and mutual respect, allowing both partners to feel valued and understood.

4. Engage in Shared Spiritual Activities
Participating in shared spiritual practices, such as prayer, meditation, or attending worship services together, strengthens the

spiritual connection between partners. These activities reinforce the role of faith in the partnership, offering shared moments of peace, joy, and reflection that deepen the relationship.

5. Address Conflicts with Patience and Understanding

Approach conflicts with a mindset prioritizing resolution and growth. Instead of dwelling on disagreements, seek to understand each other's perspectives and find common ground. Use prayer and reflection as tools for patience and understanding, ensuring conflicts are resolved in ways that align with shared values and faith.

6. Celebrate Milestones and Achievements

Acknowledge and celebrate achievements and milestones within the relationship, both personal and collective. Celebrations reinforce positive behaviors and actions, creating lasting memories and strengthening the connection. These moments of joy and recognition highlight the importance of individual and shared journeys within the partnership.

7. Encourage Individual Growth

Support each other's personal growth and spiritual development, encouraging pursuits that align with each individual's talents and callings. A purpose-driven partnership recognizes the value of individuality, allowing each person to thrive while contributing to the strength and unity of the relationship.

By integrating these tips into daily interactions and commitments, faith-based partnerships can flourish, embodying love, understanding, and shared purpose. These efforts foster a nurturing environment where both individuals can grow spiritually and personally, reinforcing the relationship's alignment with divine purpose and mutual fulfillment.

Purpose-Driven Relationships Examples

In the realm of purpose-driven relationships, numerous examples highlight the principles of accountability, growth, and conflict resolution, serving as inspirations for modern faith-based partnerships.

1. Paul and Timothy (Biblical Example):

- The mentorship between Paul and Timothy in the New Testament exemplifies a profound relationship grounded in faith and spiritual development. Paul offered guidance, wisdom, and encouragement to Timothy, helping him grow as a leader in the early Church. This example illustrates how mentorship and accountability can foster spiritual growth and resilience in the face of challenges.

2. Franklin D. Roosevelt and Winston Churchill (Historical Example):

- During World War II, the alliance between Franklin D. Roosevelt and Winston Churchill proved pivotal. Despite their differing political and cultural backgrounds, their partnership was characterized by a shared vision to defeat the Axis powers. They maintained strong communication, demonstrating how aligned purpose and mutual respect can overcome conflict and drive significant change during times of crisis. Some connections are divine intersections—God places them strategically when your journey requires a reroute through relationship.

3. Bill Gates and Warren Buffett (Contemporary Example):

- Bill Gates and Warren Buffett exemplify a contemporary purpose-driven relationship through their philanthropic efforts. Rooted in shared values and a commitment to improving the world via the Giving Pledge, their partnership highlights how mutual goals and accountability can lead to impactful change. Their collaboration underscores the relevance of purpose-driven relationships today, just as in the past.

These examples collectively illustrate the transformative potential of relationships centered on shared purpose and principles, enhancing both individual and collective achievements within a faith-based framework.

Nurturing Purpose-Driven Marriage Relationships

Purpose-driven marriages are founded on shared values, goals, and spiritual aspirations, creating a strong base that sustains the relationship while enhancing individual growth and fulfillment. Here's a guide to nurturing such a marriage effectively:

1. Establish Shared Vision and Goals
Begin by defining a vision that aligns with both partners' spiritual and personal aspirations. Take time to discuss each other's

dreams, ensuring they complement one another. Although the man may set the direction based on purpose, being complementary is vital. Use this as a foundation to establish joint goals that advance both individual desires and the relational purpose. Reflect on Proverbs 29:18, which states, *"Where there is no vision, the people perish,"* emphasizing the importance of a unified direction in marriage.

2. Foster Open and Faithful Communication

Healthy marriages thrive on honest communication. Prioritize regular discussions about your hopes, concerns, and spiritual journeys. Active listening and empathy are crucial, allowing each partner to feel heard and valued. This reinforces trust and facilitates a deeper emotional connection, essential for a purpose-driven bond.

3. Incorporate Spiritual Practices Together

Engage in shared spiritual practices such as prayer, meditation, or attending faith-based events. These activities strengthen the spiritual bond and align the marriage with God's purpose. By committing to spiritual practices as a couple, you create a supportive environment for mutual encouragement and accountability in spiritual growth.

4. Celebrate Each Other's Strengths and Achievements

Acknowledge and affirm each other's strengths and contributions to the marriage and shared goals. Celebrating successes—no matter how small—builds a reservoir of positivity and motivation. This practice fosters appreciation, vital for maintaining a healthy, loving relationship.

5. Navigate Conflicts with Grace and Understanding

Conflict is inevitable, but resolving it with grace ensures it strengthens rather than weakens the relationship. Approach disagreements with a spirit of understanding, prioritizing reconciliation and unity over being right. Employ prayer and seek divine guidance during conflicts, remembering James 1:19's wisdom to be *"quick to listen, slow to speak, and slow to become angry."*

6. Support Each Other's Individual Growth

While shared goals are essential, supporting each partner's personal growth is equally important. Encourage pursuits that nurture individual talents and spiritual gifts, fostering a sense of fulfillment and individuality. Such support strengthens the partnership by allowing both people to thrive.

7. Commit to a Life of Service Together

Participating in shared service projects, whether within the community or faith group, can enhance spiritual and relational bonds. Collaboratively serving others fulfills a shared purpose and deeply connects partners through acts of compassion and love.

By implementing these strategies, couples can ensure their marriage is not only a partnership of love but also a profoundly purpose-driven union. Nurturing such relationships fulfills God's call to live a life steeped in faith, unity, and shared purpose, reflecting His love through their journey together.

As you contemplate cultivating purpose-driven relationships, consider forming new connections with people who share your values and can guide you on your spiritual path. Attend faith-based events, participate in community service, and seek out networks that align with your vision.

Let Lisa and James's inspiring journey fuel your commitment to build networks that uplift and celebrate shared purposes. Today is the day to take proactive steps toward cultivating purpose-driven relationships that are not just supportive but transformative. Begin by identifying one relationship that aligns with your spiritual goals and think of ways to deepen that connection through shared activities and open, faith-centered dialogues. Embrace the opportunity to grow together, rooted in trust and understanding.

Prepare to embark on an enriching exploration in "Chapter 20: Learning from Spiritual Mentors and Leaders." This upcoming chapter will guide you in drawing wisdom from those who have trodden similar paths, equipping you with the insights needed to navigate your own journey of purpose with renewed faith. Engage eagerly with the lessons and insights that await, positioning yourself for a life infused with purpose, resilience, and divine alignment.

Rerouted Truth: *The right relationships won't just support your purpose—they'll sharpen it, stretch it, and sanctify it.*

CHAPTER 20
Learning from Spiritual Mentors and Leaders

Reverend Thomas sat cocooned in the soft, golden glow of his reading lamp, a beacon of serenity amid the deepening shadows of night. The muted hum of nighttime sounds filtered through the walls, yet his thoughts drifted back to the formative words spoken by his mentor years ago: "True purpose is not found in solitude but in the footprints we leave for others to follow." This wisdom resonated like a gentle bell, clear and compelling, during a turbulent period when uncertainties clouded his path. Thomas vividly recalled the calming presence of his mentor, whose guidance felt like a warm embrace, steering him back to his core beliefs.

This simple yet profound encouragement transformed Thomas's journey. It was not merely advice but a compass that realigned him with his calling—a role shaped not only by his aspirations but amplified through the lives he touched. With each step on this new path, he felt the weight of indecision lift, replaced by a burgeoning sense of purpose that radiated through his ministry and interactions. The counsel he had received became the bedrock of his spiritual evolution, illustrating the transformative power and profound impact a mentor can have on one's journey toward divine fulfillment.

The presence of spiritual mentors is essential for those seeking to deepen their purpose. They serve as lighthouses of wisdom, illuminating paths yet to be traveled. Their insights, borne of experience and spiritual maturity, grant us the courage and clarity to pursue our callings with greater conviction.

Identifying and choosing the right mentors requires discernment and focus. Seek individuals whose lives reflect spiritual virtues and align with your goals. These mentors should exhibit qualities like compassion, humility, and a commitment to personal and communal growth. Find them through community engagements, spiritual gatherings, or personal networks.

How Mentors Shaped My Journey

I can say with certainty that I wouldn't be who I am today without the voices of godly mentors and leaders in my life. At key crossroads, it was their wisdom—spoken in truth and love—that gave me the clarity I needed to move forward.

There was one particular conversation I'll never forget. I was struggling to make a difficult decision that would affect not just my career but my calling. I sat across from a mentor who had walked through similar seasons. He didn't give me a quick answer. Instead, he asked me questions that made me wrestle. He challenged my motives. And most importantly, he prayed with me—not just for direction, but for strength.

That kind of mentorship didn't feel like control—it felt like covering. Over the years, I've learned to lean into that kind of leadership. I've sought out people who weren't impressed by my potential but were committed to my process. They've corrected me when needed, affirmed me when discouraged, and reminded me that spiritual growth always precedes platform.

I now carry their voices with me—scripture they've shared, prayers they've spoken, lessons they've lived. And it's made me more intentional about how I pour into others. Because what they gave me was more than advice—it was legacy. Mentors don't just offer wisdom; they serve as divine road signs when your purpose journey hits a bend or blind curve.

Practical Steps for Finding and Approaching Mentors

Finding and approaching a mentor is a significant step in enhancing personal and spiritual growth. A mentor provides guidance, wisdom, and support on your journey, helping to align your goals with divine purpose. Here is a practical guide for connecting with potential mentors:

1. **Understand Your Needs and Goals**
- **Exercise:** Reflect on your current needs and goals. Consider which aspects of your spiritual or personal development require guidance. Clarifying these areas helps you identify the type of mentor best suited to support your journey.
- **Outcome:** Understanding your specific needs ensures you seek a mentor whose strengths align with your

growth objectives, facilitating a productive mentoring relationship.

2. **Identify Potential Mentors**
- **Exercise:** Make a list of potential mentors based on their experience, expertise, and values. Consider individuals within your community and network, such as leaders in your church, professional circles, or local organizations.
- **Outcome:** This targeted list focuses your outreach on individuals who resonate with your aspirations, increasing the likelihood of a successful mentor-mentee match.

3. **Utilize Social and Professional Platforms**
- **Exercise:** Explore platforms like LinkedIn, mentorship programs, or faith-based community forums where potential mentors are active. These spaces offer opportunities to connect with experienced individuals open to guiding others.
- **Outcome:** Utilizing these platforms expands your reach and access to diverse mentors who can offer valuable perspectives and guidance in your field of interest.

4. **Attend Networking Events**
- **Exercise:** Participate in networking events, workshops, or conferences related to your goals. Engage with speakers and participants who demonstrate expertise

and insight, approaching conversations with genuine curiosity.
- **Outcome:** These events provide a chance to connect with new contacts in your field, fostering relationships that could lead to meaningful mentorship opportunities.

5. **Approach with Respect and Clarity**
- **Exercise:** When reaching out to potential mentors, clearly articulate your goals, why you seek their guidance, and how you believe they can assist your journey. Be courteous and concise, respecting their time and demonstrating genuine interest in their insights.
- **Outcome:** A clear, respectful approach increases the likelihood of a positive response and lays the foundation for potential mentorship.

6. **Establish Mutual Expectations**
- **Exercise:** Once a mentor agrees to guide you, discuss mutual expectations, including communication frequency, key focus areas, and goals for the relationship.
- **Outcome:** Clearly defined expectations foster a structured and productive mentoring relationship, facilitating effective growth and development.

7. **Demonstrate Commitment**
- **Exercise:** Actively engage in learning, ask thoughtful questions, and diligently apply the mentor's advice in

your personal and spiritual life. Regularly express gratitude for their time and insights.
- **Outcome**: Demonstrating commitment and appreciation reinforces the mentoring relationship, motivating continued support and shared effort toward achieving your goals.

By following these steps, you can find and connect with a mentor who will guide and support your journey toward a more purpose-driven life. Cultivating a mentorship relationship enriches personal growth, providing clarity, direction, and wisdom aligned with your spiritual and personal aspirations.

As you embark on the journey of finding a mentor, consider the profound biblical example of Elijah and Elisha. Their relationship epitomizes the principles outlined in these practical steps. Just as Elisha recognized his need for Elijah's wisdom and actively pursued his guidance, you too are encouraged to clarify your goals and identify mentors who embody the expertise and spiritual insight you seek.

Elisha's unwavering dedication to learning from Elijah underscores the importance of a proactive and committed approach in nurturing meaningful mentorship. Reflecting on their enduring relationship can inspire you to foster connections that are spiritually enriching and growth-oriented, aligning with the divine purpose in your life.

The Reciprocal Nature of Mentorship

The mentor-mentee relationship is more than guidance—it's a dynamic exchange where both parties grow. Here's how this reciprocal nature unfolds:

For Mentors:

- **Fresh Insights:** Mentees provide new perspectives, challenging mentors to remain agile and innovative.
- **Fulfillment and Purpose:** Mentors often find personal satisfaction in guiding others, reinforcing their life's work.
- **Enhanced Leadership:** The mentoring process hones communication and empathy, enhancing leadership abilities.
- **Legacy Building:** Sharing experiences with mentees allows mentors to establish a lasting legacy.
- **Renewed Enthusiasm:** Helping mentees progress often rekindles mentors' passion for their field.

For Mentees:

- **Knowledge Access:** Mentees gain valuable insights, helping them navigate challenges efficiently.
- **Expanded Networks:** Mentorship opens doors to new resources and connections.
- **Increased Confidence:** With a mentor's support, mentees develop confidence in their abilities.

- **Holistic Growth:** Mentors aid in personal and professional development, equipping mentees with skills for future challenges.

This mutually rewarding framework ensures both mentor and mentee evolve, fostering a vibrant, purpose-driven relationship.

Creating a Reciprocal Bond

To fully harness the benefits of a reciprocal mentorship relationship, both mentors and mentees should engage with dedication and openness. Here's how to cultivate this bond:

- **Commitment to Open Communication:** Create a safe environment for honest dialogue, encouraging the sharing of insights and feedback.
- **Shared Goal Setting:** Identify mutual objectives that align with each person's growth and aspirations, ensuring focus and dedication.
- **Regular Reflection:** Both mentors and mentees should regularly reflect on their learning and how the relationship continues to evolve.
- **Celebrating Collective Achievements:** Acknowledge and celebrate both individual and joint successes, reinforcing the benefits of collaboration.

By understanding and embracing the reciprocal nature of mentorship, both parties can experience growth that enriches their personal and professional lives. This dynamic partnership holds the potential for profound impact, building bridges of understanding and progress through shared purpose and humility.

Mentorship profoundly influences personal and spiritual growth, as illustrated by Sarah's journey. Under her pastor's guidance, she evolved from hesitant beginnings to establishing a community-focused ministry. Her transformation demonstrates how mentorship can unlock potential and create significant impact, encouraging us to learn from those with more experience.

To effectively integrate mentorship into your life, start by identifying the areas in which you seek guidance—whether emotional, spiritual, or career-related. Approach potential mentors with respect, inviting their wisdom and recognizing their experiences. Be ready to listen attentively, act on their counsel, and contribute your unique perspective to the conversation.

Such mentorship relationships are reciprocal, allowing both parties to experience mutual growth and a deeper understanding of their paths. Reverend Thomas emphasizes that spiritual mentorship is not just guidance; it's a shared journey toward realizing God's purpose in our lives.

Guide on Identifying and Approaching a Spiritual Mentor

Finding a spiritual mentor requires thoughtful consideration and a respectful approach. A spiritual mentor provides invaluable guidance rooted in faith, helping navigate spiritual, personal, and sometimes professional challenges. Here is a comprehensive guide to help you identify and connect with a spiritual mentor:

1. **Define Your Spiritual and Personal Objectives**
- **Exercise:** Start by clarifying your aspirations for spiritual and personal growth. Identify the areas where you seek guidance, such as deepening your faith, understanding scripture, or developing a prayer life.
- **Outcome:** Knowing your objectives helps determine the type of mentor you need and allows you to articulate these needs when reaching out to potential mentors.

2. **Identify Potential Mentors**
- **Exercise:** Create a list of individuals who embody the spiritual maturity and qualities you admire. Consider leaders within your church, community, or faith-based organizations who are respected and dedicated to spiritual growth.
- **Outcome:** This focused list guides your approach, ensuring you seek mentors who align with your values and have the experience to support your journey.

3. **Observe and Engage**
- **Exercise:** Watch how potential mentors interact and teach in community settings, noting how they embody their faith. Engage with their work—sermons, books, or public discussions—to understand their perspectives.

- **Outcome:** Observing mentors in action provides insights into their approach and how it aligns with your needs.

4. **Approach with Respect and Purpose**
- **Exercise:** Contact potential mentors with a clear purpose and a respectful demeanor. Explain your goals and how you believe they can assist in your spiritual journey, highlighting specific areas of interest.
- **Outcome:** Clearly communicating your purpose and respect shows sincerity and eagerness to learn, fostering a positive initial interaction.

5. **Establish Clear Expectations**
- **Exercise:** Once a mentor agrees to guide you, discuss the structure of the mentoring relationship, including frequency, communication methods, and goal-setting. Clarify mutual expectations to ensure a productive and goal-oriented relationship.
- **Outcome:** Setting clear expectations fosters a focused, effective mentoring relationship that benefits both mentor and mentee.

6. **Demonstrate Commitment and Gratitude**
- **Exercise:** Engage actively in the mentoring process by participating in suggested readings, exercises, or discussions. Regularly express gratitude for your mentor's guidance and time.

- **Outcome:** Commitment and gratitude strengthen the mentor-mentee relationship, ensuring ongoing support and encouragement.

7. **Reflect and Reassess**
- **Exercise:** Regularly reflect on your progress and the effectiveness of the mentoring relationship. Be open to reassessment and adaptations to ensure alignment with your spiritual growth goals.
- **Outcome:** Continuous reflection keeps the relationship dynamic and responsive to emerging needs and challenges.

By following this guide, you can establish a fruitful relationship with a spiritual mentor, significantly enhancing your spiritual journey. A mentor's support and guidance can catalyze personal and spiritual growth, providing clarity and insight as you pursue a purposeful life.

Mentorship Reflection Questions for Self-Growth

Engaging with spiritual mentors offers rich opportunities for personal and spiritual growth. Regular reflection enhances the mentoring experience, providing insights and a deeper understanding of the lessons learned. To make the most of your mentoring experience, use these specific and action-oriented reflection questions:

1. Assessing Personal and Spiritual Growth

- What tangible changes have I noticed in my spiritual practices since working with my mentor?
- Identify a scenario where you successfully applied your mentor's advice. What was the outcome?
- Reflect on a moment that deepened your understanding of faith and purpose.

2. Understanding Mentor-Mentee Dynamics

- Rate your communication with your mentor on a scale of 1-10. What steps can you take to enhance this interaction?
- Identify one aspect of your relationship that has significantly contributed to your growth.

3. Setting and Achieving Goals

- List two specific goals achieved through this mentorship and the strategies employed.
- What is one pending goal? Outline the next steps to progress, utilizing your mentor's insights.

4. Learning from Challenges

- Describe a challenge faced in this mentorship. What did you learn from overcoming it?
- How can you better integrate feedback received from your mentor moving forward?

5. Deepening Spiritual Practices

- Identify a new spiritual discipline introduced by your mentor and your progress in integrating it.
- Set a goal to enhance a spiritual practice influenced by your mentorship.

6. Building Community and Support Networks

- Name a new connection made through your mentor and its impact on your spiritual journey.
- Plan one action to contribute to your faith community, inspired by your mentor's guidance.

7. Evaluating Mentorship Outcomes

- What are the top three lessons learned from this mentorship, and how do they align with your long-term goals?
- Decide whether continuing with your current mentor or seeking a new one better aligns with your current needs.

These questions aim to keep your mentorship dynamic and purposeful, ensuring continuous personal and spiritual development.

Mentorship is a lifelong journey, an evolving path that shapes your spiritual and personal growth over time. By incorporating these reflection questions into your mentoring experience, you enhance dialogue, deepen self-awareness, and foster spiritual development. Let this reflective practice guide you as you build a more purpose-driven life, grounded in wisdom and understanding.

Rerouted Truth: *Mentors are mirrors and guides—divine connections that help you see more clearly what God sees in you.*

CHAPTER 21
Cultivating Humility in Purpose

"Humble people don't think less of themselves; they just think of themselves less." C.S. Lewis captured the essence of humility with these words, illustrating it as a virtue integral to a purposeful life. Humility does not diminish one's worth but amplifies one's capacity for service, enriching both the individual and those they encounter.

Within the Christian framework, humility holds profound significance. It is exemplified through Jesus washing the disciples' feet, teaching that true greatness is rooted in serving others. This act defied societal norms, inviting followers to recognize humility not as a weakness but as profound strength.

What Humility Really Taught Me

I used to think humility was just about being modest—keeping my head down and letting my work speak for itself. But the more I walked in purpose, the more God revealed that true humility isn't about thinking less of myself; it's about thinking of myself less.

There was a point in my journey where I was doing well externally—doors were opening, people were affirming me—but internally, I was starting to believe I had something to prove. I didn't realize how subtly pride can show up: in how I responded to feedback, in how I carried success, even in how I compared my journey to others.

It wasn't until I found myself in a moment of quiet conviction during prayer that the shift began. God showed me that the weight I was feeling wasn't from His calling—it was from trying to protect an image. That realization was sobering.

I began to ask for help more often. I started listening more and talking less. I paid attention to how I responded when someone else was celebrated or promoted. And slowly, God started teaching me that humility is actually freedom—freedom from performing, from competing, from having to be the answer.

Now, I measure my growth not by applause, but by how easily I can serve without being seen. Not by how well I lead, but by how quickly I repent. And not by how much I do—but by how surrendered I stay.

Practical Ways to Develop Humility in Daily Life

Cultivating humility is a continuous journey that enriches spiritual and personal growth, aligning individuals more closely with divine purpose. This virtue fosters a deeper understanding of oneself and others, promotes empathy, and enhances one's ability to serve. Here are practical ways to nurture humility in daily life:

1. **Practice Self-Reflection**
- **Activity:** Dedicate time each day to reflect on your thoughts, actions, and decisions. Evaluate them in light of their impacts on others and your personal growth. Use journaling to document these reflections, focusing on identifying areas of pride that require humbling.
- **Outcome:** Self-reflection fosters self-awareness and honesty, revealing moments of arrogance and providing opportunities to cultivate a more humble outlook.

2. **Acknowledge Strengths and Weaknesses with Balance**
- **Activity:** Regularly assess your strengths and weaknesses without embellishment or self-deprecation. Recognize achievements honestly while embracing areas for improvement as opportunities for growth.
- **Outcome:** Acceptance of your complete self promotes a balanced self-view, reducing ego and inviting humility by acknowledging your dependence on others and God for true strength and wisdom.

3. **Engage in Active Listening**
- **Activity:** Practice active listening by giving others your full attention during conversations. Resist the urge to interrupt or formulate responses while others are speaking. Validate their perspectives through questions and affirmations.

- **Outcome:** Active listening fosters respect and understanding, diminishing pride by prioritizing others' voices and deepening connections.

4. **Serve Others Selflessly**
- **Activity:** Participate in acts of service without expecting recognition or reward. Volunteer regularly in community service or assist individuals in need, focusing on the act of giving rather than receiving thanks.
- **Outcome:** Service cultivates humility by shifting focus from oneself to the needs and dignity of others, echoing the examples set by humble leaders like Mother Teresa.

5. **Embrace Feedback and Criticism**
- **Activity:** Accept constructive criticism graciously, viewing it as an opportunity for refinement and learning. Seek feedback from trusted mentors or peers to gain insights on areas needing growth.
- **Outcome:** Openness to criticism nurtures a humble spirit by recognizing that growth is a collaborative effort that benefits from external insights and guidance.

6. **Celebrate Others' Successes**
- **Activity:** Genuinely celebrate and appreciate the achievements of others. Offer congratulations and share in their joy while avoiding comparisons or jealousy.

- **Outcome:** Celebrating others redirects focus from self-centeredness to collective well-being, reinforcing community spirit and personal humility.

7. **Cultivate Gratitude**
- **Activity:** Maintain a daily gratitude journal, noting things you are thankful for each day, including contributions from others to your success and happiness.
- **Outcome:** Gratitude enhances humility by acknowledging the role of others and divine grace in personal achievements, fostering a mindset rooted in appreciation rather than entitlement.

8. **Pray for Humility**
- **Activity:** Integrate prayers for humility into your daily spiritual practices. Ask God to help you cultivate a humble heart and guide you away from prideful tendencies.
- **Outcome:** Praying for humility invites divine guidance and support in becoming more modest, fostering a reliance on God's wisdom and grace.

Incorporating these practices into daily life enables individuals to cultivate humility effectively, enriching their spiritual journey and enhancing interactions with others. Humility aligns with a purpose-driven life, opening hearts to deeper relationships with God and community, fostering growth, and exemplifying the teachings of Christ through everyday actions.

Balancing humility with confidence requires clearly distinguishing between confidence and arrogance. *Confidence* is exemplified by individuals who acknowledge their God-given talents and strive to use them for the greater good, similar to a leader who empowers their team by recognizing each member's strengths to achieve collective goals.

In contrast, *arrogance* arises when someone prioritizes self-promotion over teamwork, as seen in a manager who takes credit for their team's successes while ignoring their contributions. Confidence, when aligned with humility, becomes a powerful force that inspires trust and respect, fostering an atmosphere of mutual growth and learning. Conversely, when arrogance intrudes, it disrupts harmony and impedes communal progress, highlighting the importance of maintaining this delicate balance.

Transitioning to the concept of balancing these virtues, it is essential to explore how nurturing both humility and confidence can lead to a fulfilling and robust personal and spiritual life.

The Balance Between Humility and Confidence

Cultivating the virtues of humility and confidence together in one's personal and spiritual journey is crucial for achieving a healthy, purposeful life. While humility teaches us to recognize and honor the contributions of others, confidence empowers us to assert ourselves, pursue goals, and make impactful decisions. Here's how one can find balance between these seemingly contrasting virtues:

1. **Embrace Self-Awareness**
- **Practice:** Develop a deep understanding of your strengths and areas needing growth. This involves regular self-reflection and a keen understanding that we can do nothing apart from Christ, identifying where confidence can elevate your abilities without overshadowing humility. Keep in mind on a daily basis that we can do nothing without Jesus (John 15:5: *"I am the vine, ye are the branches: He that abideth in me, and I in him, the same bringeth forth much fruit: for without me ye can do nothing"*). Document daily successes and lessons learned, attributing growth to both personal efforts and external influences, such as mentors or community support.
- **Outcome:** Self-awareness fosters an accurate self-assessment, allowing individuals to appreciate achievements without veering into arrogance.

2. **Recognize and Celebrate Collective Efforts**
- **Practice:** Acknowledge the role of teamwork and support in personal or professional accomplishments. Share successes by celebrating collaborators and focusing on the collective contributions that enabled success.
- **Outcome:** Celebrating collective efforts cultivates humility by demonstrating appreciation for others and contextualizing personal achievements within broader community achievements.

3. **Assert While Listening and Learning**
- **Practice:** Cultivate an assertive communication style that allows you to express ideas confidently while remaining open to the perspectives of others. Practice active listening, aiming to learn and empathize with different viewpoints during discussions or collaborations.
- **Outcome:** This balance enhances both confidence in personal input and the humility required to grow from external insights, fostering enriched dialogue and mutual respect.

4. **Make Informed Decisions with Empathy**
- **Practice:** When making decisions, balance rational analysis with empathy and understanding of potential impacts on others. Consider how your decisions might be perceived and how they align with both your values and the interests of involved parties.
- **Outcome:** Informed decision-making strengthens confidence in leadership roles while grounding actions in the empathetic principles of humility.

5. **Maintain a Gratitude Practice**
- **Practice:** Incorporate gratitude into everyday activities, taking time to reflect on and give thanks for the opportunities, support, and achievements encountered along your journey. Gratitude journals or regular reflection sessions can be effective tools for this practice.

- **Outcome:** Gratitude highlights the contributions of others and fosters humility, reminding us of the interconnectedness of our successes with the community and divine support.

6. **Seek Continuous Learning and Growth**
- **Practice:** Actively pursue learning opportunities and mentorships to enhance skills and understanding. Approach new challenges with eagerness to expand your expertise, balancing self-confidence with a willingness to explore uncharted territory.
- **Outcome:** Continuous learning cultivates confidence in evolving capabilities while humility remains rooted in the acknowledgment of endless growth possibilities.

By integrating these practices into daily life, individuals achieve a harmonious balance between humility and confidence, enriching their spiritual journey and enhancing interactions with others. In this balance, they reflect the teachings of Jesus, who embodied servant leadership with courage and grace. Such equilibrium not only enhances personal development but also serves as a foundation for purpose-driven actions and relationships rooted in both empathy and assertive faith.

The story of a humble leader transforming an organization exemplifies this virtue in action. Esther, a school principal, revitalized a struggling school through patient listening and empowerment. Her approach was rooted in quiet guidance rather than dominance, fostering a thriving environment for both students and teachers. Esther's success highlights how humility in leadership can drive meaningful transformation and upliftment.

Practical applications of humility can begin with daily reflection and prayer, asking God to reveal where self-interest overshadows His purpose. Practice active listening, seek feedback from your surroundings, and engage in acts of service, viewing them as opportunities to express Christ-like love.

Consider routine exercises to cultivate humility: offering your time to those in need, acknowledging and addressing personal faults without defensiveness, and celebrating others' achievements genuinely. These actions reinforce humility and contribute to a life aligned with a higher purpose.

Exercises on Practicing Humility in Different Contexts

Developing Humility through Consistent Practice

Cultivating humility requires ongoing self-improvement in personal, professional, and communal contexts. Here are combined exercises to nurture service and modesty:

Reflection and Gratitude Exercise

- **Activity:** Dedicate time each evening for personal reflection, asking, "How did I practice humility today?" and "Where could I improve?" Complement this with expressing gratitude to those who supported or influenced your day.

- **Application:** Use a journal to reflect on your actions and write gratitude notes or messages to peers, mentors, and loved ones.
- **Outcome:** This practice enhances self-awareness, encourages personal growth, and fosters a spirit of thanksgiving, providing a broader perspective on your interactions and achievements.

Community and Empathetic Engagement Exercise

- **Activity:** Engage in community service while practicing empathetic listening. Focus on roles that prioritize helping others, such as serving meals, and make understanding the primary goal during interactions.
- **Application:** Volunteer for local organizations in roles that allow you to listen to and value others' stories and experiences during service.
- **Outcome:** This dual approach cultivates humility by centering on service and attentive empathy, strengthening community bonds and reducing self-centeredness in communication.

Professional Collaboration and Growth Exercise

- **Activity:** Avoid dominating in professional settings; instead, promote shared leadership and collaboration. Encourage team members to voice their ideas and acknowledge their contributions.

- **Application:** During team meetings or projects, ensure all voices are heard and valued, emphasizing collective rather than individual success.
- **Outcome:** By fostering an inclusive environment, this exercise highlights the importance of humility in teamwork and nurtures a supportive professional atmosphere conducive to growth and innovation.

By integrating these exercises into your routine, you can deepen your practice of humility across various settings, resulting in more enriching relationships and a purpose-driven life.

Humility remains a steadfast foundation for a life dedicated to purpose. As demonstrated by Jesus, genuine greatness blossoms when ambition is shaped by a desire to serve beyond oneself.

Real-Life Stories of Leaders Who Embody Humility

Leadership rooted in humility offers profound lessons in effectively serving others while maintaining a modest and selfless demeanor. Here are inspiring stories of leaders whose lives exemplify humility, providing rich illustrations of this virtue in action.

Nelson Mandela: A Beacon of Reconciliation

Nelson Mandela, the iconic leader of South Africa's anti-apartheid movement, embodied humility during his decades-long struggle for equality and justice. After 27 years in prison, Mandela emerged not with resentment but with forgiveness, championing reconciliation over retribution. His leadership style emphasized listening, unity, and service, focusing on rebuilding a fractured nation with compassion and generosity. Mandela consistently downplayed his role, attributing achievements to collective efforts underpinned by hope and perseverance. His humble approach earned him global respect and underscored that true leadership involves elevating those around you, reinforcing humility as a cornerstone of enduring influence.

Mother Teresa: A Missionary of Charity

Mother Teresa's life was a testament to humility through her unwavering dedication to serving the marginalized and forgotten. Founding the Missionaries of Charity primarily to care for "the poorest of the poor," she served those in greatest need with profound respect and empathy. Often performing the most menial tasks, she led by example and demonstrated dignity in service. Even when receiving accolades, including the Nobel Peace Prize, Mother Teresa redirected praise to the people she served and the communal efforts of her organization. Her humility inspired countless others to look beyond personal gain and serve with a spirit of love and selflessness.

Fred Rogers: An Advocate of Kindness

Fred Rogers, beloved host of the educational television series "Mister Rogers' Neighborhood," modeled humility through his gentle demeanor and genuine interest in every person he met. He never sought celebrity for himself but used his platform to communicate love, kindness, and understanding, treating everyone—from children to adults—with respect and warmth. He saw potential and dignity in every person, guiding them to embrace authenticity and compassion in everyday interactions. Rogers's humility was evident in his efforts to respond personally to every letter he received, fostering a sense of connection and community through simple, humble gestures.

These leaders demonstrate how humility enhances effective service and the meaningful impact one can have on others. Their stories echo a powerful truth: the greatest leaders serve by lifting others, encouraging empathy, connection, and growth. Emulating their humility allows individuals to contribute to broader, lasting change, aligning with a purpose-driven life that reflects God's love and grace through service.

Guidance on How Humility Can Strengthen Purpose-Driven Leadership

Integrating Humility in Leadership

Incorporating humility into leadership significantly enhances the authenticity and effectiveness of a purpose-driven approach. It fosters deeper connections and respect, encouraging leaders to serve with integrity and dedication.

Promoting Self-Awareness and Growth

Humility drives leaders to remain aware of their strengths and limitations, promoting honesty and openness. By recognizing areas in need of improvement, leaders create a culture that values continuous learning. This approach builds credibility and serves as the foundation for both personal and professional development.

Enhancing Relational Dynamics

Humility sparks a collaborative environment where trust and respect flourish. Humble leaders prioritize active listening and value diverse perspectives, strengthening team dynamics. Team members feel respected and engaged, cultivating an atmosphere of shared purpose and mutual support.

Encouraging Resilience and Adaptability

In today's rapidly changing world, adaptability is crucial. Humble leaders are open to feedback and willing to change course when needed, recognizing that leadership requires flexibility. This adaptability enhances problem-solving and decision-making, aligning actions with evolving organizational needs.

Building Trust and Engagement

Humble leaders earn their teams' trust and loyalty by putting others' needs ahead of personal gain and recognizing contributions from all levels. This builds an inclusive environment, fostering engagement and motivation. Such trust bolsters team loyalty and strengthens broader organizational and community relationships.

Prioritizing Service Over Status

Purpose-driven leaders practicing humility emphasize serving others over personal advancement. They focus on community needs, using their influence to empower others. This service-oriented approach aligns with ethical values, enhancing their capacity to drive meaningful change.

Inspiring Authentic Leadership

Authenticity is a cornerstone of leadership, and humility allows leaders to be genuine and transparent. By admitting mistakes and showing vulnerability, humble leaders inspire openness and authenticity in others, encouraging a learning environment without the fear of failure.

Conclusion

Incorporating humility into leadership practices enriches the overall experience, fostering a culture rooted in respect, growth, and service. This balanced approach enhances a leader's influence while empowering teams and communities, driving collective success in alignment with spiritual and ethical principles. By leading with humility, leaders become catalysts for positive change, embodying a purpose that resonates beyond personal and organizational boundaries. Humility is the U-turn of the soul—it reroutes pride into surrender and postures us to follow God's lead.

As we conclude this chapter, let humility guide your journey toward a purpose-filled life. With open hearts and minds, we can transform each day into an opportunity to act with intentional humility. I encourage you to start today—integrate humility into your daily routine and witness its profound impact on your interactions and decisions.

Rerouted Truth: *Humility isn't weakness—it's the posture that positions you for God's elevation in His perfect timing.*

CHAPTER 22
Stewardship of Resources

In a corner of the city, on what was once an abandoned lot, lies a thriving community garden—a testament to responsible stewardship and the transformative power of collective effort. This is a story of a neighborhood united in turning a neglected space into a source of sustenance, community, and education. The garden symbolizes environmental rejuvenation and reflects how purpose-driven living encompasses the responsible management of God's gifts and blessings.

From a Christian perspective, stewardship means diligently managing the resources God has entrusted to us—our time, talents, and treasures—to serve His purpose and benefit others. The parable of the talents illustrates this principle. In this parable, servants entrusted with sums of money are rewarded for wisely investing their master's wealth. The lesson is clear: stewardship involves both safeguarding and growing what has been given.

What I've Learned About Stewardship

For me, stewardship has become more than just managing money—it's about managing trust. I've learned that everything I've been given—finances, time, relationships, influence—is a resource God expects me to hold with care and purpose, not control.

There were times when I thought stewardship meant saving more or spending less. But over time, I began to realize it's really about alignment. Am I using what I've been given in ways that reflect the heart of the One who gave it? Am I multiplying impact or just maintaining comfort?

One principle I've held onto is this: ownership leads to pressure, but stewardship leads to peace. When I started viewing my finances and opportunities through that lens, things shifted. Decisions became less about gain and more about obedience. I stopped asking, *"What's the return?"* and started asking, *"What's the assignment?"*

I've also had to wrestle with generosity—not just giving when it's easy, but when it stretches me. That's where faith meets finance. And I've seen firsthand how God responds to open hands and a willing heart.

Stewardship has taught me to pause, to pray, and to hold everything loosely. Because in the end, it's not about how much I had—it's about how faithfully I managed what was entrusted to me.

Modern Applications of Stewardship Beyond Finances

Stewardship in today's world stretches well beyond the boundaries of financial management. It calls for a broader consciousness—an intentional care for the time we're given, the talents we possess, the world we inhabit, and the communities we influence. This perspective isn't just practical; it's deeply spiritual. It reflects a recognition that every facet of our lives—how we think, act, and contribute—matters to God and has the potential to reflect His purpose.

Consider time. In a culture that equates busyness with significance, the way we steward our hours speaks volumes about our values. It's not just about scheduling and productivity—it's about choosing to spend time in ways that align with our calling, our relationships, and our personal renewal. Time stewardship requires discernment: learning to say yes with intention and no without guilt, recognizing that rest, reflection, and spiritual growth are not luxuries but necessities.

Then there's the matter of our talents and skills—gifts uniquely embedded within us, not for personal elevation, but for the benefit of others. Stewarding our abilities involves both recognizing and refining them. It's a commitment to lifelong growth, not to gain status, but to offer meaningful contributions in service to others, whether through our vocation, ministry, or personal interactions.

Environmental stewardship, though often politicized, is deeply theological. It stems from the Genesis mandate to "keep and cultivate" the earth. Caring for creation—whether through small lifestyle changes or broader advocacy—is an act of gratitude and responsibility. It acknowledges that the world is not ours to exploit, but ours to tend.

Relational stewardship is perhaps one of the most overlooked dimensions. How we engage with those around us—our families, neighbors, coworkers, and faith communities—reveals the depth of our commitment to unity, empathy, and mutual uplift. Healthy relationships are not automatic; they're cultivated with time, presence, and grace. Choosing reconciliation over resentment, listening over reacting, and service over self-interest transforms ordinary interactions into sacred exchanges.

In the digital age, even information becomes a matter of stewardship. With access to limitless knowledge also comes the responsibility to discern truth, engage critically, and share wisely. Choosing to be trustworthy in how we consume and communicate ideas reflects a deeper commitment to integrity, especially when misinformation has the power to mislead entire communities.

Each of these areas—time, talent, environment, relationships, and knowledge—presents both opportunity and challenge. But woven together, they paint a picture of holistic stewardship: a life that is attentively managed not for personal control, but for divine alignment. This approach doesn't rely on rigid checklists but invites ongoing reflection on how our everyday decisions honor God and serve others. It becomes less about what we have and more about how faithfully we handle what we've been given.

Case Study: Ethical Business Practices at Patagonia

Takeaway: Applying Patagonia's Stewardship Model Beyond the Corporate World

Overview for Context

Patagonia, founded in 1973 by Yvon Chouinard, is more than just a successful outdoor apparel company. It is widely recognized for pioneering ethical business practices that prioritize environmental stewardship, social responsibility, and radical transparency. What sets Patagonia apart is not only its commitment to producing sustainable products but also its bold willingness to challenge conventional corporate norms.

From the beginning, Patagonia embedded environmental ethics into its mission, famously pledging, "We're in business to save our home planet." Its initiatives include using organic cotton, recycled polyester, and fair trade-certified factories, as well as launching the Worn Wear program to encourage product repair and reuse. Patagonia's dedication reached a historic milestone in 2022 when Chouinard transferred ownership of the company to a trust and nonprofit, ensuring that all future profits (around $100 million annually) would be used to combat climate change and protect undeveloped land globally.

Transparency as a Guiding Principle

Patagonia's operations exemplify radical transparency. The company openly publishes detailed information about its supply chain, including the locations of its factories, the environmental impact of its materials, and the labor conditions of its workers. It even discloses its shortcomings—such as the environmental trade-offs of certain manufacturing decisions—demonstrating a rare corporate humility.

This level of openness fosters deep trust with consumers and stakeholders and sets a powerful precedent: that being honest about flaws is not a liability but a strength. Patagonia's Footprint Chronicles, an interactive website feature, lets customers trace the origins of their garments and understand the broader impact of their purchases.

Applying Patagonia's Model Beyond the Corporate World

Patagonia's example offers a powerful stewardship model that individuals, ministries, and organizations—whether corporate or grassroots—can adopt. Here's how:

Takeaway: Living Out Stewardship Like Patagonia

1. Prioritize Sustainability in Everyday Decisions
Just as Patagonia uses organic and recycled materials to reduce its environmental footprint, individuals can choose products and practices that support sustainability. This might look like buying secondhand goods, reducing plastic use, or supporting ethical brands. Stewardship means managing God's creation wisely—personally and collectively.

2. Practice Radical Transparency
In your personal life or ministry, commit to honesty, especially when facing setbacks or difficult truths. Whether you're sharing financial updates, teaching a Bible study, or leading a team, open

communication builds trust. Like Patagonia, don't shy away from disclosing challenges—doing so cultivates integrity and resilience.

3. Engage and Support Your Community

Patagonia contributes to local activism and nonprofit efforts around conservation. Similarly, you can get involved in your neighborhood by volunteering, hosting community dialogues, or supporting local small businesses. Stewardship isn't just about resources—it's about relationship and shared responsibility.

4. Be an Advocate for Righteousness

Patagonia doesn't just make clothes—it uses its platform to speak boldly on climate change and systemic injustice. In your own sphere, use your voice to elevate truth and justice. Whether through social media, conversations, or voting, align your influence with values that reflect God's kingdom.

Lessons for Faith-Driven Leaders and Entrepreneurs

- **Integrate Purpose and Profit:** Make mission the heartbeat of your work. Let your values shape your strategy, not just your marketing.
- **Be Accountable to More Than the Bottom Line:** Like Patagonia, build in systems that reflect accountability—to your team, your community, and to creation itself.
- **Lead with Humility:** Acknowledge failures and pursue better solutions. This humility not only strengthens your testimony but also deepens your impact.

Spiritual Stewardship Reflection

To evaluate how well you're stewarding your resources in alignment with God's purposes, ask:

- Am I transparent with how I spend my time, money, and influence?
- Are my consumer choices reflecting care for creation and people?
- How do my daily decisions reflect God's justice, mercy, and truth?

Let Patagonia's story serve not as a secular success tale but as a vivid example of what happens when conviction, courage, and creativity intersect in service of a greater mission.

Steps for Integrating Stewardship into Daily Decision-Making

Adopting stewardship as a guiding principle in daily decision-making encourages effective resource management and alignment with ethical and spiritual values. This approach fosters a sustainable lifestyle that reflects responsibility, gratitude, and commitment to serving broader community and environmental goals. Here are steps to seamlessly incorporate stewardship into everyday choices:

1. **Cultivate Gratefulness and Purpose**
- **Exercise:** Begin each day with a moment of gratitude and purpose-setting. Reflect on how your actions can embody stewardship, focusing on time management, resource conservation, and interpersonal interactions.

- **Outcome:** Establishing gratitude ensures decisions are purposeful and aligned with stewardship values, promoting a day shaped by conscious and considerate actions.

2. **Prioritize Time Effectively**
- **Exercise:** Create a balanced schedule that aligns with your personal and professional priorities. Allocate time for productive tasks, personal growth, spiritual practices, and rest, acknowledging that time is a finite and valuable resource.
- **Outcome:** Effective time management reflects stewardship by ensuring this precious resource is used purposefully, enhancing well-being and productivity.

3. **Establish Environmental Responsibility**
- **Exercise:** Integrate sustainable practices into daily routines, such as recycling, reducing energy consumption, and choosing eco-friendly products.
- **Outcome:** Environmental stewardship supports planetary health, demonstrating a commitment to preserving resources for future generations while living responsibly.

4. **Foster Relationship Stewardship**
- **Exercise:** Invest in maintaining and nurturing relationships by actively listening, providing support, and communicating honestly. Prioritize relational health by

regularly connecting with loved ones and community members.
- **Outcome:** Stewardship of relationships strengthens social connections and community bonds, fostering environments of trust and mutual support.

5. **Implement Financial Stewardship**
- **Exercise:** Regularly review and adjust financial practices—budgeting, saving, and spending in alignment with stewardship principles. Allocate resources to causes and initiatives that reflect personal values and positively contribute to society.
- **Outcome:** Financial stewardship ensures resources are managed wisely, enhancing personal stability and providing opportunities to support the greater good.

6. **Embrace Lifelong Learning and Development**
- **Exercise:** Commit to continual learning and personal or professional development. Seek educational opportunities, attend workshops, and engage in mentorship to refine skills and expand knowledge.
- **Outcome:** Investing in self-improvement represents stewardship of talents and abilities, enhancing capabilities to contribute meaningfully to various areas of life.

7. **Reflect Regularly and Adjust**
- **Exercise:** Set aside regular intervals for reflection on your stewardship practices. Assess areas of success and

identify aspects requiring improvement, allowing room for adjustments.
- **Outcome:** Continuous reflection and adaptation reinforce stewardship, ensuring growth and alignment with evolving values and objectives.

By embedding these steps into daily life, individuals can actively demonstrate stewardship across diverse domains, cultivating a lifestyle that prioritizes responsible and ethical resource management. This holistic integration not only highlights personal growth but also contributes positively to societal and ecological well-being, fostering a legacy of purposeful living rooted in stewardship. True stewardship is recognizing that the Owner of the route may also change the road, and trusting Him with the wheel.

As you consider these reflections, recognize that each stewardship decision contributes to the lasting legacy you are crafting. Whether through daily actions or significant choices, your practice of stewardship accumulates into a testament of purpose-filled living. This legacy not only reflects your values and priorities but also influences future generations.

Rerouted Truth: *When you treat everything you have as God's, you'll live with less pressure and more peace—and multiply impact, not just income.*

CHAPTER 23
Legacy and the Future

"What will be the legacy of your purposeful life?" This question serves as a reflective prompt to envision the long-lasting impact of a life dedicated to divine purpose. Such a life naturally transmits a legacy of influence and faith, shaping the future well beyond its immediate reach. A legacy is more than memories; it is the enduring impact of one's actions on others and the world.

Understanding legacy through a biblical lens, we look at Hannah, who fervently prayed for and dedicated her son, Samuel, to the service of the Lord. Her commitment not only shaped his life but led to profound spiritual contributions to Israel. This highlights how a life's purpose, aligned with faith, extends its influence far beyond personal horizons.

Cultivating a legacy of purpose involves everyday actions that reflect intentional living. Simple gestures, such as acts of kindness, consistent community involvement, and nurturing relationships grounded in love and respect, significantly contribute to a meaningful legacy. Engage daily in activities that align with your core values and spiritual goals to maintain this trajectory.

Building a Legacy That Outlives Me

I've thought a lot about legacy—not just what I want to leave behind, but who I want to become while I'm still here. For a long time, I assumed legacy was about accomplishments, achievements, and what people would remember me for. But now I see it differently. Legacy is not what I build for myself—it's what God builds through me.

I've come to believe that the most enduring legacy I can leave is the impact I make on people—the encouragement I give, the truth I speak, the love I live out daily. If my life doesn't point others toward hope, healing, or purpose, then it doesn't matter how many titles I've held or how much I've achieved.

The future I'm building now is shaped more by faith than ambition. I'm asking God regularly, *"How can I invest my time, my words, and my life into something eternal?"* That question has guided how I lead, how I serve, and how I show up for my family, my community, and those I'm called to reach.

I don't know every detail of what the future holds, but I do know this: I want to be known more for my obedience than my outcomes. I want to be remembered not just for what I did—but for who I helped others become.

And when it's all said and done, I want my legacy to echo this simple truth: he lived on purpose, with purpose, for something greater than himself.

The Heart Check for Purpose: Matthew 6:21

In navigating the concept of legacy and the future, understanding the intersection of our hearts and values becomes crucial. One foundational scripture that addresses this idea is found in Matthew 6:21: *"For where your treasure is, there your heart will be also."* This verse invites us to perform a "heart check" to assess where our true priorities lie, especially concerning purpose and resources.

Understanding Treasures and the Heart

At its core, Matthew 6:21 emphasizes the alignment between our investments and our spiritual state. Treasures, in this context, aren't limited to financial assets but encompass anything we prioritize—time, talents, relationships, and experiences. These treasures become the tangible expressions of what we truly value. As we consider our legacy and the future, this verse prompts us to scrutinize how well our investments reflect our spiritual goals and aspirations.

The Role of Treasures in Purpose

A key aspect of living purposefully involves being deliberate about where and how we allocate our resources. When we channel our efforts and assets into pursuits that align with our purpose, we cultivate a life that fulfills our immediate desires while contributing to a lasting legacy. This alignment ensures that our actions echo our values, creating congruency between what we profess and what we practice.

For example, investing time in mentoring others reflects a treasure of knowledge and guidance, prioritizing human connection and lasting influence. Similarly, directing financial resources into philanthropic endeavors demonstrates a commitment to service and compassion—the core tenets of many spiritual beliefs.

Conducting a Heart Check

To apply this biblical principle effectively, regular "heart checks" are invaluable. Such assessments involve reflecting on the following questions:

- What are my primary treasures, and do they reflect my values and purpose?
- How do my daily actions align with my spiritual and personal goals?
- Are there areas in my life where my investments might be misaligned with my stated priorities?

Engaging in this introspection facilitates awareness, allowing you to recalibrate your focus and redirect energies toward goals that resonate with divine and personal purposes.

Reflecting on what we hold dear inevitably illuminates our underlying values, inviting a deeper inquiry into what truly shapes our principles and drives our actions. As we evaluate our treasures, we uncover not only what we cherish but also why we cherish it, revealing the core beliefs that guide our lives and urging us toward necessary self-examination.

Implementing Change and Alignment

After assessing the current alignment of your activities with your values, consider practical steps for change. Start by reallocating time from tasks that don't contribute to your goals to activities that enhance your spiritual growth or community connections. For example, reduce time spent on social media and instead volunteer at a local charity or attend community events.

Additionally, simplify your life by identifying and removing distractions, such as unnecessary subscriptions or clutter, to better focus on what strengthens your purpose. Addressing such adjustments may involve tangible changes in habit or spiritual practices. Consider integrating new activities that align with treasured values, such as volunteering for causes that matter to you or setting aside daily time for meditation or study that grounds you.

Conclusion

Matthew 6:21 challenges each of us to examine where our hearts and treasures truly lie. By conducting regular heart checks and making conscious adjustments to align our resources with our purpose, we cultivate a more authentic, value-driven life. This alignment enriches our personal fulfillment and spiritual growth while laying a foundation for a meaningful legacy that positively impacts future generations. Through conscientious stewardship, we ensure our treasures are invested in what truly matters, echoing the eternal significance of our values and beliefs.

As you reflect on building a legacy, consider these questions to guide your thoughts:

- What key contributions should define your life?
- In what ways do your current actions align with your core values and desired legacy?
- How does your faith shape your vision and plans for the future?

Engage with these questions through journaling or meditation to effectively anchor a purpose-driven life.

Building a Faith-Based Legacy and Passing Values to Future Generations

Creating a legacy grounded in faith means living and leading in ways that reflect spiritual truth, moral clarity, and kingdom purpose. It's about imprinting eternal values on the lives you touch, particularly on the next generation. Below is a practical and transformational guide to building and passing on a legacy that honors God.

1. **Live with Purpose and Integrity**
- **Action:** Define your core spiritual values and craft a personal mission statement.
- **Exercise:** Reflect on how your faith influences daily decisions and long-term goals. Write them down.
- **Impact:** A purpose-driven life becomes a compass for others, creating a consistent, authentic model of faith.

2. **Model Christ-Centered Values in Everyday Life**
- **Action:** Demonstrate principles like kindness, humility, and patience through daily behavior.
- **Exercise:** Volunteer regularly and share your life with those in need.
- **Impact:** Your faith lived out in real time becomes the most powerful sermon your family and community will ever witness.

3. **Cultivate and Nurture Relationships**
- **Action:** Invest intentionally in your family, friendships, and spiritual community.

- **Exercise:** Schedule regular time for meaningful conversations and acts of service.
- **Impact:** Relationships act as vessels for transmitting love, faith, and shared wisdom.

4. **Mentor, Teach, and Encourage Growth**
- **Action:** Guide others through mentorship, teaching, and storytelling.
- **Exercise:** Share your testimony, lead study groups, and provide spiritual counsel.
- **Impact:** Mentorship creates generational continuity and helps others walk more confidently in faith.

5. **Foster a Culture of Open Dialogue**
- **Action:** Encourage honest discussions about values, faith, and life's challenges.
- **Exercise:** Use family dinners, group devotionals, or walks as times to talk openly and spiritually.
- **Impact:** Conversations reinforce values and help younger generations internalize spiritual truths.

6. **Establish and Celebrate Traditions**
- **Action:** Build and maintain faith-based and cultural traditions within your home and community.
- **Exercise:** Celebrate spiritual milestones, holidays, or service days together.
- **Impact:** Traditions anchor identity and pass on values with meaning and joy.

7. **Engage in Service and Community Projects**
- **Action:** Regularly participate in activities that bless others and reflect kingdom values.
- **Exercise:** Involve younger generations in outreach efforts and mission-driven work.
- **Impact:** Service builds empathy and provides a hands-on way to embody Christ's love.

8. **Document and Preserve Your Faith Journey**
- **Action:** Record your spiritual journey, insights, and lessons for those who follow.
- **Exercise:** Keep a journal, write letters to loved ones, or create digital archives.
- **Impact:** These become timeless resources that extend your influence long after you're gone.

9. **Support Kingdom Causes and Steward Resources Well**
- **Action:** Invest your time, talents, and finances in ministries and movements that reflect your values.
- **Exercise:** Teach your family about tithing, generosity, and supporting impactful causes.
- **Impact:** You cultivate a legacy of generosity, vision, and purpose-driven impact.

10. **Use Teachable Moments and Real-Life Examples**
- **Action:** Leverage daily situations to demonstrate spiritual principles.

- **Exercise:** After a challenge or conflict, ask reflective questions like, "What do you think God wanted us to learn here?"
- **Impact:** This reinforces spiritual thinking and helps values stick in practical, relatable ways.

11. Create a Spiritually Accountable Environment
- **Action:** Invite accountability through community, mentors, and faith-based standards.
- **Exercise:** Establish regular check-ins with family members or mentees for spiritual growth.
- **Impact:** Accountability keeps everyone aligned and encouraged on the journey of faith.

12. Let Your Life Be the Testimony
- **Action:** Live a life so aligned with God that it speaks louder than words.
- **Exercise:** Pray daily that your actions reflect the character of Christ more than your opinions or preferences.
- **Impact:** The most enduring legacies aren't spoken—they're lived.

Building a faith-based legacy is not about perfection—it's about intentionality. It is the quiet, consistent weaving of eternal values into the fabric of everyday life. It is about making decisions that echo beyond your lifetime, inspiring those who come after you to walk in truth, courage, and purpose. Your legacy is not measured by material wealth, but by how your life points to something greater than yourself: the kingdom of God.

Every prayer whispered over your children, every story of God's faithfulness shared at the dinner table, every act of forgiveness, generosity, and obedience adds another layer to the legacy you're building. You're not simply preparing your family for the future—you're preparing them to stand firm in a world that constantly shifts, by anchoring them in something unshakable.

The future is uncertain, but your legacy can bring clarity. In a culture obsessed with success and self, a life that leaves behind faith, integrity, and purpose is both countercultural and eternal. You are writing a living letter with your life—one that will be read long after your voice goes silent.

So live today with the future in mind. Let the seeds of faith you plant now grow into trees that provide shelter, guidance, and spiritual nourishment for generations to come. Let your life testify not just to what you accomplished, but to whom you trusted, what you believed, and how deeply you loved.

In the end, the truest legacy is one that leads others not merely to remember you—but to follow Jesus.

Stories of Individuals Whose Faith Legacies Shaped Communities

Faith-driven individuals often leave profound legacies, shaping personal lives and entire communities. Their dedication to living out core values rooted in faith inspires transformative change, setting lasting precedents for generations to follow. Here are stories of three individuals whose legacies hinged on their steadfast faith and service to others, making impactful contributions to their communities.

Martin Luther King Jr.: A Legacy of Justice and Nonviolence

Dr. Martin Luther King Jr., one of the most influential civil rights leaders, remains a beacon of faith-based courage and activism. Deeply rooted in Christian theology, King advocated for justice and equality through nonviolence and love. He spearheaded initiatives across the United States, leading to significant legislative changes such as the Civil Rights Act of 1964 and the Voting Rights Act of 1965. His legacy, built on faith and moral resilience, reshaped societal norms and continues to inspire advocacy for human rights worldwide. King's vision of a "beloved community" remains within reach, encouraging collective compassion and unity against injustice.

Fred Rogers: Fostering Love and Understanding

Fred Rogers, best known for his TV show "Mister Rogers' Neighborhood," dedicated his life to nurturing kindness and emotional health in children. A Presbyterian minister, Rogers used television to impart lessons of empathy, acceptance, and unconditional love. Through simple yet profound messages, he emphasized the importance of self-worth and respect for others, addressing complex emotions and difficult topics with compassion. His faith-based initiatives left a significant cultural and spiritual impact, influencing generations to embrace empathy and gentle strength in facing personal and communal challenges.

Jean Vanier: Building Inclusive Communities

Jean Vanier, a Canadian philosopher and theologian, founded the L'Arche communities, an international network that promotes inclusive living situations for individuals with disabilities and their supporters. Rooted in Christian values, Vanier's work emphasized the inherent dignity of every person, advocating that community and relationships enrich lives beyond societal capacities. Under his leadership, L'Arche evolved into a global movement that fosters acceptance, love, and friendship while shifting perceptions around disability and valuing diversity as strength. His commitment to faith-driven living illuminated paths toward inclusive societies aligned with spiritual unity.

Jacinda Ardern: Contemporary Faith-Driven Leader

Jacinda Ardern, the former Prime Minister of New Zealand, is a contemporary leader who has significantly influenced communities through her faith-driven approach. Renowned for her compassionate leadership, Ardern draws on her values to promote inclusivity, kindness, and social justice. During her tenure, her empathetic response to the Christchurch mosque shootings highlighted her dedication to unity and peace. Her leadership style, rooted in sincerity and collective well-being, continues to inspire global audiences, demonstrating the transformative power of faith in public service.

These examples illustrate how individuals deeply rooted in their faith can drive transformative community changes, leaving a lasting impact through compassionate action and dedicated service. This legacy influences societal norms, fostering enriched communities and inspiring future generations, emphasizing faith's enduring power in shaping the world.

Family Legacy Planning Guide

Creating a family legacy plan involves intentionally shaping the values, beliefs, and practices that members pass down through generations. Understanding that there are many rerouted believers who don't have family situations that can benefit from this directly, some of these same principles apply to extended families as well.

Family legacy plans transcend wealth; they focus on instilling principles that guide and influence future generations. Here's a comprehensive guide to crafting a meaningful family legacy:

1. Defining and Documenting Family Values

- **Define and Discuss Values**
  - **Exercise:** Gather your family to discuss core values and the vision you wish to establish for the future. Reflect on questions like, "What principles do we stand by?" and "What impact do we want to have on society?"
  - **Outcome:** Clearly articulated values provide a guiding framework for decision-making, aligning with the family's overarching objectives.

- **Document Family History**
  - **Exercise:** Create a family history book or digital archive that includes stories, photos, and reflections on key family moments, principles, and decisions.
  - **Outcome:** This documentation becomes a cherished legacy, preserving family wisdom and

experiences for future generations as a source of reference and inspiration.

2. Set Long-Term Goals

- **Exercise:** Involve family members in establishing long-term goals that align with your defined values and vision, such as educational aspirations, philanthropic efforts, or community involvement.
- **Outcome:** Setting these goals instills a sense of purpose and direction, guiding family actions and decisions over the years.

3. Develop Family Traditions

- **Exercise:** Create regular family traditions that reinforce shared values, such as annual service projects, celebrations of cultural or religious holidays, or storytelling sessions.
- **Outcome:** Traditions strengthen family bonds, preserve culture, and reinforce the values you wish to impart, fostering unity and continuity.

4. Create a Financial Strategy Aligned with Values

- **Exercise:** Develop a financial plan that reflects the family's values, including investments in education, charitable giving, and responsible spending.
- **Outcome:** This strategy ensures financial resources are managed in a way that supports the family's vision and

principles, promoting stewardship and long-term sustainability.

5. Foster Open Communication Across Generations

- **Exercise:** Maintain open lines of communication across generations, discussing plans, expectations, and adaptations to evolving circumstances. Encourage younger members to voice ideas and concerns.
- **Outcome:** Dialogue fosters mutual understanding and respect, empowering each generation to contribute to the legacy's ongoing evolution and success.

6. Engage in Philanthropic Activities

- **Exercise:** Identify causes and charitable activities as a family that align with your values and commit to regular involvement or support.
- **Outcome:** Active participation in philanthropy emphasizes the importance of giving back, embedding a sense of responsibility and empathy within the legacy.

7. Regularly Revisit and Revise the Legacy Plan

- **Exercise:** Schedule regular family meetings to review and update the legacy plan, adapting it to life changes and new insights while reaffirming core values.
- **Outcome:** Regular updates ensure the plan remains relevant and effective, perpetuating a dynamic legacy

that evolves with changing times while staying true to foundational values.

By implementing these strategies, families and extended families can craft a legacy that resonates through generations, leaving a lasting mark of values and principles. This approach fosters a deep sense of connection and purpose, empowering family members to continue building upon the life work established by previous generations, ensuring the legacy remains vibrant, relevant, and impactful. Legacy isn't built on how straight the road was but how faithfully we followed when God rerouted us toward others.

Returning to the initial question about legacy, consider how each intentional action today builds a foundation for tomorrow. This ongoing reflection should serve to realign daily pursuits with the divine path intended for you, fostering a legacy that transcends personal narrative.

As you ponder these insights, prepare to embrace the concluding chapter of this book, which will synthesize the journey you've undertaken and invite you to continue walking a path that aligns with faith and purpose.

Rerouted Truth: *Legacy is not what you leave behind—it's what you build now, one obedient step and one intentional seed at a time.*

CHAPTER 24
Continuing Your Purposeful Journey

Back in Chapter One, I opened the door to my story—not just as an introduction, but as a living thread woven through every chapter. It wasn't just about a failed business or a rough season. It was about how brokenness can become the birthplace of something far more beautiful than what we planned. That journey didn't end with a revelation—it evolved into a steady rhythm of surrender, obedience, and rediscovery. And as we continue walking together, that rhythm will pulse through each theme we explore.

Embracing Change on the Path

When the walls of my business crumbled, I faced what many of us fear: change that wasn't chosen. I didn't want a detour—I wanted recovery. But God was writing something deeper into my story. He was reshaping how I saw my gifts. What once looked like loss became an invitation to reimagine how those same talents could serve something eternal. That pivot—choosing to align my entrepreneurship with God's assignment—wasn't easy. But it became a declaration: change isn't the end; it's often the beginning of clarity.

Redefining Personal Success

My old definition of success? It was loud. It looked good on paper, but it left my soul quiet—and not in the peaceful way. Over time, God redefined what "winning" meant. It was no longer about status or a stacked bank account. It became about obedience, about showing up with integrity and pouring into people rather than platforms. That shift wasn't just for me; it's for anyone ready to measure their life by impact instead of applause. I didn't lose success—I found the version that lasts.

Growth in Communal and Spiritual Dimensions

Isolation can make pain feel permanent. But when I allowed my private struggles to become shared conversations, healing began. Re-engaging with community wasn't just therapeutic—it was transformative. My purpose expanded as I stopped asking, "What can I rebuild for myself?" and started asking, "What can we build together?" The more I poured into others, the more God multiplied my reach. That shift from me-centered to we-centered purpose continues to shape everything I do.

Overcoming Fear and Resistance

Fear has a subtle voice. It often sounds like reason, like protection. But I've learned that God's whispers don't shout over fear—they invite us to lean in and trust anyway. I had to face the voices telling me I had nothing left, that I'd missed my moment. But when I chose to act anyway, faith stepped in where certainty couldn't. If you've ever felt paralyzed by what-ifs, know this: courage isn't the absence of fear. It's the decision to move anyway, anchored in trust.

The Continuous Journey of Faith

This story? It's still unfolding. That's the beauty of walking with God. There's no finish line to purpose—just deeper layers, new assignments, and constant growth. Even now, I remain in process. I still ask questions. I still get rerouted. But the more I walk, the more I realize this journey isn't about arriving—it's about abiding. And every step forward is one more reminder that God doesn't waste anything—not the pain, not the process, and certainly not the purpose.

By reflecting on my journey across these pages—not as a spotlight but as a mirror—I hope you see more than just my story. I hope you see your own possibilities. That every loss can lead to redefinition. That God can repurpose anything surrendered into something sacred.

So, as you continue through this book and beyond, hold tight to what's unfolding in your life. The Purpose Paradigm System is more than a framework—it's a compass. One rooted in calling, driven by service, and anchored in the truth that your life was never random. It's a masterpiece in motion, designed by a Creator who's not finished yet.

Introducing the Purpose Paradigm System for Ongoing Growth

Living with purpose isn't a one-time decision—it's a continuous process of aligning with God's will and growing intentionally. The Purpose Paradigm System was created to support that journey. It's a structured framework that integrates your passion, leadership potential, and entrepreneurial spirit across three core dimensions: spirit, soul, and body. This system doesn't just help you grow—it keeps your growth aligned with your God-given purpose, offering practical tools to walk it out every day.

Passion & Purpose (Serve) - *Spirit*

Anchoring Passion in Purpose:

Passion alone can lead to burnout or unproductive busyness. But when passion is rooted in prayer and directed toward service, it becomes fruitful. I discovered that focusing on "why" over "what" brought clarity and strength to my purpose.

- **Vision Blueprint:**
  Start by crafting a Vision Blueprint—your spiritual GPS. Use visual mapping and prayer to envision goals that reflect God's purpose. For example, if you feel called to serve your community, picture the impact you want to make over the next five years. Journal regularly to track progress and stay aligned.

- **Motivation Mastery:**
  Identify what energizes you. Reflect on past moments of fulfillment—like mentoring or volunteering—and use them to drive you forward. Reinforce your motivation with

Scripture, such as Philippians 4:13, to maintain spiritual momentum.

- **Clarity Playbook:**
  Eliminate distractions and focus on what truly matters. Regularly assess your schedule. Replace time-wasters (like excessive social media) with prayer, skill-building, or purposeful rest. Let your Clarity Playbook guide how you spend your time.

Personal Leadership (Lead) - *Soul*

Becoming a Leader Worth Following:

Leadership begins in private before it shows in public. I grew by submitting to mentorship, humbling myself to learn from others, and allowing God to shape my character as deeply as He shaped my calling.

- **Development Evolution:**
  Invest in your leadership. Attend faith-based workshops, find mentors, and study servant leadership. Apply what you learn to foster humility, empathy, and strength.

- **Cycle of Excellence:**
  Create a feedback loop of growth. Set stretching goals, like speaking in front of small groups. Read, take courses, and reflect on your progress. Keep evolving.

- **Action Matrix:**
  Stay accountable by creating a system to track your goals. For instance, commit to monthly workshops to sharpen your communication. Celebrate progress, adjust when needed, and let consistency build integrity.

Entrepreneurial Mindset (Execute) – *Body*

Executing with God, Not Just for God:

I had the drive to build, but I had to surrender control. Only then did the "how" become clear. I learned to invite the Holy Spirit into my planning, productivity, and partnerships. Entrepreneurial mindset is not exclusively for entrepreneurs, it's for professionals and those that work in ministry also.

- **Skills Toolkit:**

    Build expertise in areas aligned with your calling. Take industry-specific courses. Hone the talents God has given you—so they serve your vision with excellence.

- **Momentum Map:**

    Streamline your daily activities for mission alignment. Use tools like Trello to manage tasks, but start each day with purpose-driven planning. Let productivity serve your purpose.

- **Trailblazing Framework:**

    Develop systems that support sustainable, God-aligned execution. Write a plan or structure your partnerships with Kingdom values in mind. Build to last—and to serve.

The Intersections: Where Spirit, Soul, and Body Unite

Clarity came when I saw how all three areas worked together. Passion without leadership loses direction. Leadership without execution stalls. Execution without God's purpose exhausts. But when they intersect—anchored in faith—you gain momentum and clarity.

- **Personal Purpose:**

  Your purpose emerges at the intersection of passion, leadership, and execution. When these elements align with God's will, your life becomes whole and meaningful.

- **Leadership Mindset:**

  Real leadership is resilient, humble, and anchored in spiritual insight. Lead with empathy, serve others, and let your life reflect Kingdom values.

- **Entrepreneurial Passion:**

  Your business, vision, or project should do more than succeed—it should serve. When you build from purpose, success becomes a byproduct, not the goal.

The Purpose Paradigm System isn't about perfection—it's about obedience. Growth happens one surrendered, purposeful step at a time. My encouragement to you is this: Take what God has shown you and walk it out. The path will unfold as you do.

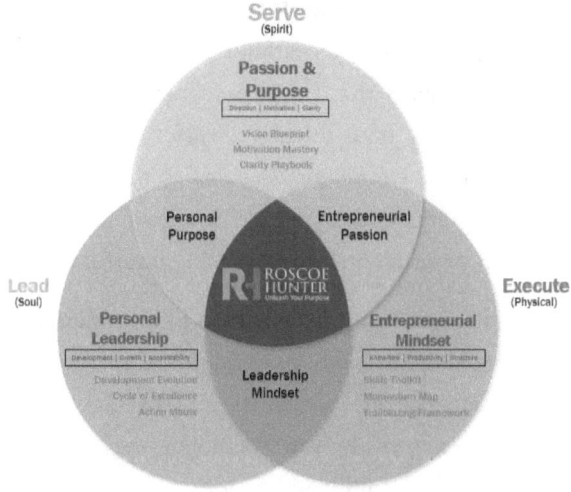

The 5 A's of Execution: A Biblical Blueprint for Purpose

Success, in the eyes of the world, is often measured by wealth, power, or recognition. However, in the kingdom of God, success is defined not by what we accumulate but by how faithfully we fulfill our divine calling. True success lies in alignment with God's purpose, walking in obedience, and bearing fruit that lasts beyond our time on earth.

Proverbs 3:5-6 (ESV) reminds us, "Trust in the Lord with all your heart and lean not on your own understanding; in all your ways submit to him, and he will make your paths straight." This verse establishes the foundation for biblical success—relying on God's wisdom instead of our limited perspective. As we embark on this journey of purposeful living, we must embrace five key principles—The 5 A's of Execution—which serve as guideposts for fulfilling our God-given destiny.

1. Assembly – Planning with Purpose

Before any great endeavor, preparation is essential. The principle of assembly highlights that purpose requires intentional planning. In Luke 14:28, Jesus teaches, *"Suppose one of you wants to build a tower. Won't you first sit down and estimate the cost to see if you have enough money to complete it?"* Success in life and ministry does not occur by accident; it results from prayerful preparation.

Consider Nehemiah, who did not rush into rebuilding Jerusalem's walls. He sought God in prayer, assessed the situation, and developed a strategic plan (Nehemiah 2:11-18). Likewise, we are called to seek God's wisdom in assembling the right plans, resources, and people to fulfill our mission.

Action Steps for Assembly:

- Spend time in prayer before setting goals.
- Seek wise counsel (Proverbs 15:22 (ESV): *"Plans fail for lack of counsel, but with many advisers they succeed."*)
- Create a clear, written vision that aligns with God's will for your life.

2. Action – Faith in Motion

While planning is vital, faith demands action. James 2:17 reminds us, *"Faith by itself, if it is not accompanied by action, is dead."* Success does not stem from good intentions alone but from diligently implementing the plans God has provided.

Consider the story of Joshua. After Moses' death, God instructed Joshua to lead Israel into the Promised Land. However, the Jordan River stood in their way. It wasn't until the priests stepped into the water that the river parted (Joshua 3:15-17). Their faith required movement.

In our own lives, action means stepping out despite uncertainty. Whether launching a new ministry, pursuing a calling, or making bold decisions, we must trust that God will meet us as we move forward in faith.

Action Steps for Taking Bold Steps:

- Ask God, "What step of faith am I avoiding due to fear?"
- Commit to one courageous action each week that aligns with your God-given purpose.

- Remember Philippians 4:13: *"I can do all things through Christ who strengthens me."*

3. Accountability – The Power of Community

No one achieves success alone. God designed us for relationships, and accountability is vital for sustaining a purpose-driven life. Ecclesiastes 4:9-10 (ESV) states, *"Two are better than one because they have a good return for their labor: If either of them falls down, one can help the other up."*

Consider Paul and Timothy. Paul mentored Timothy and held him accountable in his spiritual journey, encouraging him to remain faithful despite challenges (2 Timothy 1:6-7). Similarly, we all need individuals in our lives who will challenge, encourage, and help us stay steadfast.

Ways to Build Accountability:

- Find a mentor or spiritual leader for guidance.
- Join a faith-based group that promotes growth and transparency.
- Regularly check in with a trusted friend to discuss your faith journey.

4. Assessment – Reflecting with Purpose

In business and leadership, progress is measured through regular evaluations. Likewise, in our spiritual lives, we must assess our growth and alignment with God's plan. 2 Corinthians 13:5 (ESV) urges, *"Examine yourselves to see whether you are in the faith; test yourselves."*

King David practiced this principle. In Psalm 139:23-24 (ESV), he prayed, "Search me, God, and know my heart; test me and know my anxious thoughts. See if there is any offensive way in me, and lead me in the way everlasting." Regular self-reflection enables us to course-correct and refine our approach to fulfilling God's purpose.

Action Steps for Spiritual Assessment:

- Set aside time each month to reflect on your progress toward goals.
- Ask yourself: "Is what I'm doing bringing glory to God?"
- Pray for discernment in areas where you need to grow or adjust.

5. Adjustments – The Willingness to Change

Success requires flexibility. Even the best plans must be adapted based on God's timing and direction. Proverbs 16:9 tells us, *"In their hearts humans plan their course, but the Lord establishes their steps."*

A biblical example of necessary adjustment is Peter. Initially resistant to preaching to Gentiles, he ultimately embraced a greater plan revealed by God (Acts 10:9-16). Peter had to shift his mindset to align with God's broader vision.

Likewise, we must remain open to change. Sometimes, God closes doors to guide us toward better opportunities. At other times, He challenges us to step into new, uncomfortable territories for His glory.

How to Make Spirit-Led Adjustments:

Fulfilling your divine purpose requires continuous alignment with spiritual directives. Here's how you can actively tune into these adjustments and take meaningful steps:

- **Constant Communication with God:** Engage in regular prayer to keep your heart and mind receptive to divine guidance.
- **Embrace Change as Growth:** View change not as a setback but as an essential part of your spiritual and personal development. Each transformation brings you closer to your God-given potential.
- **Seek Confirmation Through Scripture:** Before making significant shifts, confirm your path through scripture study and seek advice from wise counsel to ensure your decisions align with God's will.

Take Action Now

Implementing these principles immediately can transform your spiritual journey. Don't wait—begin today by setting aside time for reflection and prayer. Use these moments to clarify your direction and commit to necessary changes. Remember, every step you take in faith brings you closer to a more purpose-driven life. Your dedication to these adjustments not only enriches your life but also inspires those around you to pursue their paths with courage and clarity.

Essential Resources for a Purpose-Filled Life

Books and Literature

- **"The Purpose Driven Life" by Rick Warren:** A foundational text offering daily devotions and reflections for those seeking God's purpose.
- **"Mere Christianity" by C.S. Lewis:** Clarifies core Christian beliefs, aiding those looking to strengthen their faith.
- **"Knowing God" by J.I. Packer:** Delves into the nature of God, enhancing your understanding of the divine.

Online Courses and Communities

- **Rerouted Nation:** Offers courses and community engagement for navigating a purpose-filled life.
- **BibleProject.com:** Provides free videos to aid in a comprehensive understanding of the Bible.
- **Desiring God by John Piper:** Features sermons, articles, and podcasts on practical Christian living.
- **Alpha Course:** A series exploring Christian faith, fostering conversations about life's big questions.

Podcasts and Audio Resources

- **The Rerouted Life Podcast:** For Christians seeking effectiveness in their spiritual walk.

- **The Bible Project Podcast:** Engages listeners with a comprehensive understanding of the Bible.
- **"Unbelievable?":** Explores challenging topics to foster understanding and deepen faith.

Community and Fellowship Opportunities

- **Local Church Bible Study Groups:** Provides fellowship and structured scriptural engagement.
- **SmallGroups.com:** Connect with local Christian groups for fellowship and community service.
- **The Navigators:** Offers discipleship and Bible study resources for spiritual growth.

Journals and Reflection Tools

- **"The Daily Kairos Journal":** Supports daily spiritual reflection, gratitude, and prayer practices.
- **"Open Windows: A 60-Day Journal":** Guides reflection on your spiritual journey with prompts for scripture and personal insights.

Platforms and Tools

- RightNow Media (Christian Netflix for small group studies)
- Glorify App (daily devotion, journaling, scripture, and music)

Spiritual Gifts Discovery Tools:

- SpiritualGiftsTest.com

- Every Nation Spiritual Gifts Survey

By utilizing these resources, you are equipped to deepen your spiritual journey, enhancing your connection to God and refining your purpose. Engaging with a variety of Christian-based materials enriches your understanding and provides diverse perspectives, promoting both personal and spiritual growth. As you incorporate these tools into your life, may your faith be continually nurtured, leading to a deeper and more fulfilling spiritual journey.

Group Discussion Prompts for Engaging with Your Community

Designed for Book Clubs, Small Groups, and Spiritual Communities

Fostering a deeper connection through meaningful conversation not only nurtures individual growth but strengthens collective unity. These revised prompts follow the thematic arc of the book—highlighting surrender, alignment, resilience, purpose, and spiritual community. Each question is paired with suggested reflections to encourage authenticity and spiritual depth.

1. **Recognizing God's Reroutes (Ch. 1–5)**
   Prompt: Reflect on a time when your plans were completely rerouted. What did that experience teach you about surrendering control to God?

   Follow-up: How did this shift affect your identity, sense of direction, or view of God's involvement in your life?

2. **Cultivating a Christ-Centered Mindset (Ch. 6–7)**
   Prompt: What practical steps have you taken—or need to take—to shift from self-centered thinking to Christ-centered living?

   Follow-up: What distractions challenge your focus, and how can you anchor yourself in spiritual disciplines to stay grounded?

3. **Committing to Your Purpose (Ch. 8–9)**
   Prompt: What internal resistance have you faced when trying to commit fully to your God-given purpose?

   Follow-up: Share how scriptures like Proverbs 16:3 or 1 Corinthians 3:5–10 have shaped your view of divine alignment.

4. **Overcoming Setbacks and Burnout (Ch. 10–14)**
   Prompt: When purpose no longer felt motivating, what helped you persevere?

   Follow-up: How do you distinguish between needing rest and needing to realign with purpose?

5. **Rebuilding Identity Through Trials (Ch. 15–17)**
   Prompt: How has adversity clarified your true identity in Christ?

   Follow-up: Reflect on how "success" has been redefined for you—what does it mean now in light of your faith?

6. **Strengthening Relationships for Purpose (Ch. 18–20)**
   Prompt: Which relationships have sharpened your purpose, and which ones have distracted you from it?

   Follow-up: How can we cultivate more spiritually accountable and honest relationships in our group?

7. **Leading and Serving in Alignment (Ch. 21–22)**
   Prompt: How do you embody servant leadership in your home, workplace, or church?

   Follow-up: Share a time when leading through service brought clarity to your mission or healed division.

8. **Unity and Impact in Community (Ch. 23)**
   Prompt: In what ways can our group reflect the unity described in Ephesians 4:2–3 and Romans 12:10?

   Follow-up: What are some tangible actions we can take to promote reconciliation and spiritual growth in our community?

9. **Reflecting on Your Legacy (Ch. 24)**
   Prompt: What legacy do you hope to leave behind as you live out your divine purpose?

   Follow-up: How can your daily decisions today plant seeds of impact for future generations?

10. **Walking Boldly into the Final Stretch (Ch. 25)**
    Prompt: In light of the urgency described in the final chapter, what areas of your life need immediate spiritual attention?

    Follow-up: What is one "next right step" God is prompting you to take as you finish this book?

These prompts are not merely for discussion—they're an invitation into deeper transformation. Use them to foster vulnerability, build authentic fellowship, and challenge each other toward action rooted in faith. As your community shares, listens, and prays together, may the Spirit move powerfully in your midst, guiding each heart toward purpose and legacy.

Embracing Your Eternal Journey

As you stand on the threshold of your ongoing spiritual journey, remember that true purpose is not a destination but a constant, evolving dialogue between your soul and God's grand design. Each step you take is significant, and every action carries the weight of potential transformation—not just for your own life, but for those around you. Embrace this journey with hope and faith, knowing that your path is divinely guided.

Take the inspiration gathered from these chapters and channel it into purposeful steps forward. Dare to pursue your dreams with conviction, integrating your passions with divine service while touching others as you navigate the world. Let your actions serve as a testament to a life well-lived, a beacon of light reflecting the unique divine purpose crafted for you.

Life is an open canvas, where each act of faith and every decision adds new colors and shapes to the masterpiece God envisions. Embed in your heart the courage to face challenges, the humility to learn from every experience, and the wisdom to recognize the signs that guide your way. Your legacy lies not only in what you leave behind but also in the seeds of inspiration you plant, nurturing growth and goodness that continue to bloom in the hearts of others long after you have moved on. Every chapter of your story may not make sense until you trace the reroutes—and realize they were divine redirections, not detours.

Step boldly into this future, assured that with God as your guide and faith as your compass, every journey will find its rightful course. Let this call to action solidify your commitment to live a life that celebrates the divine voice within, extending that celebration in all you do. As you navigate your ongoing journey, may your heart remain steadfast, your spirit resilient, and your life a resonant echo of the purpose you embrace.

May God bless you on this enduring journey of discovery and fulfillment.

Rerouted Truth: *Purpose isn't a destination—it's a daily declaration that your life still carries divine weight, even when the path changes.*

CHAPTER 25
Equipped for the Final Stretch – Readiness in a Rerouted World

We've come full circle.

From the broken places where dreams were shattered to the sacred places where surrender gave birth to purpose—your journey has been nothing short of divine interruption. But this isn't the end of your story. In fact, it's just the beginning of what God is preparing you for.

This final chapter isn't a closing thought—it's a commissioning. A divine handoff. A sending. Because while rerouting helped you reclaim your identity and realign your path, now you must walk it out with urgency and precision.

Why?

Because we are in the final stretch.

Living in Urgency Without Fear

If you've ever sensed that time is accelerating, you're not alone. Scripture warned us that in the last days, deception would increase, truth would be traded for opinion, and the love of many would grow cold. And here we are—watching prophecy play out like headlines.

But here's the encouragement: **God never places His people in a time without also placing purpose inside of them.**

This is not a moment to survive—it's a moment to *thrive* spiritually. The rerouted believer doesn't just wait for the storm to pass—they **build in the rain**, **lead with fire**, and **serve with precision**.

The world is unraveling, but God's plan for your life is unfolding.

The enemy is loud, but God's voice is still leading.

Now is the time to walk with the confidence of Heaven and the focus of eternity.

Activate the Qualities of the Ready

Peter gives us a checklist that isn't just helpful—it's urgent.

"Make every effort to supplement your faith..." (2 Peter 1:5)

Faith is the launchpad, but it's the virtues we build upon it that sustain us in turbulent times. This is not religion—it's *readiness through relationship*.

Here's what readiness looks like when the world is shaking:

- **Virtue** – Living in a way that honors God even when no one's applauding. Integrity is your insulation in a morally bankrupt culture.
- **Knowledge** – Growing in the Word and knowing what God sounds like. When the noise increases, discernment becomes your compass.
- **Self-Control** – The ability to remain composed when everything around you invites chaos. The flesh reacts, but the Spirit responds.
- **Steadfastness** – The kind of patience that doesn't quit. Even when results are slow, even when emotions are raw—you stay.
- **Godliness** – Living with a sense of sacredness. A daily awareness that your life is on display as a testimony of who God is.
- **Brotherly Affection** – Love that is fiercely loyal. It's easy to criticize the Church—God is calling you to cover it in love.
- **Agape Love** – The kind of love that stays when it's inconvenient, forgives when it hurts, and gives when nothing comes back.

These are more than spiritual goals. They are the survival tools of the **end-time remnant**—the believers who won't bow, won't burn out, and won't back down.

Remember Where You've Come From

Peter also issues a warning:

"Whoever lacks these qualities is so nearsighted that he is blind, having forgotten that he was cleansed from his former sins." (2 Peter 1:9 ESV)

Spiritual amnesia is the beginning of spiritual apathy. When we forget the Cross, we stop carrying ours. When we forget what we've been delivered from, we drift toward the very chains we were freed from.

Your story of being rerouted is a sacred reminder: **you've been cleansed**. You were rescued from a life of confusion, self-reliance, and aimless striving. Don't forget. Let your gratitude for grace fuel your pursuit of godliness.

Diligence in a Time of Deception

"Be all the more diligent to confirm your calling and election..." (2 Peter 1:10 ESV)

In a world where spiritual attention spans are shrinking, you are called to be **diligent**.

Not busy. Diligent.

Not distracted. Focused.

Not just inspired. *Intentional.*

Your rerouting has taught you to tune into God's voice, trust His timing, and obey without full clarity. That same posture is what will sustain you in the days ahead. You don't need the whole map when you walk with the One who holds the future.

Peter's promise? *"If you practice these qualities, you will never fall."*

That's not hype. That's holy assurance.

The Rerouted End-Time Strategy: Your New Lifestyle

What we've learned in this book wasn't just for survival. It was for execution. As you step into the final stretch of your assignment, this process becomes your roadmap:

1. **Gain knowledge and understanding** – Anchor yourself in the Word. Let the Holy Spirit be your interpreter.
2. **Determine God's plan** – Don't just do what looks good. Do what is God.
3. **Be patient about the process** – God's pause is prelude. Let patience have its perfect work.
4. **Don't get anxious for anything** – Peace is your weapon. Guard it fiercely.
5. **Be diligent in the process** – Excellence honors God.
6. **Take emotion out of decision-making** – Let your spirit lead, not your flesh.
7. **Have a narrow vision for what it looks like** – Focus brings fruit.
8. **Put on blinders** – Comparison is a thief. Stay in your lane.
9. **Resist distraction and redirection** – Recognize when the enemy is trying to pull you off course.
10. **Don't take the credit** – Glory belongs to God alone.
11. **Uproot pride** – Stay humble. Stay usable.
12. **Remember you are clay** – You are not the potter. You are the masterpiece in progress.

Here's what executing purpose looks like now:

Step	Strategy Point	Spiritual Focus
1	Gain knowledge and understanding	Biblical Insight
2	Determine God's plan	Divine Direction
3	Be patient about the process	Endurance
4	Don't get anxious for anything	Peace
5	Be diligent in the process	Excellence
6	Take emotion out of decision-making	Discernment
7	Have a narrow vision for what it looks like	Focus
8	Put on blinders	Faithfulness
9	Resist distraction and redirection	Alertness
10	Don't take the credit	Humility
11	Uproot pride	Surrender
12	Remember you are clay	Obedience

This is not just strategy. This is **spiritual architecture** for building a life that will stand when everything else falls.

Let this chart live on your mirror, in your journal, or as a bookmark in your Bible. Refer to it not just when you're confused—but when you're clear and committed. Because these habits will carry you through both the drought and the downpour.

Your Eternal Entrance is Coming

"There will be richly provided for you an entrance into the eternal kingdom of our Lord and Savior Jesus Christ." (2 Peter 1:11 ESV)

Can you imagine that moment?

When your earthly assignment ends...

When your rerouted path meets Heaven's welcome...

When the gates swing open—not just because you believed, but because you *lived* like you believed.

There will be a celebration. An affirmation. A Father saying, *"Well done."* And all the pain, confusion, loss, and surrender will suddenly make sense.

You weren't just rerouted for restoration.

You were rerouted for **eternal impact**.

Final Words: This Is Your Call to Execution

Now is not the time to retreat.
Now is not the time to wait for perfect conditions.
And now is certainly not the time to shrink back into the shadows of uncertainty.

You are not the same person who picked up this book.
You've been rerouted. Reframed. Refined.
And now—you're being released.

You weren't rerouted just to reflect.
You were rerouted to rebuild. To rise.
To lead. To speak. To serve. To execute. To endure.

This isn't just your invitation.
It's your commissioning.

- Don't just walk away inspired. Walk away ignited.
- Don't just wait for Heaven. Make Earth ready for it.
- Don't just survive. Live as if eternity is already unfolding—because it is.

Obedience in this hour is not optional—it is eternal.
Every step of surrender you take echoes far beyond your own life.
It shapes legacy. It establishes divine fingerprints in broken places.
It testifies.

So build what only you can build.
Speak what only you can say.
And love like your story depends on it—because someone else's might.

The journey doesn't end here.
This is the threshold of your assignment.
This is where the rerouted become relentless.

So walk boldly.
Love radically.
Lead faithfully.

The final stretch isn't your ending.
It's your finest hour.

Go.
Execute with purpose.

Heaven is watching—and history is waiting.

Rerouted Truth: *You weren't rerouted for convenience—you were rerouted for the Kingdom, and the world needs your obedience now more than ever.*

EPILOGUE
The Time is Now

You've made it to the end of this book—but not the end of your journey.

We are living in a divine moment—a window of grace before the return of our King. All around us, the world groans with urgency. Truth is blurred, hearts are hardened, and the noise of culture grows louder by the day. But even now, God is whispering to His people: *"Awake, O sleeper, and arise from the dead, and Christ will shine on you."* (Ephesians 5:14 ESV)

This is not the hour for hesitation. This is the time for clarity. For courage. For divine resolve. You weren't rerouted for convenience—you were rerouted for the Kingdom. Your story, your scars, your surrendered steps—they matter now more than ever.

If you feel discouraged, stuck, or unsure of how your life fits into God's grand design, don't let despair speak louder than His promise. **You are not too far behind. You are not too wounded. You are not too late.** God specializes in resurrecting what we thought was ruined. And He is faithful to complete the work He began in you. If you have breath in your body and blood running warm through your veins, it is not finished for you yet.

Let your purpose become the pathway by which God's glory is revealed on the earth. Every act of obedience, every seed sown in faith, every quiet yes—it all counts. In a world racing toward its end, your alignment with God's plan carries eternal consequences.

Scripture Meditation

"The Lord will fulfill His purpose for me; your steadfast love, O Lord, endures forever. Do not forsake the work of your hands."

—Psalm 138:8 (ESV)

Let these words be your anchor when the way feels unclear. He will finish what He started. His love is enduring. And you are still the work of His hands.

So go—live rerouted. Live ready. Live like He's coming back.

Because He is.

Acknowledgements

First and foremost, I want to thank my beautiful wife, Waleska. Your unwavering support, godly wisdom, and ability to see me fully—even when I couldn't see myself—have carried me through more seasons than I can count. Your insight and strength have been a pillar throughout my entire career, and without you, this book and the calling behind it wouldn't be what they are.

To my church family at Tree of Life Christian Ministries—thank you for being a space of growth, grace, and accountability. You have not only supported me but given me room to become the man, leader, and servant God has called me to be.

To the many people who've walked alongside me—thank you for your feedback, encouragement, and truth, often spoken when I needed it most. Some of you have read early drafts, challenged my thoughts, or simply listened. Many of you have witnessed me live out the very lessons described in this book—sometimes triumphantly, sometimes with tears—but always with the conviction that God was rerouting me for His glory.

A special and heartfelt thanks goes to Kristen Adams, a dear friend and invaluable contributor to this project. Your guidance on the structure, flow, and narration helped bring this message to life in a way that is clear, impactful, and honest. You have truly been a Godsend in this process.

Lastly, to all of you—my friends, brothers, sisters, mentors, and mentees—thank you for sharpening me through conversation, correction, and love. I am grateful for every voice that helped me find my own. You are the iron that God has used to refine this vessel.

This book is as much yours as it is mine.

Thank you for being part of the journey.

—Roscoe Hunter

Scripture References by Chapter

Chapter 1: The Call to Purpose

Jeremiah 1:5-10 (ESV)

Before I formed you in the womb I knew you, and before you were born I consecrated you;

I appointed you a prophet to the nations.

Then I said, "Ah, Lord GOD! Behold, I do not know how to speak, for I am only a youth."

But the LORD said to me, "Do not say, 'I am only a youth';

for to all to whom I send you, you shall go,

and whatever I command you, you shall speak.

Do not be afraid of them,

for I am with you to deliver you,

declares the LORD."

Then the LORD put out his hand and touched my mouth. And the LORD said to me,

"Behold, I have put my words in your mouth.

See, I have set you this day over nations and over kingdoms,

to pluck up and to break down,

to destroy and to overthrow,

to build and to plant.

Chapter 2: The Source of Purpose

Jeremiah 1:5 (ESV)

Before I formed you in the womb I knew you, and before you were born I consecrated you;

I appointed you a prophet to the nations.

Proverbs 19:21 (ESV)

Many are the plans in the mind of a man,

but it is the purpose of the LORD that will stand.

Ephesians 4:16 (ESV)

From whom the whole body, joined and held together by every joint with which it is equipped,

when each part is working properly, makes the body grow so that it builds itself up in love.

1 Corinthians 12:12 (ESV)

For just as the body is one and has many members, and all the members of the body,

though many, are one body, so it is with Christ.

Matthew 28:18-20 (ESV)

And Jesus came and said to them, "All authority in heaven and on earth has been given to me.

Go therefore and make disciples of all nations, baptizing them in the name of the Father

and of the Son and of the Holy Spirit, teaching them to observe all that I have commanded you.

And behold, I am with you always, to the end of the age.

1 Timothy 2:4 (ESV)

Who desires all people to be saved and to come to the knowledge of the truth.

Genesis 18:14 (ESV)

Is anything too hard for the LORD? At the appointed time I will return to you,

about this time next year, and Sarah shall have a son.

Exodus 3:11-12 (ESV)

But Moses said to God, "Who am I that I should go to Pharaoh and bring the children of Israel out of Egypt?

He said, "But I will be with you, and this shall be the sign for you, that I have sent you:

when you have brought the people out of Egypt, you shall serve God on this mountain.

Chapter 3: Uncovering Your Gifts and Talents

1 Samuel 17:36 (ESV)

Your servant has struck down both lions and bears, and this uncircumcised Philistine

shall be like one of them, for he has defied the armies of the living God.

Chapter 4: Passion vs. Purpose

Proverbs 16:3 (ESV)

Commit your work to the LORD, and your plans will be established.

1 Corinthians 3:5-10 (ESV)

What then is Apollos? What is Paul? Servants through whom you believed, as the Lord assigned to each.

I planted, Apollos watered, but God gave the growth.

So neither he who plants nor he who waters is anything, but only God who gives the growth.

He who plants and he who waters are one, and each will receive his wages according to his labor.

For we are God's fellow workers. You are God's field, God's building.

According to the grace of God given to me, like a skilled master builder I laid a foundation,

and someone else is building upon it. Let each one take care how he builds upon it.

1 Corinthians 3:10-15 (ESV)

According to the grace of God given to me, like a skilled master builder I laid a foundation,

and someone else is building upon it. Let each one take care how he builds upon it.

For no one can lay a foundation other than that which is laid, which is Jesus Christ.

Now if anyone builds on the foundation with gold, silver, precious stones, wood, hay, straw—

each one's work will become manifest, for the Day will disclose it,

because it will be revealed by fire, and the fire will test what sort of work each one has done.

If the work that anyone has built on the foundation survives, he will receive a reward.

If anyone's work is burned up, he will suffer loss, though he himself will be saved,

but only as through fire.

Mark 12:41-44 (ESV)

And he sat down opposite the treasury and watched the people putting money into the offering box.

Many rich people put in large sums.

And a poor widow came and put in two small copper coins, which make a penny.

And he called his disciples to him and said to them,

Truly, I say to you, this poor widow has put in more than all those who are contributing to the offering box.

For they all contributed out of their abundance, but she out of her poverty has put in everything she had,

all she had to live on.

Proverbs 15:21-22 (ESV)

Folly is a joy to him who lacks sense,

but a man of understanding walks straight ahead.

Without counsel plans fail,

but with many advisers they succeed.

Romans 12:2 (ESV)

Do not be conformed to this world, but be transformed by the renewal of your mind,

that by testing you may discern what is the will of God, what is good and acceptable and perfect.

Matthew 7:15-20 (ESV)

Beware of false prophets, who come to you in sheep's clothing but inwardly are ravenous wolves.

You will recognize them by their fruits. Are grapes gathered from thornbushes, or figs from thistles?

So, every healthy tree bears good fruit, but the diseased tree bears bad fruit.

A healthy tree cannot bear bad fruit, nor can a diseased tree bear good fruit.

Every tree that does not bear good fruit is cut down and thrown into the fire.

Thus you will recognize them by their fruits.

Colossians 3:23 (ESV)

Whatever you do, work heartily, as for the Lord and not for men,

Chapter 5: The Role of Patience in Discovering Purpose

Habakkuk 3:2 (ESV)

For still the vision awaits its appointed time; it hastens to the end— it will not lie. If it seems slow, wait for it; it will surely come; it will not delay.

John 11:5-6 (ESV)

Now Jesus loved Martha and her sister and Lazarus. So, when he heard that Lazarus was ill, he stayed two days longer in the place where he was.

Romans 8:28-31 (ESV)

And we know that for those who love God all things work together for good, for those who are called according to his purpose. For those whom he foreknew he also predestined to be conformed to the image of his Son, in order that he might be the firstborn among many brothers. And those whom he predestined he also called, and those whom he called he also justified, and those whom he justified he also glorified. What then shall we say to these things? If God is for us, who can be against us?

Romans 8:28 (ESV)

And we know that for those who love God all things work together for good, for those who are called according to his purpose.

Romans 8:29-30 (ESV)

For those whom he foreknew he also predestined to be conformed to the image of his Son, in order that he might be the firstborn among many brothers. And those whom he predestined he also called, and those whom he called he also justified, and those whom he justified he also glorified.

Romans 8:31 (ESV)

What then shall we say to these things? If God is for us, who can be against us?

Chapter 6: Cultivating a Christ-Centered Mindset

Colossians 3:1-2 (ESV)

If then you have been raised with Christ, seek the things that are above, where Christ is, seated at the right hand of God. 2 Set your minds on things that are above, not on things that are on earth.

Romans 12:2 (ESV)

Do not be conformed to this world, but be transformed by the renewal of your mind, that by testing you may discern what is the will of God, what is good and acceptable and perfect.

Chapter 7: Staying Focused and Avoiding Distractions

2 Corinthians 12:9

But he said to me, "My grace is sufficient for you, for my power is made perfect in weakness."

Therefore I will boast all the more gladly of my weaknesses, so that the power of Christ may rest upon me.

Matthew 14:29-31 (ESV)

He said, "Come." So Peter got out of the boat and walked on the water and came to Jesus.

But when he saw the wind, he was afraid, and beginning to sink he cried out, "Lord, save me."

Jesus immediately reached out his hand and took hold of him, saying to him,

"O you of little faith, why did you doubt?

Philippians 4:6-7 (ESV)

Do not be anxious about anything, but in everything by prayer and supplication with thanksgiving

let your requests be made known to God.

And the peace of God, which surpasses all understanding, will guard your hearts and your minds in Christ Jesus.

Philippians 4:13 (ESV)

I can do all things through him who strengthens me.

Nehemiah 6:3 (ESV)

And I sent messengers to them, saying, I am doing a great work and I cannot come down.

Why should the work stop while I leave it and come down to you?

Philippians 3:14 (ESV)

I press on toward the goal for the prize of the upward call of God in Christ Jesus.

Ecclesiastes 3:1 (ESV)

For everything there is a season, and a time for every matter under heaven:

Proverbs 4:20-22 (ESV)

My son, be attentive to my words; incline your ear to my sayings.

Let them not escape from your sight; keep them within your heart.

For they are life to those who find them, and healing to all their flesh.

Romans 8:13 (ESV)

For if you live according to the flesh you will die, but if by the Spirit you put to death the deeds of the body, you will live.

Proverbs 4:23 (ESV)

Keep your heart with all vigilance, for from it flow the springs of life.

Proverbs 3:5-6 (ESV)

Trust in the LORD with all your heart, and do not lean on your own understanding.

In all your ways acknowledge him, and he will make straight your paths.

Hebrews 12:1-2 (ESV)

Therefore, since we are surrounded by so great a cloud of witnesses, let us also lay aside every weight, and sin which clings so closely, and let us run with endurance the race that is set before us, looking to Jesus, the founder and perfecter of our faith, who for the joy that was set before him endured the cross, despising the shame, and is seated at the right hand of the throne of God.

Chapter 8: Committing to Your Purpose

Proverbs 16:3 (ESV)

Commit your work to the LORD, and your plans will be established.

1 Corinthians 3:5-10 (ESV)

What then is Apollos? What is Paul? Servants through whom you believed, as the Lord assigned to each. I planted, Apollos watered, but God gave the growth...

(Full passage as quoted in Chapter 4 — see above for extended excerpt.)

1 Corinthians 3:10-15 (ESV)

According to the grace of God given to me, like a skilled master builder I laid a foundation, and someone else is building upon it...

(See full quotation in Chapter 4.)

Mark 12:41-44 (ESV)

And he sat down opposite the treasury and watched the people putting money into the offering box. Many rich people put in large sums. And a poor widow came and put in two small copper coins, which make a penny. And he called his disciples to him and said to them, "Truly, I say to you, this poor widow has put in more than all those who are contributing to the offering box. For they all contributed out of their abundance, but she out of her poverty has put in everything she had, all she had to live on.

Proverbs 15:21-22 (ESV)

Folly is a joy to him who lacks sense,

but a man of understanding walks straight ahead.

Without counsel plans fail,

but with many advisers they succeed.

Romans 12:2 (ESV)

Do not be conformed to this world, but be transformed by the renewal of your mind.

Matthew 7:15-20 (ESV)

Beware of false prophets... Thus you will recognize them by their fruits.

(See full quotation in Chapter 4.)

Psalm 139:23-24 (ESV)

Search me, O God, and know my heart! Try me and know my thoughts!

And see if there be any grievous way in me, and lead me in the way everlasting!

Matthew 6:33 (ESV)

But seek first the kingdom of God and his righteousness, and all these things will be added to you.

Ephesians 2:10 (ESV)

For we are his workmanship, created in Christ Jesus for good works, which God prepared beforehand, that we should walk in them.

James 2:17 (ESV)

So also faith by itself, if it does not have works, is dead.

Proverbs 27:17 (ESV)

Iron sharpens iron, and one man sharpens another.

Chapter 9: Why God's Purpose is Important

Jeremiah 29:11 (ESV)

For I know the plans I have for you, declares the LORD, plans for welfare and not for evil, to give you a future and a hope.

Romans 8:28 (ESV)

And we know that for those who love God all things work together for good, for those who are called according to his purpose.

1 Corinthians 12:12-14 (ESV)

For just as the body is one and has many members, and all the members of the body, though many, are one body, so it is with Christ. For in one Spirit we were all baptized into one body—Jews or Greeks, slaves or free— and all were made to drink of one Spirit. For the body does not consist of one member but of many.

Matthew 25:14-30 (ESV)

For it will be like a man going on a journey, who called his servants and entrusted to them his property...

(This is the Parable of the Talents; for brevity, refer to full passage in Matthew 25:14–30.)

Ecclesiastes 3:1 (ESV)

For everything there is a season, and a time for every matter under heaven:

Philippians 4:7 (ESV)

And the peace of God, which surpasses all understanding, will guard your hearts and your minds in Christ Jesus.

2 Timothy 3:2 (ESV)

For people will be lovers of self, lovers of money, proud, arrogant, abusive, disobedient to their parents, ungrateful, unholy...

1 Peter 5:8 (ESV)

Be sober-minded; be watchful. Your adversary the devil prowls around like a roaring lion, seeking someone to devour.

Ecclesiastes 4:12 (ESV)

And though a man might prevail against one who is alone, two will withstand him—a threefold cord is not quickly broken.

Chapter 10: Applying God's Wisdom in Leadership

Proverbs 22:1 (ESV)

A good name is to be chosen rather than great riches,

and favor is better than silver or gold.

Proverbs 10:9 (ESV)

Whoever walks in integrity walks securely,

but he who makes his ways crooked will be found out.

Philippians 4:13 (ESV)

I can do all things through him who strengthens me.

Galatians 6:2 (ESV)

Bear one another's burdens, and so fulfill the law of Christ.

Proverbs 3:13 (ESV)

Blessed is the one who finds wisdom,

and the one who gets understanding.

Proverbs 22:6 (ESV)

Train up a child in the way he should go;

even when he is old he will not depart from it.

Ephesians 4:11-13 (ESV)

And he gave the apostles, the prophets, the evangelists, the shepherds and teachers, to equip the saints for the work of ministry, for building up the body of Christ, until we all attain to the unity of the faith and of the knowledge of the Son of God, to mature manhood, to the measure of the stature of the fullness of Christ.

Colossians 3:23-24 (ESV)

Whatever you do, work heartily, as for the Lord and not for men, knowing that from the Lord you will receive the inheritance as your reward. You are serving the Lord Christ.

John 13:34-35 (ESV)

A new commandment I give to you, that you love one another: just as I have loved you, you also are to love one another. By this all people will know that you are my disciples, if you have love for one another."

Proverbs 11:3 (ESV)

The integrity of the upright guides them,

but the crookedness of the treacherous destroys them.

Philippians 2:3 (ESV)

Do nothing from selfish ambition or conceit, but in humility count others more significant than yourselves.

Micah 6:8 (ESV)

He has told you, O man, what is good; and what does the LORD require of you but to do justice, and to love kindness, and to walk humbly with your God?

1 Peter 4:10 (ESV)

As each has received a gift, use it to serve one another, as good stewards of God's varied grace.

Galatians 6:9 (ESV)

And let us not grow weary of doing good, for in due season we will reap, if we do not give up.

Ephesians 4:32 (ESV)

Be kind to one another, tenderhearted, forgiving one another, as God in Christ forgave you.

Chapter 11: Setting and Achieving Faith-Driven Goals

Proverbs 16:3 (ESV)

Commit your work to the LORD, and your plans will be established.

1 Corinthians 10:31 (ESV)

So, whether you eat or drink, or whatever you do, do all to the glory of God.

Proverbs 16:9 (ESV)

The heart of man plans his way, but the LORD establishes his steps.

Isaiah 58:12 (ESV)

And your ancient ruins shall be rebuilt; you shall raise up the foundations of many generations; you shall be called the repairer of the breach, the restorer of streets to dwell in.

Ephesians 6:12 (ESV)

For we do not wrestle against flesh and blood, but against the rulers, against the authorities, against the cosmic powers over this present darkness, against the spiritual forces of evil in the heavenly places.

Philippians 4:19 (ESV)

And my God will supply every need of yours according to his riches in glory in Christ Jesus.

Galatians 6:9 (ESV)

And let us not grow weary of doing good, for in due season we will reap, if we do not give up.

Luke 14:28 (ESV)

For which of you, desiring to build a tower, does not first sit down and count the cost...

Chapter 12: Fostering Unity Across Communities

Acts 4:32 (ESV)

Now the full number of those who believed were of one heart and soul, and no one said that any of the things that belonged to him was his own, but they had everything in common.

Ephesians 4:3 (ESV)

Eager to maintain the unity of the Spirit in the bond of peace.

1 Corinthians 12:12-14 (ESV)

For just as the body is one and has many members, and all the members of the body, though many, are one body, so it is with Christ. For in one Spirit we were all baptized into one body—Jews or Greeks, slaves or free—and all were made to drink of one Spirit.

(See full quote in Chapter 9)

Romans 12:10 (ESV)

Love one another with brotherly affection. Outdo one another in showing honor.

Ephesians 4:2-3 (ESV)

With all humility and gentleness, with patience, bearing with one another in love, eager to maintain the unity of the Spirit in the bond of peace.

Galatians 6:2 (ESV)

Bear one another's burdens, and so fulfill the law of Christ.

Colossians 3:13 (ESV)

Bearing with one another and, if one has a complaint against another, forgiving each other; as the Lord has forgiven you, so you also must forgive.

Matthew 18:19-20 (ESV)

Again I say to you, if two of you agree on earth about anything they ask, it will be done for them by my Father in heaven. For where two or three are gathered in my name, there am I among them.

Chapter 13: Embracing a Life of Service

Galatians 5:13 (ESV)

For you were called to freedom, brothers. Only do not use your freedom as an opportunity for the flesh, but through love serve one another.

Chapter 14: Overcoming Burnout in a Purpose-Driven Life

Mark 1:35 (ESV)

And rising very early in the morning, while it was still dark, he departed and went out to a desolate place, and there he prayed.

Genesis 2:2-3 (ESV)

And on the seventh day God finished his work that he had done, and he rested on the seventh day from all his work that he had done. So God blessed the seventh day and made it holy, because on it God rested from all his work that he had done in creation.

Chapter 16: Embarking on Your Purposeful Journey

2 Timothy 1:7 (ESV)

For God gave us a spirit not of fear but of power and love and self-control.

Jeremiah 29:11 (ESV)

For I know the plans I have for you, declares the LORD, plans for welfare and not for evil, to give you a future and a hope.

Chapter 17: Embracing Change as Part of Purpose

Romans 12:2 (ESV)

Do not be conformed to this world,[a] but be transformed by the renewal of your mind, that by testing you may discern what is the will of God, what is good and acceptable and perfect.

Ruth 1:16 (ESV)

But Ruth said, "Do not urge me to leave you or to return from following you. For where you go I will go, and where you lodge I will lodge. Your people shall be my people, and your God my God."

Jeremiah 29:11 (ESV)

For I know the plans I have for you, declares the Lord, plans for welfare[a] and not for evil, to give you a future and a hope.

Romans 8:28 (ESV)

And we know that for those who love God all things work together for good, for those who are called according to his purpose.

Hebrews 10:24-25 (ESV)

And let us consider how to stir up one another to love and good works, not neglecting to meet together, as is the habit of some, but encouraging one another, and all the more as you see the Day drawing near.

Chapter 18: Navigating Challenges on the Path

Proverbs 19:21 (ESV)

Many are the plans in the mind of a man,

but it is the purpose of the LORD that will stand.

Philippians 4:13 (ESV)

I can do all things through him who strengthens me.

Isaiah 40:31 (ESV)

But they who wait for the LORD shall renew their strength; they shall mount up with wings like eagles; they shall run and not be weary; they shall walk and not faint.

Romans 8:28 (ESV)

And we know that for those who love God all things work together for good, for those who are called according to his purpose.

James 1:2-4 (ESV)

Count it all joy, my brothers, when you meet trials of various kinds, for you know that the testing of your faith produces steadfastness.

And let steadfastness have its full effect, that you may be perfect and complete, lacking in nothing.

1 Peter 5:7 (ESV)

Casting all your anxieties on him, because he cares for you.

Joshua 1:9 (ESV)

Have I not commanded you? Be strong and courageous. Do not be frightened, and do not be dismayed, for the LORD your God is with you wherever you go.

Proverbs 3:5-6 (ESV)

(See full quote in Chapter 7.)

Proverbs 15:22 (ESV)

Without counsel plans fail,

but with many advisers they succeed.

Psalm 107:1 (ESV)

Oh give thanks to the LORD, for he is good,

for his steadfast love endures forever!

Psalm 42:11 (ESV)

Why are you cast down, O my soul, and why are you in turmoil within me?

Hope in God; for I shall again praise him, my salvation and my God.

1 Samuel 7:12 (ESV)

Then Samuel took a stone and set it up between Mizpah and Shen and called its name Ebenezer; for he said, "Till now the LORD has helped us."

1 Thessalonians 5:18 (ESV)

Give thanks in all circumstances; for this is the will of God in Christ Jesus for you.

Proverbs 16:9 (ESV)

The heart of man plans his way, but the Lord establishes his steps.

Psalm 23:4 (ESV)

Even though I walk through the valley of the shadow of death, I will fear no evil, for you are with me; your rod and your staff, they comfort me....

Chapter 19: Purpose-Driven Relationships

James 1:5 (ESV)

If any of you lacks wisdom, let him ask God, who gives generously to all without reproach, and it will be given him.

Proverbs 29:18 (ESV)

Where there is no prophetic vision the people cast off restraint,

but blessed is he who keeps the law.

James 1:19 (ESV)

Know this, my beloved brothers: let every person be quick to hear, slow to speak, slow to anger.

Ecclesiastes 4:9-12 (ESV)

Two are better than one, because they have a good reward for their toil. For if they fall, one will lift up his fellow. But woe to him who is alone when he falls and has not another to lift him up! Again, if two lie together, they keep warm, but how can one keep warm alone? And though a man might prevail against one who is alone, two will withstand him—a threefold cord is not quickly broken.

Proverbs 13:20 (ESV)

Whoever walks with the wise becomes wise...

Chapter 20: learning from Spiritual Mentors and Leaders

2 Kings 2:2

And Elijah said to Elisha, "Please stay here, for the LORD has sent me as far as Bethel." But Elisha said, "As the LORD lives, and as you yourself live, I will not leave you." So they went down to Bethel.

Proverbs 11:14

Where there is no guidance, a people falls, but in an abundance of counselors there is safety.

Proverbs 27:17

Iron sharpens iron, and one man sharpens another.

Hebrews 13:7

Remember your leaders, those who spoke to you the word of God. Consider the outcome of their way of life, and imitate their faith.

1 Thessalonians 5:11

Therefore encourage one another and build one another up, just as you are doing.

2 Timothy 2:2

Entrust to faithful men who will be able to teach others also

Chapter 21: Cultivating Humility in Purpose

John 13:14-15

If I then, your Lord and Teacher, have washed your feet, you also ought to wash one another's feet. For I have given you an example, that you also should do just as I have done to you.

Philippians 2:3-4

Do nothing from selfish ambition or conceit, but in humility count others more significant than yourselves. Let each of you look not only to his own interests, but also to the interests of others.

James 4:10

Humble yourselves before the Lord, and he will exalt you.

1 Peter 5:5-6

Likewise, you who are younger, be subject to the elders. Clothe yourselves, all of you, with humility toward one another, for "God opposes the proud but gives grace to the humble." Humble yourselves, therefore, under the mighty hand of God so that at the proper time he may exalt you.

Micah 6:8

He has told you, O man, what is good; and what does the Lord require of you but to do justice, and to love kindness, and to walk humbly with your God?

Proverbs 22:4

The reward for humility and fear of the Lord is riches and honor and life.

Luke 14:11

For everyone who exalts himself will be humbled, and he who humbles himself will be exalted.

Chapter 22: Stewardship of Resources

Psalm 24:1 (ESV)

The earth is the LORD's and the fullness thereof,

the world and those who dwell therein.

Proverbs 21:5 (ESV)

The plans of the diligent lead surely to abundance,

but everyone who is hasty comes only to poverty.

Proverbs 6:6-8 (ESV)

Go to the ant, O sluggard; consider her ways, and be wise.

Without having any chief, officer, or ruler,

she prepares her bread in summer and gathers her food in harvest.

Malachi 3:10 (ESV)

Bring the full tithe into the storehouse, that there may be food in my house. And thereby put me to the test, says the LORD of hosts, if I will not open the windows of heaven for you and pour down for you a blessing until there is no more need.

Romans 13:8 (ESV)

Owe no one anything, except to love each other, for the one who loves another has fulfilled the law.

2 Corinthians 9:6-7 (ESV)

The point is this: whoever sows sparingly will also reap sparingly, and whoever sows bountifully will also reap bountifully. Each one must give as he has decided in his heart, not reluctantly or under compulsion, for God loves a cheerful giver.

Proverbs 13:11 (ESV)

Wealth gained hastily will dwindle,

but whoever gathers little by little will increase it.

Luke 16:10 (ESV)

One who is faithful in a very little is also faithful in much, and one who is dishonest in a very little is also dishonest in much.

Chapter 23: Legacy and the Future

Matthew 6:21 (ESV)

For where your treasure is, there your heart will be also.

Chapter 24: Continuing Your Purposeful Journey

Philippians 4:13 (ESV)

I can do all things through him who strengthens me.

2 Peter 1:3-11 (ESV)

His divine power has granted to us all things that pertain to life and godliness, through the knowledge of him who called us to his own glory and excellence...

(This passage continues extensively; please see 2 Peter 1:3–11 for full reading.)

Hosea 4:6 (ESV)

My people are destroyed for lack of knowledge;

because you have rejected knowledge,

I reject you from being a priest to me.

Proverbs 25:28 (ESV)

A man without self-control is like a city broken into and left without walls.

James 1:12 (ESV)

Blessed is the man who remains steadfast under trial, for when he has stood the test he will receive the crown of life, which God has promised to those who love him.

Romans 5:3-4 (ESV)

Not only that, but we rejoice in our sufferings, knowing that suffering produces endurance, and endurance produces character, and character produces hope.

1 Timothy 4:8 (ESV)

For while bodily training is of some value, godliness is of value in every way, as it holds promise for the present life and also for the life to come.

Romans 12:10 (ESV)

Love one another with brotherly affection. Outdo one another in showing honor.

John 13:35 (ESV)

By this all people will know that you are my disciples, if you have love for one another."

2 Peter 1:8-10 (ESV)

For if these qualities are yours and are increasing, they keep you from being ineffective or unfruitful in the knowledge of our Lord Jesus Christ. For whoever lacks these qualities is so nearsighted that he is blind, having forgotten that he was cleansed from his former sins. Therefore, brothers, be all the more diligent to confirm your calling and election, for if you practice these qualities you will never fall.

Proverbs 3:5-6 (ESV)

Trust in the Lord with all your heart, and do not lean on your own understanding. In all your ways acknowledge him, and he will make straight your paths.

Luke 14:28 (ESV)

For which of you, desiring to build a tower, does not first sit down and count the cost, whether he has enough to complete it?

Nehemiah 2:11-18 (ESV)

(Nehemiah surveys Jerusalem and inspires the people to rebuild the wall—see passage for full context.)

Proverbs 15:22 (ESV)

Without counsel plans fail, but with many advisers they succeed.

James 2:17 (ESV)

So also faith by itself, if it does not have works, is dead.

Joshua 3:15-17 (ESV)

And as soon as those bearing the ark had come as far as the Jordan, and the feet of the priests bearing the ark were dipped in the brink of the water (now the Jordan overflows all its banks throughout the time of harvest), the waters coming down from above stood and rose up in a heap very far away, at Adam, the city that is beside Zarethan, and those flowing down toward the Sea of the Arabah, the Salt Sea, were completely cut off. And the people passed over opposite Jericho. Now the priests bearing the ark of the covenant of the Lord stood firmly on dry ground in the midst of the Jordan, and all Israel was passing over on dry ground until all the nation finished passing over the Jordan.

Ecclesiastes 4:9-10 (ESV)

Two are better than one, because they have a good reward for their toil. For if they fall, one will lift up his fellow. But woe to him who is alone when he falls and has not another to lift him up!

2 Timothy 1:6-7 (ESV)

For this reason I remind you to fan into flame the gift of God, which is in you through the laying on of my hands, for God gave us a spirit not of fear but of power and love and self-control.

2 Corinthians 13:5 (ESV)

Examine yourselves, to see whether you are in the faith. Test yourselves. Or do you not realize this about yourselves, that Jesus Christ is in you?—unless indeed you fail to meet the test!

Psalm 139:23-24 (ESV)

Search me, O God, and know my heart! Try me and know my thoughts! And see if there be any grievous way in me, and lead me in the way everlasting!

Proverbs 16:9 (ESV)

The heart of man plans his way, but the Lord establishes his steps.

Acts 10:9-16 (ESV)

The next day, as they were on their journey and approaching the city, Peter went up on the housetop about the sixth hour[a] to pray. And he became hungry and wanted something to eat, but while they were preparing it, he fell into a trance and saw the heavens opened and something like a great sheet descending, being let down by its four corners upon the earth. In it were all kinds of animals and reptiles and birds of the air. And there came a voice to him: "Rise, Peter; kill and eat." But Peter said, "By no means, Lord; for I have never eaten anything that is common or unclean." And the voice came to him again a second time, "What God has made clean, do not call common." This happened three times, and the thing was taken up at once to heaven.

Chapter 25: Equipped for the Final Stretch – Readiness in a Rerouted World

2 Peter 1:5-11 (ESV)

For this very reason, make every effort to supplement your faith with virtue,[a] and virtue with knowledge, and knowledge with self-control, and self-control with steadfastness, and steadfastness with godliness, and godliness with brotherly affection, and brotherly affection with love. For if these qualities[b] are yours and are increasing, they keep you from being ineffective or unfruitful in the knowledge of our Lord Jesus Christ. For whoever lacks these qualities is so nearsighted that he is blind, having forgotten that he was cleansed from his former sins. Therefore, brothers,[c] be all the more diligent to confirm your calling and election, for if you practice these qualities you will never fall. For in this way there will be richly provided for you an entrance into the eternal kingdom of our Lord and Savior Jesus Christ.

About the Author

Roscoe Hunter is a passionate Christian leader, seasoned business strategist, and transformational purpose coach with over 25 years of experience in professional marketing, consulting, and leadership development. His life's mission is to help people uncover, embrace, and execute God's plan—especially when their own plans fall apart.

Roscoe became a Christian at the age of 12 and has walked with God for nearly five decades. His spiritual journey—marked by both triumphs and trials—includes mentoring and coaching countless professionals and entrepreneurs, both believers and seekers. He has guided many through personal and vocational detours, helping them rediscover purpose, gain clarity, and realign with God's calling on their lives.

With a Bachelor of Science in Business, certifications in marketing consulting, AI marketing, and a range of professional business credentials, Roscoe brings a powerful blend of biblical insight and practical strategy to everything he teaches. He has invested tens of thousands of dollars into his own growth through coaching and mentorship—and now pours that wisdom into others.

From working in Corporate America and the federal government to launching and leading successful businesses, Roscoe knows what it's like to climb ladders that don't lead to purpose—and how to reroute when God calls you higher.

Alongside his wife, Roscoe has served as a ministry leader for couples at their local church since 2019. He regularly teaches Bible studies, preaches on Sunday mornings, and shares faith-based content through his YouTube channel and the Rerouted Nation community.

Through his book Rerouted, his online community, live teachings, and tiered coaching and mentorship programs, Roscoe equips others to move from confusion to clarity, from detour to destiny, and from survival to significance.

If this book stirred something in you, don't stop here. Join the free online community, take the next step in discovering your divine purpose, and walk with others who are learning to live life by design—not default. JoinRerouted.com

What Comes Next?

You've made it this far—and that means something.

If you've read these pages and felt something awaken, something stir… maybe even something heal, then you're not alone. The journey of being rerouted doesn't end with the last chapter. In fact, it's just the beginning.

You weren't meant to walk this road by yourself.

That's why I created **Rerouted Nation**—a free online community built for people just like you. It's a place for believers who've been through the valley, felt the pain of redirection, and are now choosing to walk boldly into God's plan—no matter what it costs.

Inside, you'll find:

- **Exclusive devotionals and reflections** tied to the lessons in this book.
- **Live coaching sessions** and Q&As with me and other mentors.
- **A supportive community** of people who understand your story because they're living it too.
- **Next steps** to deepen your faith, clarify your purpose, and even build the ministry, coaching business, or legacy you were created for.

This is more than a community group or another email list.

This is a movement of people being *rerouted on purpose*—and building something better with God at the center.

So don't stop here.

Don't close the book and stay where you are.

You've been rerouted... now it's time to rise.

Join the free community today at JoinRerouted.com

Let's walk this road together.

www.ingramcontent.com/pod-product-compliance
Lightning Source LLC
Chambersburg PA
CBHW030515230426
43665CB00010B/629